Supporting Reuse in Business Case Development

Bart-Jan van Putten

Supporting Reuse in Business Case Development

Bart-Jan van Putten
Wirtschaftswissenschaftliche Fakultät
Humboldt-Universität zu Berlin
Berlin, Germany

Dissertation, Humboldt-Universität zu Berlin, 2012

ISBN 978-3-658-01170-3   ISBN 978-3-658-01171-0 (eBook)
DOI 10.1007/978-3-658-01171-0

The Deutsche Nationalbibliothek lists this publication in the Deutsche Nationalbibliografie; detailed bibliographic data are available in the Internet at http://dnb.d-nb.de.

Library of Congress Control Number: 2012956331

Springer Gabler
© Springer Fachmedien Wiesbaden 2013
This work is subject to copyright. All rights are reserved by the Publisher, whether the whole or part of the material is concerned, specifically the rights of translation, reprinting, reuse of illustrations, recitation, broadcasting, reproduction on microfilms or in any other physical way, and transmission or information storage and retrieval, electronic adaptation, computer software, or by similar or dissimilar methodology now known or hereafter developed. Exempted from this legal reservation are brief excerpts in connection with reviews or scholarly analysis or material supplied specifically for the purpose of being entered and executed on a computer system, for exclusive use by the purchaser of the work. Duplication of this publication or parts thereof is permitted only under the provisions of the Copyright Law of the Publisher's location, in its current version, and permission for use must always be obtained from Springer. Permissions for use may be obtained through RightsLink at the Copyright Clearance Center. Violations are liable to prosecution under the respective Copyright Law.
The use of general descriptive names, registered names, trademarks, service marks, etc. in this publication does not imply, even in the absence of a specific statement, that such names are exempt from the relevant protective laws and regulations and therefore free for general use. While the advice and information in this book are believed to be true and accurate at the date of publication, neither the authors nor the editors nor the publisher can accept any legal responsibility for any errors or omissions that may be made. The publisher makes no warranty, express or implied, with respect to the material contained herein.

Printed on acid-free paper

Springer Gabler is a brand of Springer DE.
Springer DE is part of Springer Science+Business Media.
www.springer-gabler.de

Voor Opa, ons grote voorbeeld

in de wetenschap en vele andere aspecten van het leven.

For Grandpa, our role model

in science and many other aspects of life.

Foreword

Companies today invest more than ever into the expansion of their information and communication technology. However, in the field of IT, costs and benefits remain difficult to quantify. This creates an obvious dilemma for senior management – even if they are determined to invest into IT, how should they know into what exactly? Which investments would make them most competitive? Most profitable?

This monograph is devoted to the development of reusable business cases for information systems. With his work, Bart-Jan van Putten addresses the question head-on how the profitability of IT investments can be predicted and quantified in advance. Van Putten thus deals with a subject that is of great importance not only for technologists but for corporate strategy in general.

The research is based on modern empirical methods, yielding quite a few unexpected insights. Van Putten shows his solid methodological knowledge and analytical skills in a variety of different application contexts. His key results have already been presented at prestigious international conferences. Many of these results are of both scientific and practical value.

Therefore, I wish this work to be widely disseminated and its author all the best for his future endeavors.

Oliver Günther

Preface

After my graduation in 2008 I have interviewed at about 10 companies to find out where I really wanted to work. It was not that I did not know what I wanted – I had an extensive list of criteria – but I was trying to find the employer where I would be challenged, work with bright people and have the freedom to set and achieve my own goals.

In October 2008 I interviewed for a PhD position at SAP Research Dresden, a place recommended by my uncle Theo Dirk Meijler, who was already happily employed there. On the day when I was in the train travelling to Dresden, the economic crisis struck SAP and led to a short 'hiring freeze'. The interview took place anyhow, but because of the freeze I could not be employed. I then accepted another job at a consulting firm. Unfortunately, due to the economic crisis, there were hardly any challenging projects for academics. I was deployed at a telecom operator as an expensive helpdesk employee, connecting and disconnecting mobile phone numbers in an ancient computer system. After five weeks I had made my decision. I wanted to invest in myself and accepted a PhD position at a Dutch university. I would work on an interesting project, inline with my master's thesis research. But deep inside I knew that a more practical PhD position in industry would suit me better.

On the very same day that I had sent the e-mail accepting the position at the Dutch university, I received a call from SAP Research Dresden. SAP was warming up again and the hiring freeze had melted... The next day I decided to make a bold move. I apologized to the Dutch university and accepted the offer from SAP. Of course, this meant moving to Dresden, leaving my family, friends and girlfriend behind. Nonetheless, I have had a great time at SAP. As one of our executives puts it (year after year): "the best is yet to come". SAP has become increasingly innovative and its focus on the creation of beautiful products, design thinking and user experience is greater than ever. This fits perfectly to my professional goals and I am looking forward to helping SAP make its customers and *users* even happier. But let's talk about this dissertation first.

The research topic is inspired by the work that I did for the Semantic Product Memory project, funded by the German government, in which I was responsible for the 'Business Case Framework' work package. I also developed a business case for an SAP-internal project. Experiencing first-hand how difficult it can be to develop a sound and appealing business case eventually led to the focus on supporting business case developers, by enabling the reuse of business case components. Prof. Oliver

Günther from the Institute for Information Systems of the Humboldt University in Berlin agreed to supervise me. This also allowed me to work with some other great people at the institute and get to know Berlin, which is now one of my favorite cities.

During my third year I was looking for a second supervisor. Again, with a list of criteria, I evaluated several 'cases'. Prof.Dr. Antonio Krüger from Saarland University and the German Research Center for Artificial Intelligence (DFKI) was enthusiastic about my work and accepted my request. He shares my passion for the combination of intelligent systems and user-centered design and was therefore a great addition to the group of people supporting and challenging me during my work.

It has been three years since I read on Wikipedia what a business case is and if I would read that page again, there would probably still be something interesting to find. After more than 30 years since King and Schrems published their article on cost-benefit analysis for information systems (King & Schrems, 1978), the problems of business case development and its application to the domain of information systems investment evaluation remain largely unsolved and sometimes unexplored. My work in one of the unexplored areas has been an exciting journey. During the journey, I have applied my experience with user-centered design from my bachelor studies, my experience with modeling knowledge systems from my master studies and developed my business skills on top of that. The result is this dissertation, a (hopefully) interesting combination of 'desirability (user)', 'feasibility (technology)' and 'viability (business)', integrated by design science.

In retrospective, three years suddenly seems a long time period of time. My father got very ill and recovered, my irreplaceable grandfather passed away, a relationship ended, a relationship started, two of my close friends gave birth to a child and my cousin got married. During this time I have received a tremendous amount of love and support, for which I would like to thank:

From the university:

- My first supervisor, Prof. Günther, for giving me freedom and clear goals;
- My second supervisor, Prof. Krüger, for your enthusiasm and rightful questions;
- Prof. Mendling, for your impressive knowledge and for showing me that a professor does not need to be an old man with a beard;
- Franziska Brecht, for being a friend and a portal to the university;
- Anna-Lena Bujarek, for always being prepared to help me with arrangements at the university and for being so friendly;

From SAP:

- My uncle Theo Dirk Meijler, for being a family member, a friend, a coach, a co-author, being Dutch, taking me on hikes and cooking fish. Your intuition is strong, you have an extremely good sense for what is (un)logical and often helped me to get back to the key questions;
- Jochen Rode, for your friendly coaching and being a great team leader. My trust in you was the reason that I dared to move my life to Dresden;
- Ralf Ackermann, for giving me the necessary piece of mind, time wise and contract wise, to finish my dissertation in time;
- Barbara Schennerlein, for the freedom and trust you gave me during my SemProM work. You also showed me that after 20 years of working for one company, you still do not need to loose your honesty and independence;
- Sven Horn, for your friendship, for touring me around "Leipzsch", for your socialist viewpoints ("Wir bauen auf und reißen nieder, haben wir Arbeit immer wieder!") and especially your skill to put things into perspective:
    - Sven, after I complained about another Excel sheet that had to be filled out: "Manche kleben Fliesen; andere stehen an der Kasse. Wir füllen Excels aus, trinken Kaffee und können Sitzen. Was willst du noch mehr?"
    - Sven, after I held an 'important' monologue on business cases: "Business Käse, was ist das?" (In German, 'Käse' can be used in the sense of 'nonsense'.)
- Daniela Wünsch: for your mentoring, especially in the beginning when the path forward was not that clear yet;
- Markus Schief, for being an amazing colleague, co-author and for the good time in Italy;
- My colleagues, Christian Hengstler, Martin Rosjat and Roberto Hengst for your friendship and (un)wanted distractions in room B2.20;
- My colleagues, Ralf Zillmann, Alexander Claus and Lars Leibner for the excellent working atmosphere in room B2.19;
- Ralf Zillmann, once more, for translating the abstract to German;
- My students, Stefanie Spreer, Clarissa Romeiro, Sebastian Reuther and Nadja Schubert, for supporting me in parts of my work and for triggering new thoughts;
- Anirban Majumdar, Carsten Magerkurth, Holger Kunitz, Reiner Bildmayer, Ulf Guttmann and the countless other colleagues from Research, Solution Management and Value Engineering, who helped me in various ways;

Others:

- The SemProM, Aletheia and ADiWa project partners who participated in the interviews and experiments, among whom Anselm Blocher (DFKI), Bernd Stieger (ABB), Jörg Neidig (Siemens), Jörg Preißinger (BMW), Lothar Schuh (ABB), Markus Kückelhaus (DHL) and Torsten Schreiber (DB Schenker);
- Martijn van Heijst, for being a loyal friend, helping me move to Dresden and designing the cover of this dissertation. You should be working for Pixar or Dreamworks (or SAP ☺);
- Leonardo Azevedo, for the excellent collaborations, for the good time in Helsinki, for referring good students and for hosting me during my future Brazil visit ☺;
- Reinhard & Irmgard Laschner, meinen Nachbarn, weil Ihr großartige Menschen seid, Ihr mir das Gefühl gegeben habt, mich in Dresden zu Hause zu fühlen und weil Ihr während meiner häufigen Abwesenheiten meine Pflanzen gegossen habt;
- The German Ministry of Education and Research (BMBF) for partly funding this research under contract 01IA08002, project SemProM, from February 2009 through January 2011;
- The German Ministry of Economics and Technology (BMWi) for partly funding this research under contract 01NA10018, project RAN, from February 2011 through May 2012;

Last but not least, I want to thank my family, friends and girlfriend for supporting me in whatever I do and wherever I go.

Bart-Jan van Putten

Dresden, February 2012

Contents

List of Figures xix

List of Tables xxiii

List of Acronyms xxv

Abstract xxvii

Zusammenfassung xxix

Samenvatting xxxi

1 Introduction 1
   1.1   Context of the Topic 2
   1.2   Research Method 3
   1.3   Structure of the Dissertation 5

2 Challenges in Business Case Development and Requirements for Business Case Frameworks 8
   2.1   Introduction 9
   2.2   Background 10
   2.3   Research Approach 12
   2.4   Case Study 12
   2.5   Solution Areas 16
   2.6   Interviews 17
   2.7   Conclusion 21

3 Reuse in Business Case Development: Arguments, Challenges and Guidelines 23
   3.1   Introduction 23
   3.2   Research Method 25
   3.3   Reusable Components 26
   3.4   Reuse of Criteria and Methods 28
   3.5   Arguments for Reuse 29
   3.6   Challenges in Reuse 32
   3.7   Guidelines for Reuse 34
   3.8   Ongoing Research 35
   3.9   Conclusion 38

4 Business Case Ontology 40
   4.1   Introduction 40
   4.2   Background 42
   4.3   Requirements for Business Case Ontology and Related Work 44

	4.4	Competency Questions 46
	4.5	Design..47
	4.6	Evaluation 52
	4.7	Conclusion 55

5 Business Case Framework 57
- 5.1 Introduction 57
- 5.2 Background 59
- 5.3 Requirements 62
- 5.4 Design & Process 65
- 5.5 Evaluation..73
- 5.6 Conclusion 79

6 Supporting Dynamic Reuse in Business Case Development 81
- 6.1 Introduction 82
- 6.2 Motivation for the Reuse of BC Components 84
- 6.3 Limitations of Business Case Frameworks 84
- 6.4 Support for the Dynamic Reuse of Criteria 86
- 6.5 Method 88
- 6.6 Results..92
- 6.7 Conclusion 98

7 Exploring the Usability of Valuation Methods in Business Cases 100
- 7.1 Introduction 100
- 7.2 Business Case Frameworks 102
- 7.3 Usability Aspects of Valuation Methods............................103
- 7.4 Comparing Valuation Methods 104
- 7.5 Research Method 106
- 7.6 Results..109
- 7.7 Discussion..114
- 7.8 Conclusion 115

8 The Relation Between Dynamic Business Models and Business Cases... 118
- 8.1 Introduction 119
- 8.2 Background 120
- 8.3 Relations...123
- 8.4 Implications 130
- 8.5 Conclusion 133

9 Decision Support By Automatic Analysis of Business Process Models 134
- 9.1 Introduction 135

9.2	Method Design	136
9.3	Method Implementation	137
9.4	Validation	143
9.5	Related Work	145
9.6	Conclusion	147

10 Conclusion **149**
    10.1 Summaries of the Individual Papers 150
    10.2 Design Artifacts 153
    10.3 Contributions 154
    10.4 Limitations 155
    10.5 Recommendations & Future Work 155
    10.6 Closing Remarks 157

References **159**

A   **Interview Protocol (Ch. 2)** **173**

B   **Literature Review: Concept Matrix (Ch. 3)** **183**

C   **Applications of Business Case Ontology (Ch. 4)** **187**

D   **Laboratory Experiment: Recommender Algorithm (Ch. 6)** **195**

E   **Laboratory Experiment: Screenshots (Ch. 6, 7)** **201**

Additional appendices can be found on this book's website. Please visit www.springer.com or www.springer.de, search for the ISBN (978-3-658-01170-3), select the book and choose 'OnlinePLUS'.

List of Figures

Figure 1.1:	The design science cycle applied in this research	4
Figure 1.2:	The main chapters of the dissertation with the research questions and methods	7
Figure 2.1:	Overview of the research approach	12
Figure 2.2:	BCD story, modelled in BPMN	15
Figure 2.3:	The 15 topics structured along the three dimensions, based on the interviews	20
Figure 4.1:	The Business Case Ontology (using the UML Class Diagram notation)	47
Figure 5.1:	A part of the Scope worksheet of the Decentralized Production Control BC	66
Figure 5.2:	The definition of business processes on the Processes worksheet of the Decentralized Production Control BC	67
Figure 5.4:	The quantification method for 'Throughput' on the Methods worksheet of the Decentralized Production Control BC	71
Figure 5.5:	Selecting the reliability of the calculation step in the quantification method	72
Figure 5.6:	The cost criteria, a selection of the Results worksheet from the Decentralized Production Control BC	73
Figure 5.7:	A participant modelled the relation between criteria and business processes on the Criteria worksheet	76
Figure 5.8:	A participant quantified risks using probabilities	77
Figure 5.9:	A participant modelled two perspectives on the same BC, the provider's perspective (left) and the customer's perspective (right)	77
Figure 5.10:	A participant added a scoring approach to the Results worksheet	77
Figure 5.11:	A participant used relative values in his quantification methods	78
Figure 6.1:	Scoring criteria in the earlier BC based on matching criteria in the new BC	87
Figure 6.2:	The research model	89
Figure 7.1:	The research model	107
Figure 7.2:	Overview of the experimental design.	108
Figure 8.1:	Approach for the alignment of BM and BCs	130
Figure 9.1:	Overview of the analysis method	137

Figure 9.2:	Business process model of a smart dishwasher (DPG is the dishwasher's digital product memory). The automatic analysis result is shown in **Figure 9.3**	141
Figure 9.3:	Screenshot of the software program's user interface after parsing the business process model in **Figure 9.2**	142
Figure B.1:	The reviewed literature (1 of 3): Reusable Components and Arguments	183
Figure B.2:	The reviewed literature (2 of 3): Challenges and Guidelines	184
Figure B.3:	The reviewed literature (3 of 3): Methodology	185
Figure C.1:	IS investment criteria considered by Bacon (1992)	187
Figure C.2:	The five competitive forces that shape strategy, adopted from Porter (2008)	189
Figure C.3:	A balanced scorecard applied to IT investment evaluation at a European ferry company, adopted from Willcocks and Lester (1994)	191
Figure C.4:	An example of a (partial) benefits-dependency network for a new CRM system for a European paper manufacturer, adopted from Peppard et al. (2007)	192
Figure E.1:	The pre-test questionnaire	201
Figure E.2:	The pre-test questionnaire (continued)	202
Figure E.3:	The introduction to the task	203
Figure E.4:	The task in the recommendations-condition	204
Figure E.5:	The task in the recommendations-condition (continued)	205
Figure E.6:	The task in the recommendations-condition (continued)	206
Figure E.7:	The task in the recommendations-condition (continued)	207
Figure E.8:	The task in the recommendations-condition (continued)	208
Figure E.9:	The task in the templates-condition	209
Figure E.10:	The task in the templates-condition (continued)	210
Figure E.11:	The task in the templates-condition (continued)	211
Figure E.12:	The task in the templates-condition (continued)	212
Figure E.13:	The task in the control-condition	213
Figure E.14:	The post-test for the task	214
Figure E.15:	Method A, an FML method, in the Return-on-Investment condition	215
Figure E.16:	Method B, a VLM method, in the Return-on-Investment condition	216
Figure E.17:	Method C, a new method, in the Return-on-Investment condition	217

Figure E.18: Method A, an FML method, in the Time Reduction condition 218

Figure E.19: Method B, a VLM method, in the Time Reduction condition 219

Figure E.20: Method C, a new method, in the Time Reduction condition 220

Figure E.21: Method A, an FML method, in the Customer Satisfaction condition ... 221

Figure E.22: Method B, a VLM method, in the Customer Satisfaction condition 222

Figure E.23: Method C, a new method, in the Customer Satisfaction condition 223

List of Tables

Table 2.1:	Research topics within the solution areas and the scores from the interviews	18
Table 4.1:	A simplified comparison of existing frameworks with respect to their usefulness for modeling reusable BCs	45
Table 4.2:	Competency questions for BCO	46
Table 4.3:	Criteria stored in a relational database table	54
Table 6.1:	Simplified comparison of traditional and modern BCFs	85
Table 6.2:	Different types of participants and their completion rates	92
Table 6.3:	Analysis of variance. R=Recommendations, T=Templates, C=Control-condition, F*=Welch's F. Hypotheses are indicated as Hx_y	94
Table 6.4:	Bivariate correlations for Task 1 (Reuse of Criteria). Hypotheses are indicated as Hx_y	95
Table 6.5:	The hypotheses and results (***$p<.001$; **$p<.01$, *$p<.05$)	96
Table 7.1:	An overview of the methods that were compared and some of their properties	105
Table 7.2:	Different types of participants and their completion rates	110
Table 7.3:	Paired samples T-tests. F=FML, V=VLM, N=New	111
Table 7.4:	The hypotheses and results (***$p<.001$ one-tailed; **$p<.01$ one-tailed, *$p<.025$ one-tailed)	112
Table 7.5:	Bivariate correlations	114
Table 8.1:	Nine business model building blocks, adopted from (Alexander Osterwalder et al., 2005)	121
Table 8.2:	BM building blocks and related IS-specific BC evaluation criteria	125
Table 8.3:	Examples of BM change affecting BCs	127
Table 8.4:	Examples of BC analysis affecting the BM	129
Table 8.5:	Possible actions after a BM or BC change	131
Table 9.1:	Examples of business rules	138
Table 9.2:	Conformance of expert recommendations with business rules	144
Table 9.3:	Usefulness of the features	145
Table 9.4:	Usefulness of the indicators for indicating the features	145

List of Acronyms

BC	Business Case
BCD	Business Case Development
BCF	Business Case Framework
BCO	Business Case Ontology
BDN	Benefit Dependency Network
BM	Business Model
BMM	Business Motivation Model
BPM	Business Process Modeling
BPMN	Business Process Modeling Notation
CRM	Customer Relationship Management
CSF	Critical Success Factor
DCF	Discounted Cash Flow
DL	Description Logic
DPG	Digitales Produktgedächtnis (Digital Product Memory)
ERP	Enterprise Resource Planning
FML	Financial Metrics Lite
ICT	Information and Communication Technology
IRR	Internal Rate of Return
IS	Information System
ISE	Information Systems Evaluation
IT	Information Technology
KPI	Key Performance Indicator
M&A	Mergers & Acquisitions
NPV	Net Present Value
RFID	Radio Frequency Identification
ROI	Return on Investment
TAM	Technology Acceptance Model
VLM	Value Lifecycle Manager
XML	eXtensible Markup Language

Abstract

Determining the value of an information system for an organization is challenging, especially before the execution of the project in which the system is put into operation. Many organizations cope with problems when having to identify the potential benefits of the investment, while even more have difficulties with their quantification. An analysis, in which multiple possible investments and approaches are compared with respect to their benefits, costs and risks, is called a 'business case' (BC). The current frameworks that can be used to develop BCs offer too little support for the aforementioned challenges. Opportunities to improve BC frameworks, and thereby the efficiency and effectiveness of BC development, are therefore explored in this dissertation.

Three main solution areas were identified: (1) supporting the reuse of BC components ('reuse'), (2) supporting the adaptation of BCs to contextual factors ('adaptation'), and (3) supporting collaboration during BC development ('collaboration'). With respect to *adaptation,* two approaches were investigated: (1) the alignment of BCs with business models, and (2) decision making based on business process models. The focus of this dissertation has however been on *reuse*.

An extensive literature review showed that the idea of reuse in the context of BC development is hardly investigated. However, in practice some BC frameworks appear to support reuse by means of pre-defined templates and taxonomies from which BC developers can select components. Such BC frameworks are expensive to develop and maintain and have a limited applicability to the domain for which they were designed, which hampers reuse and learning across domains. Therefore, in this dissertation an approach was developed for 'dynamic reuse'. In that approach, a database of earlier BCs is used, rather than static structures of pre-defined components. The earlier BCs are structured according to an ontology of BC components. An algorithm then recommends components for reuse. Furthermore, a generic BC development process underlies this system. Several experiments were executed to validate these ideas and artifacts, which were developed in a design science approach.

Some of the main findings are that the dynamic reuse of investment criteria, such as benefits, costs and risks, improves the ease of use of BC frameworks, when compared to BC frameworks that support reuse from templates or taxonomies. Reuse in general, static or dynamic, improves the effectiveness of BC development. When dynamic reuse is developed further to support the reuse of valuation methods, BCs may become even more reliable and BC developers may be less tempted to creatively adjust estimates.

Keywords

Business Case, Business Model, Business Plan, Cost-benefit Analysis, Decision Making, Design Science, Economics, Evaluation, Ex-ante, Information System (IS), Information Technology (IT), Investment, Return-on-Investment (ROI), Reuse, Total Cost of Ownership (TCO), User-centered Design, Value

Zusammenfassung

Für Unternehmen ist es oftmals eine Herausforderung den Wert eines Informationssystems zu bestimmen. Viele Organisationen kämpfen, besonders vor der Inbetriebnahme eines neuen Systems mit dem Problem, den potentiellen Nutzen der Investition zu identifizieren. Noch schwieriger gestaltet sich deren Quantifizierung. Eine solche Analyse, die mehrere mögliche Investitionen und Ansätze mit Bezug zu dessen Nutzen, Kosten und Risiken vergleicht, nennt man einen „Business Case" (BC). Aktuelle Werkzeuge zur Entwicklung von Business Cases bieten nur eine geringe Unterstützung zur Bewältigung der zuvor erwähnten Herausforderungen. Diese Dissertation beschäftigt sich daher mit den Möglichkeiten, Business Case Frameworks, und damit einhergehend die Effizienz und Effektivität der Business Case Entwicklung zu verbessern.

Dabei wurden drei Lösungsansätze identifiziert: (1) Die Unterstützung der Wiederverwendung von BC Komponenten („Wiederverwendung"), (2) Unterstützung der Adaption von BCs in Bezug auf kontextuelle Faktoren („Adaption"), und die Unterstützung der Kollaboration während der BC Entwicklung („Kollaboration"). Bezüglich der *Adaption* wurden zwei Ansätze untersucht: (1) Der Abgleich von BCs mit Geschäftsmodellen und (2) die Entscheidungsfindung basierend auf Geschäftsprozessmodellen. Im Mittelpunkt dieser Dissertation steht allerdings die *Wiederverwendung*.

Eine ausführliche Literaturrecherche zeigt, dass die Idee der Wiederverwendung im Zusammenhang mit der Entwicklung von Business Cases bisher kaum untersucht wurde. Dennoch scheinen in der Praxis einige BC Werkzeuge die Wiederverwendung zu unterstützen, indem die BC Entwickler aus vordefinierten Vorlagen und Taxonomien Komponenten auswählen können. Solche BC Werkzeuge sind aufwändig zu entwickeln und zu pflegen und sind in der Verwendung auf das Einsatzgebiet beschränkt, wofür sie entworfen wurden. Dies behindert die Wiederverwendung über Domänengrenzen hinweg. Darüber hinaus wurde in dieser Dissertation der Ansatz einer „dynamischen Wiederverwendung" entwickelt. Bei dieser Herangehensweise wird eine Datenbank vorangegangener BCs genutzt und weniger auf die statischen Strukturen mit vordefinierten Komponenten Wert gelegt. Diese vorangegangenen BCs sind entsprechend einer Ontologie von BC Komponenten strukturiert. Diesem System liegt ein generischer BC Entwicklungsprozess zugrunde und mithilfe eines Algorithmus' werden anschließend Komponenten zur Wiederverwendung empfohlen. In verschiedenen durchgeführten Experimenten wurden diese Ideen und Artefakte validiert, welche in einem Ansatz des Design Science entwickelt wurden.

Diese Experimente führten zur Erkenntnis, dass die dynamischen Wiederverwendung von Investitionskriterien – wie beispielsweise Nutzen, Kosten und Risiken – die vereinfachte Nutzung von BC Werkzeugen verbessert, wenn man dies mit BC Werkzeugen vergleicht, die Wiederverwendung in Form von Vorlagen und Taxonomien unterstützen. Generell fördert Wiederverwendung, egal ob statisch oder dynamisch, die Effektivität der BC Entwicklung. Wird die dynamische Wiederverwendung weiterentwickelt, damit außerdem noch die Wiederverwendung von Bewertungsmethoden unterstützt wird, könnte die bessere Unterstützung der Entwickler für BCs zu deutlich zuverlässigeren Business Cases führen.

Samenvatting

Het bepalen van de waarde van een informatiesysteem voor een organisatie is uitdagend, met name voorafgaand aan de uitvoering van het project waarin het systeem in gebruik wordt genomen. Veel organisaties hebben problemen met het identificeren van de mogelijke voordelen van de investering, terwijl nog meer organisaties het moeilijk vinden om die voordelen te kwantificeren. Een analyse, waarin verschillende mogelijke investeringen en benaderingen worden vergeleken a.d.h.v. kosten, baten, en risico's, wordt een 'business case' (BC) genoemd. De huidige frameworks waarmee BCs ontwikkeld kunnen worden bieden echter te weinig ondersteuning voor de genoemde uitdagingen. Mogelijkheden om BC frameworks te verbeteren, en daarmee de efficiëntie en effectiviteit waarmee BCs ontwikkeld kunnen worden, zijn daarom verkend in deze dissertatie.

Drie oplossingsrichtingen zijn geidentificeerd: (1) het ondersteunen van hergebruik van BC componenten ('reuse'), (2) het ondersteunen van het aanpassen van BCs aan omgevingsfactoren ('adaptation'), en (3) het ondersteunen van samenwerking tijdens BC ontwikkeling ('collaboration'). M.b.t. *adaptation* zijn twee benaderingen onderzocht: (1) het afstemmen van BCs op business models, en (2) besluitvorming op basis van business process models. Het zwaartepunt van deze dissertatie ligt echter bij hergebruik (reuse).

Een uitvoerig literatuuronderzoek heeft uitgewezen dat het idee van hergebruik in de context van BC ontwikkeling nauwelijks onderzocht is. Echter, in de praktijk blijken sommige BC frameworks hergebruik wel te ondersteunen d.m.v. voorgedefinieerde sjablonen en taxonomiën. Daaruit kunnen BC ontwikkelaars componenten selecteren voor hergebruik. Zulke BC frameworks zijn duur om te ontwikkelen en te onderhouden en zijn slechts beperkt toepasbaar op het domein waarvoor ze ontworpen zijn. Dat maakt het moeilijk om uit andere domeinen te hergebruiken en te leren. Daarom is d.m.v. deze dissertatie een benadering ontwikkeld voor 'dynamisch hergebruik'. Daarvoor wordt een database van bestaande BCs gebruikt, in plaats van statische structuren van voorgedefinieerde componenten. De bestaande BCs zijn gestructureerd a.d.h.v. een ontologie van herbruikbare BC componenten. Een algoritme beveelt vervolgens componenten voor hergebruik aan. Verder ligt aan dit systeem een generiek BC ontwikkelingsproces ten grondslag. Verschillende experimenten zijn uitgevoerd om deze ideeën en artefacten, die d.m.v. een design science aanpak ontwikkeld zijn, te valideren.

Enige van de belangrijkste bevindingen zijn dat dynamisch hergebruik van investeringscriteria, zoals kosten, baten en risico's, de gebruiksvriendelijkheid van BC frameworks verbetert, in vergelijking tot BC frameworks die hergebruik alleen ondersteunen d.m.v. sjablonen en taxonomiën. Hergebruik in het algemeen, statisch of dynamisch, verbetert de effectiviteit van BC ontwikkeling. Als het principe van dynamisch hergebruik verder wordt ontwikkeld om ook het hergebruik van waarderingsmethoden te ondersteunen, kunnen BCs nog betrouwbaarder worden en komen BC ontwikkelaars wellicht minder snel in de verleiding om schattingen creatief aan te passen.

1 Introduction

For decades, determining the value and success of information systems (IS) has been high on the agendas of researchers, cf. (King & Schrems, 1978; Davis, 1989; Urbach, Smolnik, & Riempp, 2009; Schryen, 2010). Many IS investments are strategic in nature, have long-term, hard to quantify benefits and incur indirect costs (Irani, 2002). 68% of IS projects cope with problems when having to identify the potential benefits of the investment, while 85% have problems with their quantification (J. Ballantine & Stray, 1999). This may lead to over-investment, under-investment and makes it attractive to creatively adjust estimates, see e.g. (J. Ward, Daniel, & Peppard, 2008).

To support IS investment evaluation (ISE), in most organizations some kind of business case (BC) is developed. A BC is *"a recommendation to decision makers to take a particular course of action for the organization, supported by an analysis of benefits, costs and risks"* (Gambles, 2009). Business case development (BCD) is the process of realizing the BC as an 'artifact', by gathering and analyzing data to define and valuate evaluation *criteria* (Bacon, 1992), presenting it in documents, spreadsheets or presentations. It may take place before project execution for investment appraisal, during project execution for monitoring and control, or after project execution for organizational learning (Van Putten, Brecht, & Günther, 2011).

When trying to estimate the values of the criteria selected for use in the new BC, a BC developer may spend days on defining *methods*, i.e., ways to put a qualitative, quantitative non-financial, or financial value on these criteria, see e.g., (Renkema & Berghout, 1997). This is especially hard for the intangible benefits and indirect costs (Irani, 2002). Instead, criteria and methods may also come from databases which are specifically designed for the purpose of reuse, e.g., templates and taxonomies of criteria and methods, with browse and query functionality for their retrieval (Irani, Ghoneim, & Love, 2006).

BCD can be supported by a business case framework (BCF), which often comes in the form of a spreadsheet template with some pre-defined criteria and methods. Today's BCFs are, however, often too generic, providing little support for BC developers who need to define domain-specific criteria and methods. Other times, BCFs are sufficiently domain-specific, but are based on templates and taxonomies, which are explicitly defined by domain experts. Such BCFs are expensive to develop and maintain and have a limited applicability to the domain for which they were designed, which hampers cross-domain reuse.

This dissertation aimed to develop the knowledge for making a BCF that is generic enough to apply it to multiple domains, but at the same time specific enough to provide useful support for actual BCD in a specific domain. An approach for the *reuse* of domain-specific BC components, on top of a generic BC basis, was developed and evaluated from the perspective of the BC developer.

This way, the following general research questions are addressed in this dissertation:

RQ1: *What is the effect of different kinds of BCF-support for reuse on the efficiency and effectiveness of BCD?*

RQ2: *What is the effect of different kinds of BCF-support for reuse on the ease of use and usefulness of BCFs and the intention of BC developers to use such BCFs?*

Originally, the research started off with a more general focus on the improvement of the usability of BCFs. **Chapter 2** will show this broader view, where in addition to 'reuse', also 'adaptation' and 'collaboration' are presented as focus areas for future research.

1.1 Context of the Topic

The domain of IS investment evaluation has been subject to investigation for several decades, see e.g. (Farbey, Land, & Targett, 1999a; King & Schrems, 1978; M. M. Parker, Benson, & Trainor, 1988; Schryen, 2010). In the literature, different perspectives have shown up, which may roughly be categorized as follows:

- *Organizational perspective:* This perspective deals with portfolio management, e.g., deciding in which projects should be invested and how much risk can be taken in one project in order to keep overall company risk under control. Moreover, business processes and policies for BC development and evaluation may be defined.

- *Individual perspective:* This perspective deals with the challenges that a single BC developer faces. Issues are e.g., where the BC developer can find reliable data and how the data can be used to derive reliable estimates. This category also covers the challenge of selecting the right evaluation method and tools supporting BCD.

- *Social/political perspective:* This perspective deals with the different opinions and information that people may have who are collaborating on the development or evaluation of a BC. Exemplary issues are how tasks can be distributed, how conflicting information can be combined, how BC developers try to convince and sometimes even deceive decision makers.

This dissertation mainly deals with the individual perspective because it aims to make the life of BC developers easier, while sustaining or improving the quality of the BCs produced. There are clear signals in literature that this is relevant. According to Bacon (1992), „current capital budgeting theory does little to address the organizational and behavioral factors involved in the *practice* of capital budgeting (Hellings, 1985; Kennedy, 1986)". 13 years later, Berghout and Remenyi (2005, p. 86) still state that "Almost all studies presented at the conference evaluate the value of IT on an organizational level and (...) there are few publications regarding the lower individual level (exceptions are Bannister, 2002 and Hughes, et al., 2002)".

1.2 Research Method

To answer the proposed research questions, different BCF prototypes were developed and evaluated through a design science approach. Design science is about the creation and evaluation of IT artifacts intended to solve identified organizational problems. Such artifacts are represented in a structured form that may vary from software, formal logic, and rigorous mathematics to informal natural language descriptions (Hevner, March, Park, & Ram, 2004). Simon (1996) describes the nature of the design process as a cycle in which design alternatives are generated, tested against requirements, leading to the design of new alternatives. Hevner (2007) describes two additional cycles. The *relevance cycle* bridges the contextual environment of the research project with the design science activities. The *rigor cycle* connects the design science activities with the knowledge base of scientific foundations, experience, and expertise that informs the research project. The iterative process applied in this dissertation is based on these cycles and visualized in **Figure 1.1**. It consists of the following phases:

- *Requirements definition:* Understanding the challenges in BCD and the requirements for BCFs. This assures the relevance of the research.
- *BCF design:* Designing an improved BCF based on the requirements. The BCF may be applied in practice and/or become a 'meta-artifact' that embodies scientific insights.
- *BCF application:* Applying the BCF to the development of BCs. This assures the relevance of the research and is necessary for the following evaluation steps.
- *BC evaluation:* Evaluating the quality of the BCs. This may lead to new scientific insights.
- *BCF evaluation:* Evaluating the quality of the BCF. This may lead to new scientific insights and trigger the refinement of the requirements for the next iteration.

To further guarantee the rigor of the research, during all steps existing scientific theories and methods were applied.

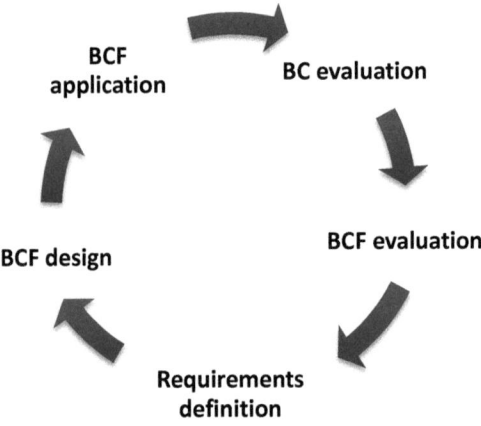

Figure 1.1: The design science cycle applied in this research

The distinction between BC evaluation and BCF evaluation is necessary because a high quality BCF does not necessarily lead to high quality BCs, nor does a low quality BCF necessarily lead to low quality BCs. The experience of the BC developer and the complexity of the task are likely to play an important role as well.

This dissertation is based on three iterations through the design science cycle. The first iteration was executed in the context of the evaluation of an SAP Research internal product idea, the 'Real World Integration Platform (RWIP)', for which a BC needed to be developed. The author's experiences during the RWIP case study led to the formulation of hypotheses which were evaluated during the practitioner interviews (**Chapter 2**). The second iteration was executed in the context of the SemProM project, for which a BCF needed to be developed. This involved the definition of a generic BCD process and a first prototype of a BCF supporting that process as well as some domain-specific components. That BCF was tested during the field experiment (**Chapter 5**). The third iteration was executed in the context of the RAN project. During that iteration, the literature review was completed (**Chapter 3**), a BC ontology was defined (**Chapter 4**), a new way to reuse domain-specific BC content was developed and tested during the first part of a laboratory experiment (**Chapter 6**). During the second part of the laboratory experiment the (re)usability of valuation methods was explored (**Chapter 7**). Within the overall design science method, several other research methods were applied as well (**Figure 1.2**).

1.3 Structure of the Dissertation

This is a cumulative dissertation, which means that it is build upon individual publications, which are represented by the **Chapters 2 to 9** (**Figure 1.2**). The chapters are highly related and each of them deals with a specific research question which contributes to the general research questions as defined in this chapter. Some overlaps between the chapters may exist, because of the cumulative nature of this dissertation. The papers are purposefully presented in their original form, i.e., just like they were published or handed in for publication. Only the formatting was changed, to give this dissertation a coherent visual appearance.

The first study, *Challenges in Business Case Development and Requirements for Business Case Frameworks*, is presented in **Chapter 2**. It shows that there are three focus areas to better support BCD:

- **Reuse:** When BC developers can reuse BC components, they may become more efficient and effective. This is the focus of the dissertation and explored in **Chapters 3 to 7**:

    3. *Reuse in Business Case Development: Arguments, Challenges and Guidelines:* This study aimed to investigate suitable components for reuse, arguments for reuse, challenges in reuse and guidelines for reuse. This way, it provides an overview of IS investment evaluation literature and reveals that the topic of reuse is largely unexplored.
    4. *Business Case Ontology:* This study aimed to develop a model of the BC as an artifact, defining the components that can be reused in a more formal manner, enabling computer-supported reuse. It can also be used by researchers and practitioners as a 'shared conceptualization of the domain'.
    5. *Business Case Framework:* This study aimed to develop a first version of a BCF, based on a generic BCD process, extensible with domain specific components. At this point, those components still had to be pre-defined by domain experts. The BCF was applied to the development of several BCs for the Semantic Product Memory (SemProM) project and evaluated during a field experiment.
    6. *Supporting Dynamic Reuse in Business Case Development:* This study aimed to compare dynamic and static reuse of BC components. In the dynamic

approach, the reusable, domain-specific criteria and methods do not need to be pre-defined by experts in templates and taxonomies (like in **Chapter 5**), but can be reused from earlier BCs. A recommender system proposes criteria that fit the new BC under development.

7. *Exploring the Usability of Valuation Methods in Business Cases:* According to the literature review (**Chapter 3**), one of the challenges for (re)using a valuation method is its 'usability'. This study explores how the 'Perceived Ease of Use' and the 'Perceived Usefulness' affect the intention of BC developers to (re)use certain methods. This knowledge can be used to improve systems that recommend methods for reuse.

- **Adaptation:** When BCs become adaptive to other sources of strategic information in the enterprise, such as business models and business process models, it is easier to maintain them and use them on a continuous basis for decision making. Some explorative research is included in this dissertation and described in **Chapters 8 and 9**:

    8. *The Relation Between Dynamic Business Models and Business Cases:* This study aimed to clarify how business models, as an implementation of a company's strategy, can be aligned with BCs, as an abstraction of a company's operations. This knowledge may help companies to decide more efficiently and effectively which BCs need to approved (before their execution) or changed (during execution).

    9. *Decision Support by Automatic Analysis of Business Process Models:* This study shows how information can be extracted automatically from business process models to support decision making in a certain domain. The original idea behind the work was to use business process models to automatically compare the 'as-is' and 'to-be' states of a BC and quantify the difference, e.g., in terms of a reduced number of processes. This study is the first step to make that possible.

- **Collaboration:** When the assumptions underlying the BC become more clear and when the sources and reliability of the information in the BC is transparent, more stakeholders of the IS project will be able to understand and influence the decision making process. This focus area has not been investigated further in the context of this dissertation.

2. Challenges in Business Case Development and Requirements for Business Case Frameworks
Research Questions: What are the challenges in business case development? What are the opportunities to improve business case frameworks?
Research Methods: Case Study (N=1), Interviews (N=8)

▶ **Reuse**

3. Reuse in Business Case Development: Arguments, Challenges and Guidelines
Research Questions: Which business case components are considered for reuse in the literature? Which arguments for reuse can be found in the domain of IS evaluation? Which challenges may hinder reuse in the domain of IS evaluation?
Research Methods: Literature Review (> 100 articles)

4. Business Case Ontology
Research Questions: How can a model of business case components be defined, in order to support their reuse?
Research Methods: Design, Literature Review

5. Business Case Framework
Research Questions: How can a business case framework be generic enough to be applicable to multiple domains and at the same time support the development of business cases for specific domains?
Research Methods: Design, Field Experiment (N=9)

6. Supporting Dynamic Reuse in Business Case Development
Research Questions: How can support for reuse improve the usefulness and usability of business case frameworks, while limiting the effort required to develop and maintain static databases of reusable components? To what extent does support for the dynamic reuse of criteria, improve the usefulness and usability of business case frameworks?
Research Methods: Design, Laboratory Experiment (N=208)

7. Exploring the Usability of Valuation Methods in Business Cases
Research Questions: Why are certain valuation methods more likely to be reused than others, from the perspective of usability?
Research Methods: Laboratory Experiment (N=199)

▶ **Adaptation**

8. The Relation Between Dynamic Business Models and Business Cases
Research Questions: What is the relation between business models and business cases? How can this understanding be incorporated in organizational processes and software tools supporting those processes?
Research Methods: Literature Review, Inductive Reasoning

9. Decision Support by Automatic Analysis of Business Process Models
Research Questions: How can business process models be analyzed automatically, in order to support decision making in a specific domain?
Research Methods: Design, Laboratory Experiment (N=6)

▶ **Collaboration**

Figure 1.2: The main chapters of the dissertation with the research questions and methods

2 Challenges in Business Case Development and Requirements for Business Case Frameworks

Bart-Jan van Putten	Humboldt-Universität zu Berlin, SAP Research Dresden
Franziska Brecht	Humboldt-Universität zu Berlin
Oliver Günther	Humboldt-Universität zu Berlin

Published as...

Van Putten, B.-J., Brecht, F., Günther, O. (2011). *Challenges in Business Case Development and Requirements for Business Case Frameworks*. Proceedings of the 5th European Conference on Information Management and Evaluation (ECIME), September 8-9, Como, Italy.

Relevance for this Dissertation

This study reveals three focus areas to better support BCD. After this study I decided to focus on the 'Reuse' area for the remainder of my dissertation.

Collaborations

- Franziska Brecht (HU Berlin) commented on the manuscript.
- Prof. Oliver Günther, PhD (HU Berlin) commented on the readiness of the paper for publication.
- The findings in the paper are partly based on interviews with BCD experts and practitioners.

Abstract

Business cases (BC) are often used to support information systems (IS) investment evaluation. Unfortunately, business case development (BCD) is a complex task, especially identifying and quantifying the benefits of a proposed investment. Although today's business case frameworks (BCF) support BCD to some extent, they have several limitations. Based on a case study and interviews with BC developers, this study further investigates challenges in BCD, describes limitations of BCF and reveals opportunities for the improvement of BCF. Thus, a starting point is provided for user-centred designers and engineers who aim to develop better tool support for BCD. The results of the study show that the general focus areas should be (1) the support for reuse of BC components, (2) enabling adaptation and maintenance of BCs over longer periods of time, and (3) improving the collaboration among BC stakeholders. More specifically, the interviewees argue that more support is needed for market potential estimation, determining information quality, clarifying reasoning, and the reuse of structure.

2.1 Introduction

Due to the high expenditures on information systems (IS), it is common practice that companies evaluate IS investment proposals. 'Cost-benefit analyses of information systems' (Sassone, 1988), 'ex-ante information system evaluations' (Walter & Spitta, 2004), and 'IT business cases' (Brugger, 2009) play an important role in supporting investment decision making.

A business case (BC) consists of qualitative and quantitative descriptions of benefits, costs and risks of each proposed investment alternative (Farbey, Land, & Targett, 1999b). Although some researchers and practitioners use different terminology, the meaning and intentions of the components are generally the same, cf. (Brugger, 2009; Gambles, 2009; Schmidt, 2009).

The development of a BC is a complex task. According to Schmidt (2003), "a short list of what it takes to produce a good IT BC holds few surprises: one needs to be thorough (track down all possible impacts, costs, and benefits), clear and logical (articulate the cause and effect chain that leads to each cost/benefit impact), objective (unbiased, including everything that is material, good or bad) and systematic (have good models and rules for finding and summarizing values). Financial talent also helps as does a solid grasp of the interplay between IT capacity, service levels, user needs, and IT resource requirements".

Today's business case frameworks (BCF), such as document guidelines and spreadsheet templates, support business case development (BCD) to some extent, but have several limitations. The aim of the study at hand is to better understand challenges in BCD, to describe the limitations of BCF and to reveal opportunities for improvement of BCF. This should provide a starting point for user-centred designers and engineers who aim to develop better tool support for BCD.

The structure of this paper is as follows: in **Section 2.2**, a background for BC, BCD and BCF is provided. In **Section 2.3**, the research approach is described. **Section 2.4** summarizes the results of the case study. Based on that, **Section 2.5** proposes three solution areas for BCD support. **Section 2.6** reports on the results of interviews with BC developers and **Section 2.7** concludes this paper.

2.2 Background

2.2.1 Business Cases

A BC is a recommendation to decision makers to take a particular course of action for the organisation, supported by an analysis of benefits, costs and risks (...), with an explanation of how it can best be implemented (Gambles, 2009). It documents the relevant facts and situational analysis, key metrics, financial analysis, allows different projects with different goals to be compared and contrasted and serves as a communication tool (Gliedman, Leganza, Visitacion, Cecere, & Brown, 2004). The BC can be seen as the successor of cost-benefit analysis (King & Schrems, 1978; Sassone, 1988). Whereas the principles of cost-benefit analysis mainly come from accounting and are thus financially oriented, BCs put additional emphasis on strategic benefits, indirect costs, risks, social and organisational factors, i.e., the 'intangible' criteria.

BCs commonly appear as spreadsheets, sometimes accompanied by presentations or explanatory documents. They may be presented by the project leader (BC 'owner' or 'champion') to senior management, which is responsible for prioritizing BCs and making investment decisions. This way, the BC can be used to decide about investment before project execution ('ex-ante'), to evaluate progress during project execution and to determine to which extent the proposed value of the investment has been realized after project execution ('ex-post') (J. Ward, Taylor, & Bond, 1996).

2.2.2 Business Case Development

To the best of the author's knowledge there is no definition of business case development (BCD) in literature. Therefore the following working definition is proposed: *Business case development is the process of realising the business case as an 'artefact', by gathering and analysing data to define and valuate evaluation criteria, presenting it in documents, spreadsheets or presentations. It may take place before project execution for investment appraisal, during project execution for continuous monitoring and control, or after project execution for organizational learning.* This definition is quite similar to the definition of IS evaluation by Farbey et al. (1999b, p. 205), but focuses on the creation of the BC as an artefact, rather than the organizational process in which it is used.

There are many problems in BCD, such as those identified by Farbey et al. (1993), and most of them are still prevalent today, cf. (J. Ballantine & Stray, 1998; Berghout & Remenyi, 2005; Farbey et al., 1999a; Irani, 2002; Walter & Spitta, 2004). Ward et al. (2008) found in a study among over 100 European companies that 65% of respondents indicated their organizations were not satisfied with their ability to identify all benefits, with 69% reporting that they do not adequately quantify and place a 'value' on the benefits for inclusion in the BC. 38% of the respondents believed their current approach led them to frequently overstate the benefits to obtain funding.

2.2.3 Business Case Frameworks

A BCF is a set of guidelines, methods, templates or tools to support BCD. *Guidelines* often come in the form of document or presentation outlines, which loosely describe the required components of a BC, e.g., (Cardin, Cullen, Symons, & Belanger, 2007; Gliedman et al., 2004), and what metrics to use, depending on the requirements of the BC evaluators of the organization in which the BCF is used. Although these guidelines can be helpful and hardly limit BC developers in their expressiveness, they mainly concern the 'what', i.e., declarative BCD knowledge, and not the 'how', i.e., procedural BCD knowledge. One of the reasons for this is that most BCF have been designed to ease the life of BC evaluators rather than BC developers. As such, guidelines often do not provide much guidance on how the BC developer should achieve the desired results.

Methods or *techniques* such as listed by Irani et al. (1997, p. 699) or Renkema and Berghout (1997, p. 10) have the potential to support BC developers in the 'how' of BCs, but are sometimes rather generic descriptions, see e.g., (J. Ward et al., 2008), and need to be combined with more specific methods, see e.g., (Love, Irani, & Edwards, 2004), to identify and quantify the benefits, costs and risks for a project in a specific industry. Moreover, it is a question which method is most suitable in which case (Farbey, Land, & Targett, 1995; Joshi & Pant, 2008).

Like guidelines, *templates* are often developed and kept company internal. Templates are built for specific types of projects, so companies may use multiple templates. Mostly they come in the form of a spreadsheet with a rigid structure and strict content requirements, thus limiting the expressiveness of the developer. However, such templates ensure the homogeneity among BCs and the investment alternatives within them. Homogeneity enables BC evaluators to work more efficiently, as they can then more easily compare and prioritize BCs.

Tools or applications often come in the form of advanced spreadsheets, e.g., with data import and export functionality, or controls that trigger changes between different worksheets of the spreadsheet. Tools mainly aim to increase the efficiency of BCD and are often highly organization and project type-specific. Public templates and tools, e.g., (BusinessCase.com, 2010; SolutionMatrix Ltd., 2010) – commercial or for free – are often generic implementations of traditional financials investment appraisal methods, such as Return-on-Investment (ROI), Net Present Value (NPV) and Payback Time (Brealey & Myers, 1988), without much support for the real challenges for BC developers: the identification of benefits and the quantification of intangible benefits and indirect costs (J. Ballantine & Stray, 1998; Irani, 2002; J. Ward et al., 2008).

2.3 Research Approach

The research approach of the study at hand is based on methodological triangulation, a concept from social science, described by Denzin (2006). **Figure 2.1** gives a simplified overview of the approach. It was an iterative process, in which the insights gradually transitioned from challenges/problems to requirements/solutions. The case study led to a better understanding of challenges in BCD (**Section 2.4**). Based on that, three high-level solution areas were defined as a vision for the development of better BCF (**Section 2.5**). Finally, interviews were conducted to refine the solution areas in more detail and to derive priorities for future research (**Section 2.6**). Each of these steps will be described in more detail in a following section.

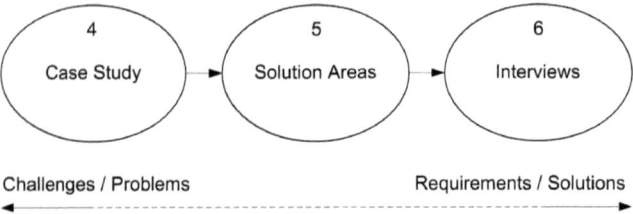

Figure 2.1: Overview of the research approach

2.4 Case Study

One of the authors was involved in the development of a BC at a global IT company. The BC proposed the 'productisation' of a concept for a new software solution, which would involve software development, marketing, sales and support of the solution. Participant observation (DeWalt, DeWalt, & Wayland, 1998; Douglas, 1976) was applied during the BCD project, which took about 14 months. Notes were taken of all meetings and telephone calls, which resulted in a large amount of case data. Particular attention was given to challenges in BCD. To communicate these challenges in an effective manner they have been incorporated in a fictional, but realistic story. Story telling is a common technique in user-centred design to better understand the needs of people and to express them concretely (Norman & Draper, 1986). The remainder of this section will first present the story and then extract the BCD challenges. **Figure 2.2** visualizes the story as a BPMN process model.

(Start of BCD story)

Marta is 35 and works as a product manager in a large IT company. Marta has an innovative idea for a new product that could potentially be sold by the company. To get approval from the company's senior management for productisation of the idea, Marta needs a BC. The BC should consist of an explanation of the benefits for the company to extend its product portfolio, a cost model and an analysis of potential risks.

As the company's senior management is most sensitive to financial arguments (e.g., potential revenue of the new product), one of the most important things to find out is how many customers would be interested in the new product. Therefore Marta asks Peter, 28, one of her team members with experience in business analysis and marketing, to collect the required information. To give Peter a head start, Marta provides him with an old BC for another idea that has been productized in the past.

Peter decides to start by analyzing the old BC. It consists of a market potential estimation and a cost model in a spreadsheet. There is also a document which explains several intangible benefits (i.e., benefits that could not be quantified) and that points to the spreadsheet for the tangible benefit: expected revenue for the new product, based on a market potential estimation.

The spreadsheet appears to contain an interesting structure to distinguish between cross-selling and up-selling opportunities. Unfortunately, Peter can not completely understand the reasoning behind the calculation methods. Therefore he asks Marta for the name of the author of the BC, but learns that 'Tim' is no longer with the company. Thus, Peter designs a new spreadsheet with an adapted calculation method that is workable for him.

After that, Peter calls David, a software developer. With David he estimates the required development effort required to turn Marta's idea into a full-fledged product. He also learns that the company currently has about 300 existing customers that would potentially be interested in the new product. As the company does not exactly know how many customers are really using the existing product, this number is an estimate that is based on the number of error messages that the company receives.

Peter then calls Eva, a sales colleague. Eva says that there are about 700 existing customers, of whom 80% would probably be interested in the new product, as long as the product is interoperable with legacy systems.

After that, Peter builds a first draft of the market potential estimation spreadsheet. As Eva has a closer relationship with the company's customers than David, Peter decides to use the numbers that Eva suggested. To calculate the revenue potential, Peter multiplies the expected number of customers with his estimation for the number of required licenses per customer and the price per license. Actually, Peter is applying a license-based pricing model, but he is not aware of that.

A few days later, Peter calls Stephan, from the pricing strategy team. Peter explains to Stephan that he now has some understanding of the market for the new product. However, to calculate the potential revenue for the company, he roughly needs to know the price that can be charged for it. Stephan explains that pricing is a complicated process and that it is more likely that a usage-based pricing model will be applied. Stephan also provides Peter with some prices of similar products that are already on the market. Finally, Peter changes the pricing model, finishes the market potential estimation and presents it to Marta.

(End of BCD story)

When analysing the story, one sees that Peter, the BC developer, would like to reuse the market potential estimation template from the earlier BC. Unfortunately he can not understand the reasoning behind it, nor get in contact with the earlier developer. Therefore he needs to change the calculation method. As a consequence, he may be using a less reliable quantification method and it will be harder to compare the new BC with the earlier one.

Peter receives inconsistent information from David and Eva regarding the number of customers. He decides to replace David's input with Eva's information, but thereby looses the perspective of David, which may be appreciated by BC evaluators later on. Another issue is that the number of customers is bound to change. In order to keep the BC accurate, Peter needs to update it continuously, based on the information that he receives.

Peter needs to apply a pricing model. At first he applies a license-based pricing model, but later on it appears that he should be using a usage-based pricing model. Such a switch is not uncommon in the iterative BCD process. However, Peter needs to develop and change the calculation methods himself. This is less efficient than if pre-defined pricing models could be applied and switched on the fly. Moreover, the 'home grown' method may be less reliable and will make the BC less comparable with other BCs.

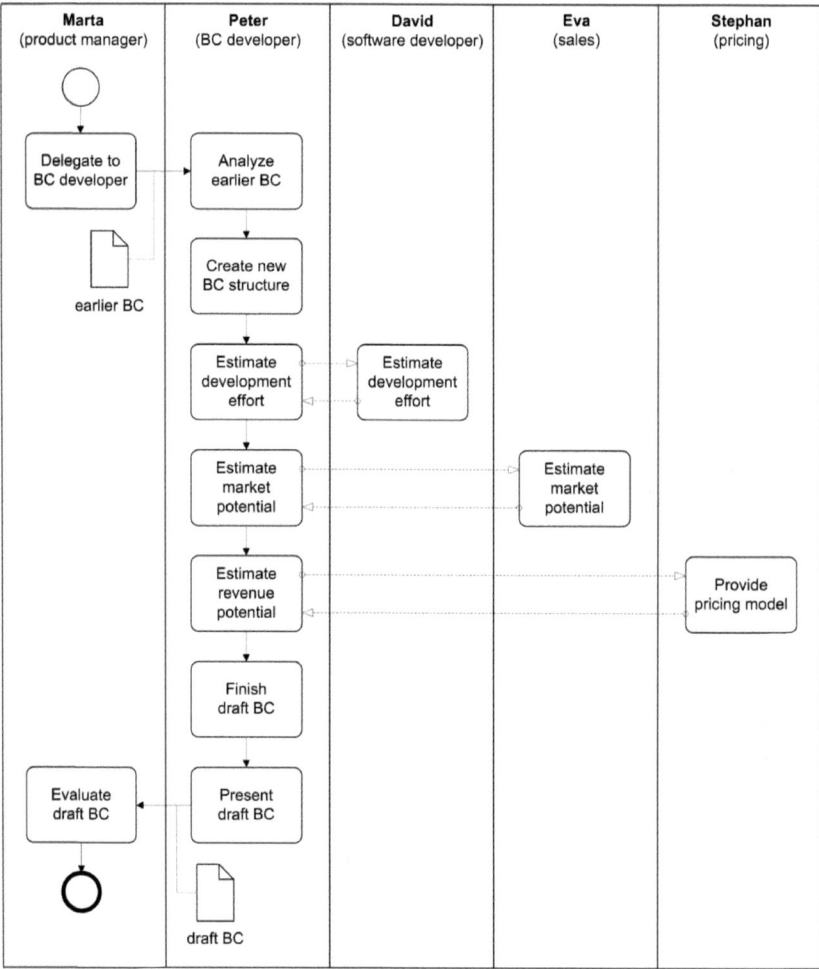

Figure 2.2: BCD story, modelled in BPMN

2.5 Solution Areas

2.5.1 Reuse

The content of earlier BCs can be valuable. For example, when estimating the payback period for an investment, it is possible to take an average of the payback periods of several earlier BCs. This way, data from earlier BCs could be used to evaluate the probability that a newer BCs is reliable. The reuse of BC content is about reusing benefit, cost and risk factors and their values. The reuse of BC structure is about reusing methods for ordering, aggregating and manipulating factors and values. Current BCF support reuse to some extent. Especially the strict spreadsheet templates enable – or enforce – the reuse of structure. However, these templates are often inflexible and unusable for unexpected applications. Moreover, the reuse of content is very limited as spreadsheets are often unconnected files, residing on a developers' individual computers. The authors envision BCF that may look and feel like ordinary spreadsheets, but which allow BC developers to interact with content that is partly stored in central databases and which support the development of reusable components of content and structure. This enables the reuse of content and structure among BCs and among BC developers.

2.5.2 Adaptation

Current BCF often only support adaptation in the sense that BC developers need to put in manual effort to do so. The authors envision BCF that support the (semi-)automatic adaptation of BCs, e.g., by standardizing user input parameters, such as the pricing model, and by synchronizing BC content with real-time dynamic data sources such as the databases in enterprise resource planning (ERP) systems. This will not just increase the efficiency of BCD, but will also make BCs more useful on the long-term, e.g., during project execution. Moreover, BCF could show the discrepancy between actual values (ex-post) and estimated values (ex-ante), facilitating project management interventions and organizational learning.

2.5.3 Collaboration

Current BCF, especially spreadsheet-based BCF that are not accompanied by explanatory text documents, hardly support collaboration. Although it is possible to send around documents and ask people for input, the chances are high that other BC developers and evaluators do not understand the underlying assumptions, the calculation methods used, or have difficulties with judging the reliability of information. The authors envision BCF that support collaborative BCD across development projects, across organizations and across time, e.g., by making assumptions explicit, by clarifying the source of content, by clarifying the quality of content, by enabling different viewpoints on the same piece of information and by providing ways to share and protect information. This will not just increase the efficiency of BCD, but will also make BCs more reliable for evaluators and support today's collaborative ways of doing business.

2.6 Interviews

To refine the identification of challenges and requirements in the reuse, adaptation and collaboration solution areas, 15 topics were identified (**Table 2.1**). Each of the topics was discussed during the eight structured interviews that were conducted with BC developers, who were invited among the industrial companies participating in three research projects (ADiWa, 2010; Aletheia, 2010; SemProM, 2010). They were selected, because they were, or would be, developing BCs for new IS that were under investigation in those research projects. The interviewees represented different industries: high tech (3x), information technology (2x), logistics (2x), automotive (1x). The interviewees had experience in BCD, but were not necessarily experts, and were representative for the population of target users of the advanced BCF.

Each interview consisted of three main parts:

- "Business cases in your organization": This part investigated the development and use of BCs in the organization and the role of the interviewee in that matter.
- "Business case frameworks in your organization": This part investigated the use of BCF in the organization, the role of the interviewee in that matter and the interest in a BCF that would be specific for the technology domain being investigated in the respective research project (Aletheia, SemProM, or ADiWa).
- "Challenges & Requirements": This part investigated the 15 topics.

The 15 topics were investigated in the interviews along three dimensions: the relevance dimension, the challenge dimension and the support dimension. The *relevance dimension* was used to investigate the required properties of BCs (not of BCF). E.g., a respondent could argue that 'information quality' is a relevant property of a BC – or not. It is assumed that relevant properties should be obtainable through the use of BCF, or in the case that they can not be obtained through the use of a BCF, the BCF should at least not prevent that.

Topic	Reuse	Adap.	Colla.	Relevance		Challenge		Support	
				Mean	SD	Mean	SD	Mean	SD
Reuse of Content	X			1,14	0,90	0,43	0,53	1,29	0,49
Reuse of Structure	X			1,63	0,52	-0,13	1,25	1,75	0,46
Aggregation	X			1,14	1,21	1,50	1,22	0,50	0,84
Comparison	X			1,50	0,76	1,13	1,13	0,86	1,07
Provider vs. Customer Persp.	X			1,38	0,74	0,88	1,36	1,13	0,99
Market Potential Estimation	X			1,75	0,46	1,50	0,53	1,00	1,31
Changing Assumptions		X		1,14	1,46	0,14	1,57	1,00	1,73
Product Innovation Lifecycle		X		1,25	0,71	0,17	0,98	0,57	0,98
Business Model Adaptivity		X		1,38	1,06	2,00	0,00	0,60	1,67
Clarifying Reasoning			X	1,88	0,35	1,25	0,89	1,38	1,06
Stakeholders' Opinions			X	1,00	1,41	0,00	0,82	0,75	1,58
Information Sources			X	1,50	0,53	1,00	1,07	1,00	0,58
Information Quality			X	1,63	0,52	1,13	0,83	1,43	0,53
Sharing			X	0,86	1,07	0,33	1,21	0,43	1,40
Security			X	1,50	0,76	-0,50	0,84	0,57	0,98

Table 2.1: Research topics within the solution areas and the scores from the interviews

The *challenge dimension* was used to investigate the complexity of the BCD task required to obtain (BC developer) or judge (BC evaluator) the respective property of the BC. E.g., irrespective of the *relevance* of the topic, the interviewee could argue that 'determining information quality' is a challenging BCD task. It is assumed that challenging tasks are good candidates for BCF support. The *support dimension* was used to investigate the need for BCF support for the respective BCD task. This dimension implicitly measured a mixture of the respondent's hope that a BCF would support the BCD task and the respondent's belief in the ability of a BCF to support the task, which in turn is based on the respondent's knowledge of state-of-the-art BCF and his/her imagination. Thus, the authors were aware of the inaccuracy of the dimension, which was therefore mainly used to provoke responses regarding which BCD tasks could/should be automated and which could/should not.

For each topic, for each dimension, a statement was defined. E.g., for the topic Information Quality the statements were:

- "The quality of information in a business case should be clear." (relevance dimension)
- "Determining the quality of information in a business case is a challenge." (challenge dimension)
- "A BCF should support the determination of the quality of information." (support dimension)

The interviewees were asked to what extent they agreed with the statements. A five point Likert-scale ranging from -2 ('strongly disagree') to +2 ('strongly agree'), including a 'no opinion' option was used. **Table 2.1** shows the mean scores and standard deviations, all with a sample size of eight. Based on the mean scores, **Figure 2.3** was drawn. Each dot represents one of the 15 topics. The size of the dot represents the relevance of the topic (note that the scores have been categorized so that there are only three different sizes, which makes it easier to see the difference in size). The vertical axis represents the challenge dimension. The challenging topics need to be understood better and thus require further investigation. The horizontal axis represents the support dimension. If BCF support is needed, supporting functionality should be implemented.

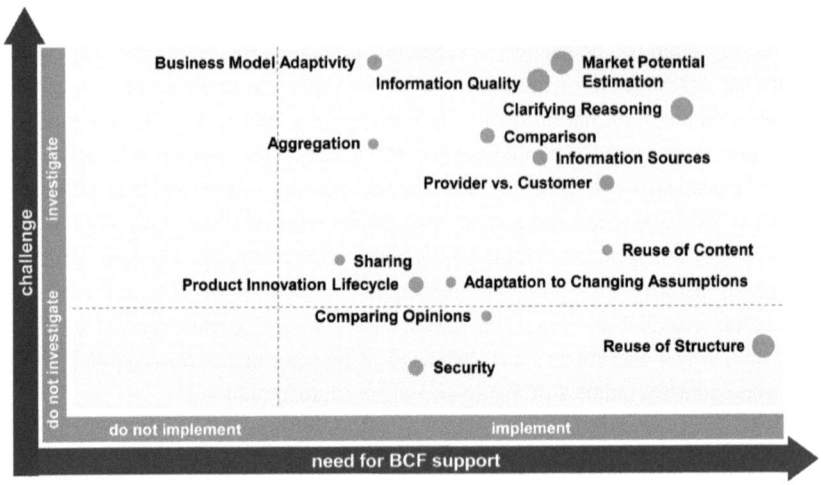

Figure 2.3: The 15 topics structured along the three dimensions, based on the interviews

Four topics, Market Potential Estimation (MPE), Information Quality (IQ), Clarifying Reasoning (CR) and Reuse of Structure (RS), fall in the highest relevance category. Three of them, MPE, IQ, CR, are both challenging and require BCF support according to the interviewees. One topic, RS, only requires BCF support but is not perceived as challenging. The remainder of this section will describe the results of the interviews regarding these four topics in more detail.

Market Potential Estimation (MPE) is about estimating the sales and revenue potential for a certain product or service, offered to a specific market segment. MPE is an issue for companies who sell products or services and thus make 'provider perspective BCs'. The interviewees strongly agreed with the relevance of the topic and stated that it can be very challenging unless you have a lot of experience in the respective market. They also strongly agreed with the need for BCF support for this challenge.

Information Quality (IQ) is about making sure that BCs are reliable and have predictive value. Gathering reliable data can be hard, doing quantifications on that data can be hard, but also determining the quality of information provided by others can be hard, e.g., a precise number may give an accurate impression, but may be a rough estimate in reality. Interviewees agree with the relevance of the topic, agree with the challenges and agree with the need for BCF support.

Clarifying Reasoning (CR) is about enabling evaluators and other stakeholders of the BC to understand the reasoning behind estimations. That way, those people may be able to better determine the quality of information and if certain estimates still hold, or if conditions have changed in such a way that estimates need to be revised. Interviewees strongly agree that this is relevant and agree that it can be very challenging, depending on the stakeholders. They also strongly agree that BCF support is needed for this.

Reuse of Structure (RS) is about enabling BC developers to reapply the same criteria and quantification methods as used in other BCs, thereby improving the efficiency of BCD and the reliability and comparability of BCs. Interviewees agree that reuse of content and structure is relevant. Although they do not see this as a challenge, they strongly agree with the need for BCF support. However, they warn that it should always remain possible to make adjustments to templates, that reuse may lead to more mistakes, that reuse may lead to the comparison of 'apples and eggs' and that reuse only works for the same types of BCs.

2.7 Conclusion

The aim of this study was to better understand challenges in BCD, to describe limitations of BCF and to reveal opportunities for improvement of BCF. In order to achieve this, participant observation was applied during a 14 month BCD project at a global IT company (the 'case study'). The derived challenges in BCD were presented in the form of a story. Next, three solution areas for improvement of BCF were defined: reuse, adaptation and collaboration. These areas were refined to 15 topics, which were investigated through interviews with BC developers along the relevance, challenge and support dimensions. The interviewees argued that more support is especially needed for market potential estimation, determining information quality, clarifying reasoning and the reuse of structure. This provides a starting point for user-centred researchers, designers, and engineers who aim to develop better tool support for BCD.

The limitations of this study are that the case study was executed with only one company and that only eight interviews were conducted. Overall, the findings presented in this paper should be considered as explorative. The existing body of knowledge on IS evaluation is relevant, despite focusing more on the organizational challenges in the evaluation of IS, than on the individual challenges of BC developers in practice.

Future work should move towards the design of an advanced BCF prototype. Usability experiments should be conducted to test whether the prototype supports the efficiency and effectiveness of BCD and if it enhances the satisfaction of BC developers when working with the BCF.

3 Reuse in Business Case Development: Arguments, Challenges and Guidelines

Bart-Jan van Putten	Humboldt-Universität zu Berlin, SAP Research Dresden
Nadja Schubert	Humboldt-Universität zu Berlin, SAP Research Dresden
Emilija Gjoncheska	Humboldt-Universität zu Berlin

Relevance for this Dissertation

This study aimed to investigate suitable components for reuse, arguments for reuse, challenges in reuse and guidelines for reuse. This way, it provides an overview of IS investment evaluation literature and reveals that the topic of reuse is largely unexplored.

Collaborations

Ms. Schubert and Ms. Gjoncheska were students participating in the Advanced Information Systems Seminar at Humboldt-Universität zu Berlin under my supervision. During the seminar they did a literature review which I used as the basis for what eventually turned into the paper at hand.

Abstract

Reusing evaluation criteria and valuation methods is a promising way to make it easier to develop reliable business cases for IS investments. Better support for reuse can support the comparison and prioritization of business cases, can make it easier for decision makers to understand them and it can facilitate learning. However, the idea of reuse seems to be rather unexplored in the IS evaluation literature. This paper therefore provides a starting point for further research by gathering what is written, either implicitly or explicitly, with respect to reusable business case components, arguments for reuse, challenges in reuse and guidelines for reuse. It also introduces three subsequent research projects that show how the challenges in reuse may be partly overcome.

3.1 Introduction

For decades, determining the value and success of information systems (IS) has been high on the agendas of researchers, cf. (King & Schrems, 1978; Davis, 1989; Urbach et al., 2009; Schryen, 2010). Many IS investments are strategic in nature, have long-term, hard to quantify benefits and incur indirect costs (Irani, 2002). 68% of IS projects cope with problems when having to identify the potential benefits of the investment, while 85% have problems with their quantification (J. Ballantine & Stray, 1999). More challenges have been identified for IS investment evaluation (ISE), in advance of investment (Walter & Spitta, 2004) as well as during and after the IS project (Brynjolfsson & Hitt, 1996). Unfortunately, ISE does not seem to have improved much: *"Many of the problems identified by Farbey et al. (1993) are still prevalent today"* (Irani & Love, 2008).

To support ISE, in most organisations some kind of business case (BC) is developed. A BC is *"a recommendation to decision makers to take a particular course of action for the organisation, supported by an analysis of benefits, costs and risks"* (Gambles, 2009). Business case development (BCD) is the process of realising the BC as an 'artefact', by gathering and analysing data to define and valuate evaluation criteria, presenting it in documents, spreadsheets or presentations. It may take place before project execution for investment appraisal, during project execution for monitoring and control, or after project execution for organizational learning (anonymized reference).

Although it would be naive to believe that the challenges in ISE can be overcome easily, it seems promising to focus research on a subset of ISE, namely the *practice* of BCD (Bacon, 1992; Serafeimidis & Smithson, 2000). In earlier research, we identified four main opportunities for supporting BC developers in addressing their challenges (anonymized reference). One of those opportunities is supporting the reuse of BC components. After analyzing the structure of BCs, it appeared that *criteria* (Bacon, 1992), such as benefits, costs and risks, see e.g., (Irani & Love, 2000), and *methods*, i.e., ways to put a qualitative, quantitative non-financial, or financial value on these criteria, see e.g., (Renkema & Berghout, 1997), are the main recurring components of BCs and thus candidates for reuse.

Imagine an old BC on the use of barcodes for tracking items in the supply chain. Due to the use of barcodes, it may become easier for warehouse workers to have fairly precise data on stock levels, which may in turn make it possible to decrease those stock levels and thus decrease warehousing costs. Criteria in this BC may be 'ease of identification', 'stock level' and 'warehousing costs'. Some years later, when developing a BC for the use of radio-frequency identification (RFID), the BC developer would again need to decide which criteria to use. Rather than defining all criteria from scratch, the developer may reuse criteria from earlier BCs. In this case, the criteria 'ease of identification', 'stock level' and 'warehousing costs' would probably also be relevant for the BC for RFID.

When trying to estimate the values of the criteria selected for use in the new BC, a BC developer may spend days on defining quantification methods, which is especially hard for the intangible benefits and indirect costs (Irani, 2002). Instead, he/she may also reuse and refine existing methods, thereby building on the knowledge of others. This way, the reused components may come from earlier BCs which are stored in a structured and accessible manner, but they may just as well come from databases which are specifically designed for the purpose of reuse, e.g., taxonomies of criteria and methods with browse and query functionality for their retrieval (Irani, Ghoneim, et al., 2006).

Researching how BC components can be made reusable thus seems to be a plausible strategy to address some of the major challenges in the field of ISE. However, the topic seems to be rather unexplored. Therefore, the objectives of the study at hand are to get a better understanding of reuse in BCD, by identifying which BC components are considered for reuse in literature (**Section 3.3**), investigating arguments for reuse (**Section 3.5**), defining the challenges that may hinder reuse (**Section 3.6**) and describing guidelines for reuse (**Section 3.7**). The research method, a literature review, is described in the next section.

3.2 Research Method

A literature review was performed, following recommendations from Webster and Watson (2002) and Vom Brocke et al. (2009). Initially, a search was done in the following databases: ACM Digital Library, IEEE Xplore, ISI Web of Knowledge, JSTOR, ScienceDirect, SpringerLink, Wiley InterScience, Emerald, and EBSCO. The following keywords were used: *business case, cost-benefit analysis, benefit-cost analysis, cost-effectiveness analysis, cost-justification, economic appraisal, investment appraisal, investment decision making, {IS, IT, ICT} evaluation, return-on-investment (ROI)*. All available database content was considered, irrespective of the year of publication. The search returned a large number of results. Many papers described business cases for specific technologies or *ex-post* IS evaluation, i.e., focusing on the performance of IS after implementation. Due to this study's focus on BCD, which mainly takes place *ex-ante*, i.e., before investment and implementation, that term was combined with the aforementioned keywords in an additional search. Many of the retrieved papers were read. Simultaneously, additional literature was retrieved through backwards searching the bibliographies of the papers and forward searching through lists of publications on the homepages of the papers' authors. This process repeated itself several times leading to a set of over 100 papers which were all read. For the literature review at hand, out of this larger corpus, a sample of papers was selected based on the following criteria:

- Relevance to the research objectives;
- Quality, determined through appearance in scholarly journals, citations, preceding publications on a similar topic by the same authors (it is assumed that authors who publish more often in a certain area have more expertise in that area), and personal judgement;
- Heterogeneity, covering different journals, authors, research methods, and topic areas.

Before re-reading the selected papers and analyzing them in detail, the initial concepts for analysis were defined and placed in the 'concept matrix' (Salipante, Notz, & Bigelow, 1982; Webster & Watson, 2002) in **Figure B.1, Figure B.2, Figure B.3**. During the analysis, changes were made to the concepts of analysis, a few were removed and a few were added. Some papers needed to be re-analyzed based on the new concepts. During the analysis, interesting explanations and citations were collected in a text document, which was structured along the concepts. By combining the findings for related concepts, e.g., 'usage' and 'acceptance' and filtering out the most relevant citations, the document finally transformed into the study at hand. It needs to be emphasized that the concepts were only investigated with respect to reuse. E.g., while many authors state that there is a need for more *effective* IS investment decision making, only few (implicitly) state that reuse could be a way to achieve that. It also needs to be noted that the Methodology columns in the concept matrix indicate the *main* methodology applied. E.g., while all papers incorporate an analysis of literature, only some present a literature review that meets the standards as defined by Webster and Watson (2002). The remainder of this paper will describe the findings from the literature review along the research objectives and concepts.

3.3 Reusable Components

There is a variety of components that can be included in a BC, among which: triggers for the proposal, a description of the solution being proposed and the problem being solved, an overview of stakeholders and responsibilities (Gliedman et al., 2004). However, the core of a BC is a set of criteria to evaluate the proposed project and the associated investment. Those criteria are commonly classified as benefits, costs, and risks. To support decision making, BC developers aim to provide a value for each of the criteria. The value may reflect the status quo or the estimated future situation, in an absolute manner, or relative to the status quo. The value can be qualitative, quantitative, financial, or non-financial. To estimate the value, a wide range of methods can be applied, such as benchmarking (J. Ward et al., 2008).

3.3.1 Criteria

A criterion is *"a standard on which a judgment or decision may be based"* (Merriam-Webster, 2011). In the context of ISE, *"criteria are concerned with the financial and non-financial justification used in proposing, evaluating, and deciding upon the project or investment. (...) [They] have significance for a number of reasons. First, the criteria used or not used, and the way in which they are applied or not applied, significantly impact the effectiveness with which IS investment decisions are made. They determine whether the 'right' projects are selected. Second, the criteria are significant for the organization's finance and management accounting function in terms of their role in maximizing return on investment and their involvement in the cost vs. benefit analysis that may precede an IST capital investment decision"* (Bacon, 1992). Bacon (1992) investigated the use of decision criteria in selecting IS investments. Fifteen criteria were used – six financial, six management, and three development – in a survey undertaken in 1990 of 80 major companies in four countries: the United States, Britain, Australia, and New Zealand. The companies were asked to indicate which criteria they use, the percentage of projects to which each criterion is applied, and the overall ranking in terms of total project value for each criterion. By determining the fifteen criteria for use in the survey, Bacon implicitly hypothesized that there would be reuse of those criteria among the different companies, coming from 11 different industries. This indeed appeared to be the case, ranging from 88% of the companies using the criterion 'Support of Explicit Business Objectives' to 8% using the criterion 'Profitability Index Method'. Later research by Ballantine and Stray (1998) had a rather similar approach in which the use of 'techniques' was surveyed among 97 companies from 12 different industry categories. The technique 'Cost-benefit Analysis' was used in 72% of the cases, while the 'Productivity Index' was one of the least popular ones with only 2% usage. **Figure B.1**, **Figure B.2**, **Figure B.3** show that most selected papers present such lists of criteria, thus (mostly implicitly) arguing that there is reuse of criteria among different companies and industries.

3.3.2 Methods

A method is *"a way, technique, or process of or for doing something"* (Merriam-Webster, 2011). In the context of ISE, we could not find a suitable definition of the term, nor does it seem to be used consistently. Some authors speak of 'techniques' rather than 'methods' (J. Ballantine & Stray, 1998). Others use the terms 'method' and 'approach' intermingled (Berghout & Remenyi, 2005). Some even alternate between the terms 'method', 'technique' and 'procedure' (Farbey, Land, & Targett, 1992), without explaining the difference between the terms, if any difference is meant to be conveyed at all. To provide some clarity for the ISE context, we propose the following working definition: *a method is a way to assign a value to a criterion*. The process of selecting criteria and combining different methods, based on the organizational context, is what we would rather call a technique.

According to Farbey et al. (1999a), *"there are a great number of methods on offer. These range from the general, for example, Return on Investment (ROI),* (Brealey & Myers, 1988) *to the IT specific, for example, Return on Management* (Strassmann, 1985). *They include methods relying on quantitative assessment of costs, benefits and risks such as Information Economics* (M. M. Parker et al., 1988). *There are also 'softer' methods for identifying and assessing benefits, for example Multi-Criteria, Multi-Objective methods* (Chandler, 1982) *as well as those based on modelling and experiments, for example systems dynamics models* (Wolstenholme, Henderson, & Gavine, 1993)*"*.

To further complicate things, there is often no clear difference between a criterion and a method. In general, a criterion deals with *what* one wants to measure, i.e., it is declarative, while a method deals with *how* it could be measured, i.e., it is procedural. For example, the term 'Return on Investment' (ROI), may be used to refer to the criterion as an indicator for the higher level criterion 'profitability', leaving the precise valuation method unspecified. However, the term may also be used to refer to the specific formula 'ROI = (return - investment) / investment * 100%'. The factors 'return' and 'investment' may in turn be seen as criteria by themselves and may be associated with other methods for their valuation. Thus, criteria and methods can be used recursively.

In the remainder of this paper, we will mainly use the term 'criterion'. Only when we explicitly mean the procedure for valuation we will use the term 'method'.

3.4 Reuse of Criteria and Methods

Reuse is the act of using something again (Merriam-Webster, 2011). In the field of computer science, software reuse is the use of existing software artefacts or knowledge to create new software. *"It is a key method for significantly improving software quality and productivity"* (Frakes & Terry, 1996). We believe that in the area of BCD, reuse can have the same effect. It has the potential to improve BCD effectiveness, i.e., the quality of the resulting BCs, as well as BCD efficiency, i.e., the ease of creating them. Different types of reuse may be defined, e.g.:

- Intra-organizational vs. inter-organizational: components may be reused from a BC in the same organization, or from another organization, such as a partner in the value chain.
- Intra-industrial vs. inter-industrial: components may be reused from a BC developed in the same industry or a different industry.
- Synchronous vs. a-synchronous: components may be reused from a BC developed simultaneously or from a BC which has been developed in the past.
- Individual vs. collective: components may be reused from a BC developed by the same BC developer or by other people.

There are probably more ways to classify reuse. However, as reuse seems to be an unexplored idea in the reviewed literature, this paper does not limit itself to any of these specific types of reuse. We investigate arguments for reuse and challenges in reuse irrespective of the aforementioned types. However, we do focus on two specific types of reusable components: criteria and methods. These components are the core of every BC and thus commonly used and also most likely to be *re*-used.

3.5 Arguments for Reuse

3.5.1 Efficiency & Effectiveness

Efficiency is about the time, effort and resources an organization needs for all processes related to the evaluation of IS. Improving BCD efficiency is an argument for reuse, as reuse may make it easier for BC developers to identify suitable criteria and methods for their BCs (Irani, Ghoneim, et al., 2006). In particular, the reuse of complex methods for uncommon criteria may avoid defining such methods from scratch. Effectiveness is about whether 'the right' decisions are taken, which may never become entirely clear due to the often late, indirect and interdependent effects (Walter & Spitta, 2004). BCD effectiveness is the degree to which the BC supports decision making, i.e., if it provides the right information and if the information is of sufficient quality, e.g., in terms of reliability and structure (Bacon, 1992). Improving BCD effectiveness is an argument for reuse, as reuse allows BC developers to build upon the work of others. Methods may be selected which have been successfully applied to other BCs in the past (L. Willcocks & Lester, 1991). Moreover, having a comprehensive collection of reusable criteria prevents important criteria from being overlooked, or from being deliberately omitted because they are too hard to quantify (Irani, Ghoneim, et al., 2006).

3.5.2 Comparison & Benchmarking

When the same criteria and methods are used during different ISE activities, the BCs that apply those criteria and methods become more homogeneous and comparable. Comparison with prior BCs and benchmarking allows decision makers to determine if the BC is realistic whereas comparison with other prospective BCs allows decision makers to set investment priorities. Comparison may be done by decision makers without any methodological guidance, but *"becomes even more feasible when there is a benefit tracking program in operation for IS projects, because there can then be feedback of cost and benefit information from prior to prospective systems investments. (...)The revenue estimates and associated costs might then be monitored, and future estimates could benefit through the data captured and learning gained from such prior projects"* (Bacon, 1992). In a similar manner, Walter and Spitta (2004) state: *"In-depth research on the integration of ex-ante and ex-post evaluation, for instance by establishing facilities for the storage of evaluation data, is also needed to enable a 'holistic' ISE"*.

When BCs use similar criteria and methods, average values may be calculated based on a collection of BCs. Such 'benchmarks' may be defined per criterion for specific companies, industries, business functions, or business processes. They can be used as proxies for more precise data which may be too costly or difficult to obtain. Moreover, decision makers may require BC developers to show the offset between their prognoses and accepted benchmarks. Although benchmarking was hardly covered in the reviewed literature, it was mentioned as a use case for the balanced scorecard, which is a performance measurement instrument, combining financial, customer, internal processes and learning perspectives (Kaplan & Norton, 1993). The balanced scorecard may also be used in the context of ISE (Milis & Mercken, 2004).

3.5.3 Usage & Acceptance

Some criteria and methods gain in importance because of their broad usage by BC developers and their acceptance by decision makers. When reusing such criteria and methods, BC discussions can focus on the actual values and recommendations, rather than on whether the right criteria and method were used. Several scholars investigated the use of criteria and methods. For example, Ballantine and Stray (1998) found that the *"majority of companies (72%) in the study used cost benefit analysis to appraise the feasibility of the most recent project, the next most popular techniques used being payback and Return on Investment (ROI)/Accounting Rate of Return (ARR)"*. Milis and Mercken (2004) reviewed the aforementioned work, as well as other empirical studies of the use of criteria and methods, and found: *"In practice, the traditional [financial techniques] are by far the most used techniques. They are well-known, well-understood and easy to use. They are primarily focused on financial gains and are developed to maximize shareholder profits. The fact that most decisions on [IS] investments are still taken by the financial department* (Hochstrasser & Griffiths, 1991) *might add to the choice for these traditional techniques"*. A possible argument *against* reuse is that it may lead to 'ritualistic' rather than conscious use of criteria and methods: *"We cannot ignore the extremely high percentage of respondents who feel that the techniques used do not rank as first, second or third in importance in terms of making the investment decision. This is obviously problematic and would seem to suggest that the techniques are being used in a ritualistic manner as opposed to adding any real value to the decision making process"* (J. Ballantine & Stray, 1998).

Rather than reusing criteria and methods because they *are* accepted, they may be reused to make sure that they *become* accepted: *"Senior executives understand that their organization's measurement system strongly affects the behavior of managers and employees"* (Kaplan & Norton, 1992). Thus, *"the scorecard is not just a measurement system; it is a management system to motivate breakthrough competitive performance"* (Kaplan & Norton, 1993). *"The scorecard gives managers a way of ensuring that all levels of the organization understand the long-term strategy and that both departmental and individual objectives are aligned with it"* (Kaplan, 1996).

3.5.4 Understanding & Learning

Certain criteria and methods may be reused because they are easier to understand for BC developers or decision makers. *"The continued use of the Payback Method and its implicit short-term orientation, notwithstanding its theoretical shortcomings, may have some justification. To begin with, it is easy to understand and use"* (Bacon, 1992). This argument may seem to be similar to the Usage & Acceptance argument, however in this case, a BC developer may decide to reuse a criterion or method for its ease of understanding rather than its acceptance. This approach could e.g., be successful when presenting a BC to an audience with little (financial) experience.

When criteria and methods are reused, the amount of new knowledge that needs to be communicated to decision makers is decreased, assuming that they have learned from evaluating similar BCs before. Moreover, because of reuse, BC developers may learn which criteria and methods are suitable for which types of BCs. Developing systems for reuse may also prevent that important criteria are overlooked: *"To carry out a robust comprehensive evaluation process, it is necessary for decision-makers to* not only integrate hidden/indirect costs into the decision-making process but also categorize such costs and ensure that this forms part of the organizational learning for future information systems adoption" (Irani, Ghoneim, et al., 2006). Finally, Kaplan (1996) describes the possibility to learn about the effect of inter-related criteria: *"By supplying a mechanism for strategic feedback and review, the balanced scorecard helps an organization foster a kind of learning often missing in companies: the ability to reflect on inferences and adjust theories about cause-and-effect relationships"*.

3.6 Challenges in Reuse

3.6.1 Formality

Reuse requires that there are earlier BCs and that they are stored in an easily accessible repository. Companies with more formal evaluation processes are more likely to produce BCs and store them for reuse. Unfortunately, formal processes are not guaranteed: *"Just under half (44%) of the respondent companies have clearly defined procedures for evaluating IS/IT investments. Comparing the extent to which formal procedures of evaluation exist with the extent to which evaluation is carried out by organizations, it would appear that informal evaluation seems to play an important role in IS/IT investment decision making within the respondent organizations. This pattern is largely confirmed by Farbey et al. (1992), who report that just over half of the organizations they studied had a formal justification procedure for evaluating IS/IT investments"* (J. A. Ballantine, Galliers, & Stray, 1996). Whereas manual reuse only requires the availability and accessibility of the BCs, tools that automatically recommend components for reuse require all BCs to be stored in a structured and standardized manner, i.e., there needs to be a common, formalized understanding of the domain (anonymized reference).

3.6.2 Reliability

BC developers should aim to reuse the most reliable methods. Those are the methods which have proven to provide estimates that were close to the values actually achieved. This involves several challenges. First, one needs to know the actual values of past projects, which means that the performance of projects needs to be tracked. Second, one needs to compare the actual values to the estimated values, which can be cumbersome without tool support. Third, there are numerous reasons why realistic estimates do not come true in the end: *"Even if the projected benefits are realized, it is difficult to prove that they are attributable to the IST investment"* (Bacon, 1992). In such cases, one may incorrectly conclude that the method was unreliable, while actually an unlikely event occurred, which caused the discrepancy between the values.

3.6.3 Familiarity

Whereas usage and acceptance are arguments for reuse, a lack of familiarity may limit reuse. When a BC developer is unfamiliar with certain criteria and methods he/she will be less likely to apply them. Even worse, when criteria or methods are completely unknown, or when the BC developer does not know where to find them, they cannot be reused. In this context, Willcocks and Lester (1991) state that: *"[Some industries] have not changed their evaluation criteria since they first introduced IT. Respondents explained this in several ways, namely they do not have the necessary techniques for alternative evaluation, or lack confidence in them, and/or prefer to keep tried and tested formulae"*. Ballantine and Stray (1998) also found that familiarity relates to use of the components: *"The reasons for the less widespread use of [sophisticated discounted cash flow techniques for IS/IT evaluation] compared to that reported earlier from the accounting and finance literature are possibly due to a combination of factors. These might include the educational backgrounds and experience of the individuals carrying out the appraisal, the number of respondents who are unfamiliar with the techniques and the fact that the organizational policy may dictate that a particular technique be used"*.

3.6.4 Usability

Usability is the extent to which a product can be used by specified users to achieve specified goals with effectiveness, efficiency and satisfaction in a specified context of use (ISO, 1998). In the context of BCD, we may consider the (re)usability of criteria and methods, i.e., the ease with which relevant criteria and methods can be identified and applied. Criteria and methods may be difficult to identify, because it is not clear yet which benefits, costs and risks the project will incur (Walter & Spitta, 2004), or because reuse is not supported with a structured repository of components used in earlier BCs. Methods may be difficult to apply, e.g., because they require specific financial knowledge, a large number of subordinate steps, or the required data may be hard to obtain: *"The difference between theory and practice in using IRR and NPV may be understandable in that (a) managers may be better able to identify with a rate of return for a project as opposed to a net present value, and (b) the NPV method predicates a (risk-adjusted) discount rate that may be difficult to determine (Butler & Schacter, 1989; Mills, 1988)"* (Bacon, 1992). This is confirmed by Milis and Mercken (2004) who explain why the less sophisticated and less accurate financial methods are used more frequently: *"Companies tend to choose for the payback period and ROI because these techniques are perceived as being 'more easy' then IRR and NPV. Consequently, it is very doubtful that techniques with adjusted cost/benefit estimates or risk sensitivity will become popular"*.

3.6.5 Applicability

Applicability is the degree to which certain criteria and methods are relevant for the new BC in which they could potentially be reused. The good news is that the traditional financial methods, such as Payback Period, Return on Investment, Internal Rate of Return, Net Present Value (Milis & Mercken, 2004), are applicable to almost any project, with the exception of non-profit projects. The bad news is that there seems to be consensus among the authors of the reviewed literature, that financial criteria alone are not enough to invest in the 'right' projects: *"Choosing an evaluation approach that seeks to go beyond the traditional boundaries of financial evaluation is increasingly important, and many factors associated with developing a robust IS requires a business, user and technology context. Therefore, providing decision-makers with direct cost analysis, cash flow projections, financial figures etc, will not be enough, as there are other strategic (grounded in long-term objectives), softer, political and social factors that need to be considered during the evaluation process"* (Irani & Love, 2008). Thus, in addition to the financial ones, other criteria and methods are needed. This is where the main challenge for reuse arises: *"There is no one method which is universally applicable and the problem is to select an appropriate technique to use in a given situation"* (Farbey et al., 1999a).

3.7 Guidelines for Reuse

Two main areas of guidelines for reuse can be distinguished in the reviewed literature. One is the well-known and frequently repeated understanding that financial criteria and methods are not sufficient for effective ISE. Therefore, non-financial criteria and methods should be (re)used as well to incorporate strategic, organizational and human factors in the BC. The other main area describes guidelines for which criteria and methods should be applied to which type of IS project: *"Organizations may need to employ many evaluation methods, each suitable for evaluating certain types of [IS] applications. Indeed, type of [IS] application and type of objective prove to be two of the most influential factors in the choice of evaluation method. Classifying the uses of information systems may therefore be of fundamental importance in selecting suitable evaluation methods"* (Farbey et al., 1995). Farbey's benefits' evaluation ladder (1995), defines eight categories of IS projects. Ranging from 'mandatory changes' to 'business transformation', the applications get more complex, risky and subject to business judgement, but also have greater potential reward: *"The rungs of the ladder reflect different levels of management complexity, uncertainty and business risk, implying in turn a different evaluation emphasis for each rung. Movement up the ladder changes the emphasis from precise quantification to more judgemental evaluation styles. This does not mean that quantification becomes irrelevant, but that it should be mediated by other techniques, for example simulation, to handle the risk. The involvement of senior management is always important but the higher the rung the more issues there are for the senior management team and the more closely involved it should be"* (Farbey et al., 1995). Joshi and Pant (2008) present a framework to help evaluate different IT projects based on the classification of IT projects along a discretionary–mandatory dimension into four types: purely discretionary, mainly discretionary, mainly mandatory, and purely mandatory. E.g., not much time should be spent on the ex-ante evaluation of a purely mandatory IT project, because it needs to be executed anyhow. Other recommendations for matching projects to evaluation approaches are described in Farbey et al., 1992, 1995, 1999; Hochstrasser, 1990; Irani et al., 2006; Milis & Mercken, 2004; M. Parker & R. Benson, 1989; Ross & Beath, 2002; Sassone, 1988; Willcocks & Lester, 1991.

3.8 Ongoing Research

There are different strategies for dealing with the challenges in reuse. Some solutions may be found in changing organizational processes, e.g., to make sure that BCs are reviewed on a regular basis, by all stakeholders, with standardized criteria and methods. Additionally, solutions may be found in improving the tools that BC developers use. We will now give three examples of our ongoing research efforts in the latter direction.

3.8.1 Business Case Ontology

In order to reuse components more easily, BC developers should be able to use existing BCs. An existing BC in a related domain can show which criteria are relevant for that domain, how they can be qualified and sometimes even which values are likely to be achieved. Especially when a BC has been reviewed during and after execution of the project and actual values have been recorded, it can be a valuable source of information. Unfortunately, in most cases, today's BCs are structured rather differently. People do not just use different terminology, but also include different components. Such flexibility is needed, because each industry, company, etc. may have specific requirements for the BC. However, it would be beneficial if the components could be described in a common way on a more abstract level. That way, BC developers could learn from earlier BCs developed by others, even when those people used different tools. It would become easier to identify the potential benefits (and other relevant criteria) of the investment and to define suitable quantification methods. Moreover, when BCs share a common model, it becomes easier for BC evaluators to compare BCs and to prioritize investments. For this purpose, Business Case Ontology (BCO) was developed (anonymized reference). Its core concepts are the criterion, the method and the value. When a database is maintained with BCs that are all structured according to BCO, BC development tools may recommend components for reuse. This idea has been investigated in the research project that will be presented next. Moreover, when different BCs are based on the same criteria and methods, benchmarks may be calculated. Those may be used for goal setting and the validation of values in new BCs.

3.8.2 Recommending Criteria by means of Collaborative Filtering

BCO was first applied during a large scale BCD experiment (anonymized reference). The goal of the experiment was to improve the usefulness and usability of BCFs, while limiting the effort required to develop and maintain man-made templates or taxonomies with reusable components. Therefore an approach was developed to support the reuse of criteria and methods directly from existing BCs.

To select criteria and methods (semi-)automatically from existing BCs, collaborative filtering was applied (Hussein & Ziegler, 2011). Collaborative filtering is common in other domains, such as online stores. For example, when looking at a certain book on Amazon, other books are recommended that were bought by other customers in combination with the book of interest. The recommender algorithm that was tested during the BCD experiment works similarly. The algorithm scores criteria in earlier BCs and recommends the highest scoring ones:

1. It identifies the criteria which have been entered into the new BC.

2. It searches the database of earlier BCs, looking for BCs in which some of these criteria appear as well. These will be called the 'matching BCs'. The criteria in these BCs need to be identifiable as such and should be structured hierarchically.

3. Each matching BC contains potentially related criteria. The strength of the relation depends on the place of the criterion in the hierarchy. Criteria that are closer in the hierarchy to the place where the new and the earlier BC matched get more points.

4. For each of the potentially related criteria, the scores are summed up over all the matching BCs. A limited set of the highest scoring criteria can then be recommended to the BC developer.

During the experiment, each of the 208 subjects had to come up with five criteria for the use of RFID in the automotive supply chain. To be able to recommend criteria for reuse, 12 BCs, consisting of 330 criteria in total, had been developed through action research with domain experts in the RFID-based Automotive Network research project (Project RAN, 2011; Reinhart, Irrenhauser, Reinhardt, Reisen, & Schellmann, 2011). Those BCs were then structured according to BCO, i.e., the criteria were listed and structured hierarchically using the 'hasEffectOn' relation and stored in a database that could be queried by the algorithm. There were different experimental conditions, which made it possible to compare subjects using the recommender algorithm with those with different types of support. The main result of the experiment was that the subjects who used the recommendations were significantly more efficient and had a higher intention to use the system than those who could not get semi-automatic support for reuse.

3.8.3 Recommending Methods by Means of an Expert Model

The selection of suitable evaluation methods can be even more challenging than selecting the right criteria for a BC (J. Ballantine & Stray, 1999). Therefore we developed an expert model that supports the BC developer in ranking methods (anonymized reference). The model consists of three main parts:

- Properties describing valuation methods, e.g., if they are financial or non-financial.
- Properties describing IS projects, e.g., if they are strategic or operational.
- Rules to weight the suitability of methods with certain properties for IS projects with certain properties.

To define the rules, several existing models for relating methods to projects have been studied, e.g., (Farbey et al., 1995; Joshi & Pant, 2008). The model, consisting of the rules and a number of common methods with assigned properties, has been used as the basis for an implementation in Microsoft Excel. The application asks the BC developer several questions concerning the nature of the IS project and then scores the methods in its database according to the BC developer's answers. The model has been evaluated with BC experts and the prototypical application has been tested with usability experts and potential end users. The preliminary results show that although the application makes it significantly easier to determine which method to use (see

Applicability) it does not yet solve the challenges of Familiarity and Usability. E.g., if the application recommends the use of a certain method and then loads an Excel template for that, it may still be unclear to the BC developer how to use it.

3.9 Conclusion

The identification and valuation of criteria top the list of challenges in information systems investment evaluation (ISE) and business case development (BCD) (J. Ballantine & Stray, 1998; J. Ward et al., 2008). The support for reuse of criteria and methods could be a solution for these challenges (anonymized reference). However, very little research seems to address this topic. This paper therefore aimed to provide a starting point for further research by gathering what is written, either implicitly or explicitly, with respect to reusable business case components, arguments for reuse, challenges in reuse and guidelines for reuse.

A literature review was performed by identifying a representative body of literature in the area of ISE and BCD. The selected papers were analyzed on the basis of a set of concepts, resulting in the concept matrix in **Figure B.1, Figure B.2, Figure B.3**.

The first research objective was to identify which BC components are considered for reuse. Criteria, in addition to the methods for valuating them, appear in most business cases. Several authors investigated the use of criteria and methods, showing that especially the simple financial criteria and methods are frequently used, in spite of many researchers calling for more focus on the strategic, organizational and human factors.

The second research objective was to investigate arguments for reuse. The main derived arguments are (1) to improve the efficiency and effectiveness of BCD, (2) to facilitate the comparison of BCs and benchmarking of values, (3) 'ritualistic' use and more deliberate use to achieve acceptance of the BC by decision makers, (4) that some criteria and methods are easier to understand and because reuse may facilitate learning.

The third research objective was to define the challenges that may hinder reuse: (1) a lack of formal evaluation procedures and a lack of easily accessible BC archives, (2) unclarity of the reliability of the methods used in earlier BCs, (3) a lack of familiarity with certain criteria and methods, (4) a low usability of certain criteria and methods, and (5) a limited applicability of certain criteria and methods.

The fourth research objective was to describe guidelines for reuse. One is the well-known and frequently repeated understanding that financial criteria and methods are not sufficient for effective ISE. Therefore, non-financial criteria and methods should be (re)used as well. In addition, there is a number of frameworks for matching IT projects to evaluation techniques.

Finally, three ongoing research endeavours were presented to show how the challenges in reuse may be partly overcome.

The findings presented in this paper have several implications. Reuse would benefit from more formal evaluation procedures including ex-post evaluation to determine whether earlier BCs have achieved what they promised. These procedures need to be supported by tools that enable BC developers to search through archived BCs in order to identify criteria and methods for reuse. To prevent ritualistic use of components and to prevent the avoidance of intangible criteria and complex methods, tools could recommend components to be reused in the specific BC that is under development and provide examples of their use. Obviously, not all challenges can be overcome by tool support. Training BC developers, changing business processes and culture may be necessary to deliver more comprehensive BCs and thus to make better investment decisions.

This work has some limitations. First, it was not feasible to analyze 'all' research in the area of ISE. Therefore a set of representative papers was identified. Second, the topic of reuse seemed to be less explored than expected. E.g., the term 'reuse' did not occur a single time in the reviewed literature in the context of BC component reuse. Therefore, quite some interpretation was needed to identify parts of the literature which are relevant to the study at hand. Third, we did not cover each and every component that could possibly be reused, nor did we describe all arguments, all challenges, or all guidelines for reuse. Rather, we tried to cluster findings along the key concepts, focusing on those findings which appeared most often and most prominently in the reviewed literature.

Among the opportunities for future work are (1) the analysis of the usability of components and how their usability could be improved, (2) the analysis of the applicability of components and the design of frameworks for matching techniques to projects: *"An eclectic approach to IT evaluation needs to be taken which matches different types of IT projects and different types of projected organizational change to specific evaluation techniques"* (Hochstrasser, 1990). Two decades later, Schryen (2010) claims that still *"only little work has been done to analyze the appropriateness of various techniques"*. Finally, future work for design science could be (3) the development of a tool which supports reuse, and its evaluation, i.e., if using the tool improves the efficiency, effectiveness and satisfaction of the BC developer.

4 Business Case Ontology

Bart-Jan van Putten   Humboldt-Universität zu Berlin, SAP Research Dresden
Virginia Dignum   Delft University of Technology
Theo Dirk Meijler   SAP Research Dresden

Relevance for this Dissertation

This study aimed to develop a model of the BC as an artifact, defining the components that can be reused in a more formal manner, enabling computer-supported reuse. It can also be used by researchers and practitioners as a 'shared conceptualization of the domain'.

Collaborations

- Dr. Virginia Dignum (TU Delft) contributed with the Description Logics.
- Dr. Theo Dirk Meijler (SAP Research) commented on the manuscript.

Abstract

Today's BCFs are not based on a standardized model of what a BC is. As a consequence, most BCFs and BCs are structured rather differently. This hampers the broader applicability of those BCFs and limits benchmarking. If however BCFs would share a common model, parts of BCs could be reused. BC developers could learn from earlier BCs developed by others, even when those people used different BCFs. This way, it may become easier to identify the potential benefits of the investment and to define suitable quantification methods. Moreover, when BCs are based on a common model, it becomes easier for BC evaluators to compare them and to prioritize investments. This paper therefore proposes an initial BC ontology (BCO). BCO may be used as a data model for BCFs and by students and scholars to build up, and build upon, a common understanding of the field of IS investment evaluation.

4.1 Introduction

To support information systems (IS) investment evaluation, organizations may develop a business case (BC). A BC is a recommendation to decision makers to take a particular course of action for the organization, supported by an analysis of benefits, costs and risks (Gambles, 2009). Those may be expressed in quantitative or qualitative, financial or non-financial terms. Business case development (BCD) is the process of realizing the BC as an 'artifact', by gathering and analyzing data to define and valuate evaluation criteria, presenting it in documents, spreadsheets or presentations. It may take place before project execution for investment appraisal, during project execution for monitoring and control, or after project execution for organizational learning (anonymized reference). BCD can be supported by a business case framework (BCF), which often comes in the form of a spreadsheet template with some predefined criteria, i.e., benefit, cost and risk factors that need to be considered during evaluation. For an example of a simple BCF, please refer to (SolutionMatrix Ltd., 2010).

There are many unresolved problems in the field of IS investment evaluation. For example, Ballantine and Stray (1999) found that 68% of IS projects cope with problems when having to identify the potential benefits of the investment, while 85% have problems with their quantification. According to more recent research, many of the problems in the field of IS investment evaluation are still prevalent today (Irani & Love, 2008). In earlier empirical research of BCD, we found that these problems may be partly attributed to a lack of support for reuse in BCFs (anonymized reference).

Today's BCFs are not based on a standardized model of what a BC is. As a consequence, most BCFs and BCs are structured rather differently. This hampers the broader applicability of those BCFs and limits benchmarking and learning. If however BCFs would share a common model, parts of BCs could be reused. BC developers could learn from earlier BCs developed by others, even when those people used different BCFs. This way, it may become easier to identify the potential benefits (and other relevant criteria) of the investment and to define suitable quantification methods. Moreover, when BCs are based on a common model, it becomes easier for BC evaluators to compare them and to prioritize investments.

To our knowledge, the standardized BC model that is needed to enable the required reuse functionality of BCFs is non-existent. This paper therefore proposes an initial BC ontology (BCO). BCO is formally defined using Description Logic (Nardi & Brachman, 2003) and presented visually using a UML Class Diagram (Object Management Group, 2011). In addition to functioning as a data model for BCFs, BCO may be used by students and scholars to build up an understanding of the field of IS investment evaluation, albeit only a small part of the field. Initially, BCO focuses on the essence of what a BC is, i.e., the BC as an 'artifact', disconnected from its organizational, social and political context.

This paper starts with a short background on reuse in BCD, ontologies and design methods for ontologies (**Section 4.2**). **Section 4.3** follows with the requirements for BCO and some related ontologies and models. **Section 4.4** describes the competency questions and **Section 4.5** the design, i.e., BCO itself. BCO is evaluated in **Section 4.6**.

Finally, **Section 4.7** describes some implications of the use of BCO and concludes this paper.

4.2 Background

4.2.1 Reuse in Business Case Development

The following scenario illustrates how reuse could take place during BCD:

Imagine an old BC on the use of barcodes for tracking parts in the supply chain. Due to the use of barcodes, it may become easier for warehouse workers to have fairly precise data on stock levels, which may in turn make it possible to decrease those stock levels and thus decrease warehousing costs. Criteria in this BC may be 'ease of identification' (qualitative), 'stock level' (quantitative, non-financial) and 'warehousing costs' (financial). Some years later, when developing a BC for the use of radio-frequency identification (RFID), the BC developer would again need to decide which criteria to use. Rather than defining all criteria from scratch, the developer may reuse criteria from earlier BCs. In this case, the criteria 'ease of identification', 'stock level' and 'warehousing costs' would probably also be relevant for the BC for RFID.

In addition to the criteria, the methods used for the valuation of those criteria may be reused. The simplest way would be to use the same methods as used in the earlier BC. Especially when methods are reused, it is possible to compare the estimated values among BCs. For example, while investment in barcodes may have led to a 10% decrease of stock levels, the investment in RFID may only lead to another 2% decrease, at even higher implementation costs. Values may also be reused, e.g., within a certain industry, the average decrease of stock levels may be 3%. When developing a new BC one could then assume that the benchmark would be a realistic value for the new BC.

The reuse of criteria, methods and values as presented in this (simplified) scenario, is only possible if a collection of earlier BCs exists, if related BCs can be identified from such a collection and if the criteria, methods and values within those BCs can easily be identified.

4.2.2 Ontologies

In philosophy, ontology is the study of 'being' or 'existence'. In computer science, *an ontology is* "a formal, explicit specification of a shared conceptualization" (Borst & Akkermans, 1997). A conceptualization is "an abstract simplified view of the world that we represent for some purpose" (Gruber, 1993). *Formal* means that the ontology should be machine-readable. *Explicit* means that the type of concepts used, and the constraints on their use are explicitly defined. *Shared* means that an ontology is often meant to capture knowledge that is accepted by a group of people, machines, or organizations.

There are several uses for ontologies, e.g., "To share common understanding of the structure of information among people or software agents.", "To enable reuse of domain knowledge." and "To make domain assumptions explicit" (Noy & McGuinness, 2001).

When used among people, the preferred way of communication is often informal (natural language) or visual, e.g., UML Class Diagrams (Object Management Group, 2011). For use by IS, such as BCFs, ontologies need to be described formally, e.g., by using Description Logic (Nardi & Brachman, 2003), RDF (W3C, 2004), or OWL 2 (W3C, 2009). Recently, UML has also become more accepted as a language for formally modeling ontologies (Kogut et al., 2002).

4.2.3 Design Methods for Ontologies

The design of an ontology should be based on a method. Corcho et al. (2003) compare several such methods. One of the main distinctions between different methods is the „degree of dependency on its final application". The aim of BCO is in the first place to facilitate the reuse of BCs by describing a BC as an artifact and decomposing it into reusable components. Thus, BCO has a high degree of dependency on its final application. Therefore, for the creation of BCO, an application-dependent method was selected: On-To-Knowledge (Staab, Studer, Schnurr, & Sure, 2001).

The On-To-Knowledge method includes the identification of goals that should be achieved by ‚knowledge management tools', i.e., the tools built on top of the ontology, and is based on an analysis of usage scenarios. The steps proposed are: ‚kick-off', where ontology requirements are captured and specified, competency questions are identified, potentially reusable ontologies are studied and a first draft version of the ontology is built; ‚refinement', where a mature and application-oriented ontology is produced; ‚evaluation', where the requirements and competency questions are checked, and the ontology is tested in the application environment; and ‚ontology maintenance'.

As a part of the kickoff phase, the ontology's goals were described (see preceding sections), requirements were identified (see following section) and the competency questions were defined (see following section).

4.3 Requirements for Business Case Ontology and Related Work

To enable the reuse of BCs among people and BCFs, an ontology is needed, which fulfills several requirements:

- It should be useful to describe a diverse range of BCs. Therefore it should consist of a comprehensive set of concepts and relations.
- It should include concepts to describe the BC as an artifact. I.e., for reuse, the focus on a management approach or business process view is of lower importance.
- It should aim to limit the number of synonyms and overlapping concepts, in order to reduce ambiguity and to facilitate human understanding.
- It should have a formal description to enable its use in BCFs as well as a semi-formal or informal description to enable human use, such as for training, learning and communication.
- It should be well-accepted in the (IS) BC community. This can be determined based on publications/citations and applications in real-world scenarios and IS.

These requirements were not only used to design BCO, but also to analyze related work in what follows.

According to Farbey at al. (1999b), a BC consists of qualitative and quantitative descriptions of benefits, costs and risks of each proposed investment alternative. Many other researchers and practitioners use different informal terminology, although the meaning and intentions of the components of a BC are generally similar, cf. (Brugger, 2009; Cardin et al., 2007; Gambles, 2009; Gliedman et al., 2004; Schmidt, 2009).

To identify more formal conceptualizations of BC, several existing models and ontologies were analyzed with respect to the requirements (**Table 4.1**). The Business Motivation Model (BMM) provides a scheme for developing, communicating, and managing business *plans*. BMM identifies factors that motivate the establishing of business plans, it identifies and defines the elements of business plans and it indicates how all these factors and elements inter-relate (Object Management Group, 2010). This model is especially strong for the modeling of the implementation of business goals (due to its focus on business *plans*). However, it falls short in describing the (financial) methods for quantifying investment criteria. It also lacks a formal description.

Val IT is a governance framework based on CobiT (ISACA, 2010). In contrast to BMM, it does focus on business *cases*. It is especially strong in describing guidelines for the development and maintenance of BCs, aiming to support executive management teams and other enterprise leaders. However, the BC is simply seen as a document and not as a set of reusable criteria, methods and values. Moreover, it does not include any (semi-)formal models which could be used by IS without human interpretation.

e^3-*value* is an approach to explore innovative e-commerce ideas with the aim to understand them thoroughly and to evaluate them for potential profitability (Gordijn & Akkermans, 2003). With e^3-value, the creation, distribution and consumption of value in a multi-actor network can be described. The approach is especially strong at demonstrating the flow of value between multiple stakeholders. However, it does not cover the reasoning (i.e., criteria, motivations) for doing so, although those are essential for the domain of investment decision making.

Osterwalder's *Business Model Ontology (BMO)* can be used to describe the value a company offers to one or several segments of customers and to describe the architecture of the firm and its network of partners for creating, marketing, and delivering this value (Alexander Osterwalder, Pigneur, & Tucci, 2005). BMO includes concepts for modeling financial aspects, such as cost structures and revenue models. However, it remains superficial in those areas and lacks (semi-)formal specifications.

As shown by **Table 4.1**, the strengths of these models and ontologies should certainly not be neglected, however there still seems to be a need for a dedicated business case ontology.

Table 4.1: A simplified comparison of existing frameworks with respect to their usefulness for modeling reusable BCs

	BMM	Val IT	e^3-value	BMO
Relevance & coverage	+/-	+/-	+/-	+/-
Business case as an artifact	+/-	-	-	-
Limited in size	+/-	-	+	+
Formal and informal	+/-	-	+	-
Accepted / shared	+	+	+/-	+/-

4.4 Competency Questions

The kick-off phase of the On To Knowledge method includes describing so-called 'competency questions', i.e., questions that should be answerable by means of the ontology, as shown in **Table 4.2**.

Table 4.2: Competency questions for BCO

CQ	Competency questions	Concepts	Relations
1	What are the criteria for business case X?	BusinessCase, Criterion	BusinessCase has Criterion
2	Which methods have been applied to valuate the criteria in business case X?	Method, MethodApplication	Method was appliedToCriterion, Method was appliedToCase
3	What types of methods were applied to valuate the criteria in business case X?	Qualification, Quantification, Indication, Scoring	Qualification is a Method, Quantification is a Method, etc.
4	Which values have been calculated in business case X?	MethodApplication, Value	MethodApplication hasResult Value
5	What kind of values resulted from the methods that were applied to the criteria in business case X?	Qualitative, Quantitative, Score	Qualitative is a Value, Quantitative is a Value, etc.
6	Are there any investment alternatives being compared in business case X?	Case	BusinessCase has Case
7	Which existing business cases are related to my new business case?	see **Section 4.6**	see **Section 4.6**
8	Which criteria, methods and values could I reuse in my new business cases?	see **Section 4.6**	see **Section 4.6**

Subsequently, existing frameworks for the modeling of BCs/business models/business plans and value were identified (see Related Work in **Section 4.3**). From these frameworks, from a set of existing BCs and from literature, a set of initial concepts for the ontology was extracted. These included concepts such as "criterion", "factor", "variable", "enabler", "objective" and "indicator".

As part of the refinement phase the initial set of concepts was reduced to a smaller set. E.g., the six aforementioned concepts were replaced by the single concept "Criterion". Next, the ontology was formalized using Description Logic. The results of this phase are presented in the next section. The evaluation phase will be described in **Section 4.6**.

4.5 Design

Each of the concepts in BCO will now be described, first in natural language and then formally, using Description Logic.

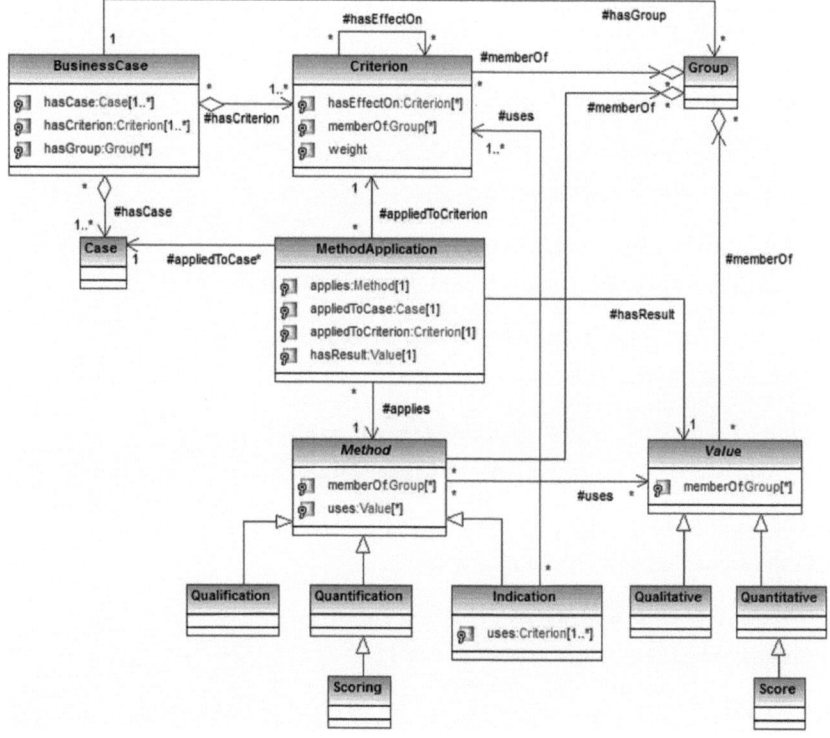

Figure 4.1: The Business Case Ontology (using the UML Class Diagram notation)

4.5.1 BusinessCase

The business case is the 'root' of the ontology: when reading the ontology it is probably the easiest to start here. A BusinessCase consists of cases ('hasCase'), criteria ('hasCriterion') and groups ('hasGroup'). Formally, using Description Logic and assuming Δ_D to be the alphabet of the domain:

`BusinessCase, Case, Criterion, Group` $\subseteq \Delta_D$
(BusinessCase, Case, Criterion, Group are concepts in the domain)

$\forall$`x,y.hasCase(x,y)` $\supset$ `BusinessCase(x)` $\wedge$ `Case(y)`
(hasCase is a relation between BusinessCase and Case)

$\forall$`x.BusinessCase(x)` $\supset$ $1 \leq$ `#{y|hasCase(x,y)}`
(a BusinessCase has at least one Case)

$\forall$`y.Case(y)` $\supset$ `#{x|hasCase(x,y)}`
(a Case belongs to any number of BusinessCases)

$\forall$`x,y.hasCriterion(x,y)` $\supset$ `BusinessCase(x)` $\wedge$ `Criterion(y)`
(hasCriterion is a relation between BusinessCase and Criterion)

$\forall$`x.BusinessCase(x)` $\supset$ $1 \leq$ `#{y|hasCriterion(x,y)}`
(a BusinessCase has at least one Criterion)

$\forall$`y.Criterion(y)` $\supset$ `#{x|hasCriterion(x,y)}`
(a Criterion belongs to any number of BusinessCases)

$\forall$`x,y.hasGroup(x,y)` $\supset$ `BusinessCase(x)` $\wedge$ `Group(y)`
(hasGroup is a relation between BusinessCase and Group)

$\forall$`x.BusinessCase(x)` $\supset$ `#{y|hasGroup(x,y)}`
(a BusinessCase has any number of Groups)

$\forall$`y.Group(y)` $\supset$ $1 \leq$ `#{x|hasGroup(x,y)}` ≤ 1
(a Group belongs to exactly one BusinessCase)

4.5.2 Case

A BC consists of one or more cases. A case can be evaluated independently and compared with other cases. Common examples of cases are the 'as-is', i.e., current situation, and the 'to-be', i.e., future situation. A time series may also be modeled by means of cases. E.g., when a BC makes a prognosis for 2014, the cases 2012, 2013, 2014 may be used to show how values change over time until 2014. Another use of the case concept is to compare alternative solutions for a certain problem, e.g., to compare 'barcode' with 'RFID'. Each case includes a value for each criterion to which a method has been applied.

4.5.3 Criterion

Each case is evaluated by means of one or more criteria. According to the Merriam-Webster dictionary, a criterion is "a standard on which a judgment or decision may be based". The BC literature often considers 'benefits', 'costs' and 'risks' as common categories of criteria, which may be refined into more specific ones. It is assumed that different cases will always be compared on the same criteria. Therefore, criteria are directly related to the BC concept and not indirectly via the case concept. Criteria may also affect other criteria, which can be modeled through the 'hasEffectOn' relation:

$\forall x,y.\text{hasEffectOn}(x,y) \supset \text{Criterion}(x) \land \text{Criterion}(y)$

4.5.4 Value

For each criterion, for each case, a value can be defined. The value can e.g., depict that the expected 'ROI for RFID' is 3.0m$ in 2014, while the 'ROI for barcode' is 2.5m$. A value can be qualitative or quantitative. A specific type of a quantitative (non-financial) value is the score. A score is often a number between 0 and 1 or between 1 and 5. Scoring methods are used to estimate a value when one wants to avoid calculating or measuring an exact value. Scores allow for easy comparison of cases and opinions of different stakeholders (Chou, Chou, & Tzeng, 2006).

Value, Qualitative, Quantitative, Score $\subseteq \Delta_D$
$\forall x.\text{Qualitative}(x) \supset \text{Value}(x)$
$\forall x.\text{Quantitative}(x) \supset \text{Value}(x)$
$\forall x.\text{Score}(x) \supset \text{Quantitative}(x)$

4.5.5 Method

A method is used to determine the value of a criterion for a case. As there are different types of values, there are also different types of methods:

- *Qualification method:* Used to define a qualitative value, often a few words in natural language.

- *Quantification method:* A formula or algorithm that is mostly used when the data for the parameters used can be obtained relatively easily.
- *Scoring method:* Used to assign a score to a criterion. It is mostly applied when it is too hard to find a reliable way of quantifying a criterion in its accepted unit of measurement. The score can then provide a quantitative value, albeit without a unit of measurement. As one criterion can have multiple method applications, it is possible to use a scoring method in addition to other methods.
- *Indicator method:* To define (more specific) criteria to be used as indicators for a (more generic) criterion. Indicators are 'proxies' for the criterion which is too hard to qualify or quantify directly. E.g., if it is too hard to determine 'customer satisfaction' directly, 'delivery time' and 'product quality' may be used as indicators. Subsequently one of the four method types should be applied for each indicator criterion. Thus, an indicator method can be used recursively. E.g., 'delivery time' is an indicator for 'customer satisfaction' and 'quality rate' is an indicator for 'delivery time'.

```
Method, Qualification, Quantification, Scoring, Indication ⊆ Δ_D
∀x.Qualification(x) ⊃ Method(x)
∀x.Quantification(x) ⊃ Method(x)
∀x.Scoring(x) ⊃ Method(x)
∀x.Indication(x) ⊃ Method(x)
```

Quantification methods may be dependent on each other by using the resulting values of method applications:

```
∀x,y.uses(x,y) ⊃ Method(x) ∧ Value(y)
```
(uses is a relation between Method and Value)

```
∀x.Method(x) ⊃ #{y|uses(x,y)}
```
(a Method uses any number of Values)

```
∀y.Value(y) ⊃ #{x|uses(x,y)}
```
(a Value is used by any number of Methods)

```
∀x,y.uses(x,y) ⊃ Indication(x) ∧ Criterion(y)
```
(uses is a relation between Indication and Criterion)

```
∀x.Method(x) ⊃ (1 ≤ #{y|uses(x,y)})
```
(an Indication method uses one or more Criteria)

$\forall y.\text{Criterion}(y) \supset \#\{x \mid \text{uses}(x,y)\}$

(a Criterion is used by any number of Indication methods)

4.5.6 Method Application

To determine the values in the BC, for each case, for each criterion, at least one method needs to be applied (the MethodApplication class in **Figure 4.1**). Different criteria often require the application of different methods. E.g., intangible benefits mostly require an indicator method, while tangible costs require the application of a quantification method. In most situations, the same method cannot be applied to the different cases for the same criterion. E.g., when comparing the current situation with the future situation, the values of the future situation often need to be estimated, requiring advanced methods, while the current situation is known and can be derived easily. However, when describing a time series, often the same method can be applied (also see 'Case', **Section 4.5.2**). The Description Logic for this quaternary association class is rather long. Basically, it defines that there is a relation between method, criterion, case and value. One or more methods can be applied to the unique combination of one criterion and one case, resulting in a value.

$\text{MethodApplication} \subseteq \Delta_D$

$\forall x,y.\text{appliedTo}(x) \land \text{r1}(x, y) \supset \text{MethodApplication}(x)$

$\forall x,y.\text{appliedTo}(x) \land \text{r2}(x, y) \supset \text{Method}(y)$

$\forall x,y,y'\text{appliedTo}(x) \land \text{r1}(x, y) \land \text{r1}(x, y') \supset y = y'$

$\forall x,y,y'\text{appliedTo}(x) \land \text{r2}(x, y) \land \text{r2}(x, y') \supset y = y'$

$\forall x,x',y1,y2.\text{appliedTo}(x) \land \text{appliedTo}(x') \land$
$(\text{r1}(x, y1) \land \text{r1}(x', y1)) \land \text{r2}(x, y2) \land \text{r2}(x', y2)) \supset x = x'$

$\forall x,y.\text{appliedToCase}(x) \land \text{r1}(x, y) \supset \text{MethodApplication}(x)$

$\forall x,y.\text{appliedToCase}(x) \land \text{r2}(x, y) \supset \text{Case}(y)$

$\forall x,y,y'\text{appliedToCase}(x) \land \text{r1}(x, y) \land \text{r1}(x, y') \supset y = y'$

$\forall x,y,y'\text{appliedToCase}(x) \land \text{r2}(x, y) \land \text{r2}(x, y') \supset y = y'$

$\forall x,x',y1,y2.\text{appliedToCase}(x) \land \text{appliedToCase}(x') \land$
$(\text{r1}(x, y1) \land \text{r1}(x', y1)) \land \text{r2}(x, y2) \land \text{r2}(x', y2)) \supset x = x'$

$\forall x,y.\text{appliedToCriterion}(x) \land \text{r1}(x, y) \supset \text{MethodApplication}(x)$

$\forall x,y.\text{appliedToCriterion}(x) \land \text{r2}(x, y) \supset \text{Case}(y)$

$\forall x,y,y'\text{appliedToCriterion}(x) \land \text{r1}(x, y) \land \text{r1}(x, y') \supset y = y'$

$\forall x,y,y'\text{appliedToCriterion}(x) \land \text{r2}(x, y) \land \text{r2}(x, y') \supset y = y'$

$\forall x,x',y1,y2.\text{appliedToCriterion}(x) \land \text{appliedToCriterion}(x') \land$

$(r1(x, y1) \land r1(x', y1)) \land r2(x, y2) \land r2(x', y2)) \supset x = x'$

4.5.7 Weight

Weight is a property of criterion and depicts its relevance for the BC. The weight may be used by scoring methods to calculate an overall score for a criterion, e.g., total score = sum of (for each criterion(weight * score)).

$\forall x, y. (\text{Criterion}(x) \land \text{weight}(x,y)) \supset \text{double}(y)$
$\forall x. \text{Criterion}(x) \supset (1 \leq \#\{y | \text{weight}(x,y)\} \leq 1)$

4.5.8 Risk & Uncertainty

BCs are often used prior to investment and project execution. Therefore, values are often predictions with a certain level of uncertainty. This can be modeled in different ways, using the concepts that have already been introduced. One way is to create a 'worst case', 'likely case' and 'best case' (using the case concept) and provide a value for each case for each criterion. This way, the risk is modeled as a variation on a criterion. Alternatively, it can be modeled as an independent criterion. For example, 'down time per year' may be a criterion, with the likely value of 10 hours. The value can also be a chance, e.g., 'risk that system will be down for more than two days per year' with a value of 5%.

4.5.9 Group

A group is a means to structure parts of a BC. Criteria, methods and groups may be grouped. Criteria, methods and groups may belong to multiple groups and groups may consist of criteria, methods and groups at the same time. This concept is not a crucial component of a BC, but has been added to BCO to be able to describe the existing models as presented in the Related Work (**Section 4.3**).

$\forall x. \text{Criterion}(x) \supset \text{Group}(x)$
$\forall x. \text{Value}(x) \supset \text{Group}(x)$
$\forall x. \text{Method}(x) \supset \text{Group}(x)$
$\forall x. \text{Group}(x) \supset \vee_{C \in \{\text{Criterion, Value, Method}\}} C(x)$

4.6 Evaluation

As proposed by the On-To-Knowledge method (Staab et al., 2001), for the evaluation of the ontology, one needs to check whether the target ontology satisfies the requirements (see Requirements, **Section 4.3**) and whether the ontology supports or answers the competency questions (**Section 4.4**).

4.6.1 Competency Questions

Competency questions 1 to 6 can easily be answered when a BC is modeled according to the ontology. But questions 7 and 8 are more difficult to answer. Actually, BCO does not explicitly support those questions. Rather, a BCF based on BCO should answer these questions. Question 7 could for example be answered by looking at similarities between criteria used in older BCs and those already entered in the newer BC. This approach has recently been investigated by the authors in related research (anonymized reference). Another approach is to explicitly model the context of the new BC, e.g., how strategic it is (Farbey et al., 1995), if it is mandatory or discretionary (Joshi & Pant, 2008). Then, the collection or database of existing BCs should be queried for BCs with similar properties. The current version of BCO only supports the former approach.

Answering question 8 would also require additional functionality in the BCF. It could for example count how often certain criteria are used in a larger number of BCs and recommend the ones which are used most often. The same could be done for methods. Other factors could be taken into account as well, such as the reliability of the methods, their ease of use and degree of acceptance by BC evaluators. However, BCO would need to be extended to support such scenarios.

4.6.2 Requirements

It can be used to describe a diverse range of business cases.

The concepts of BCO have been derived from a wide range of sources, including an analysis of existing BCs, BCFs and other models. After BCO was designed, a test was done if it could be used to describe four common conceptualizations in the domain of IS investment evaluation: (non)financial criteria (Bacon, 1992), competitive advantage (Porter, 2008), balanced scorecard (Kaplan & Norton, 1992; Milis & Mercken, 2004) and benefit-dependency network (Peppard, Ward, & Daniel, 2007). After adding the Group concept to BCO, this appeared to be the case. This activity has been described in detail in a technical report (anonymized reference).

It should include concepts to describe the business case as an artifact.

BCO consists of the core concepts of BCs and treats them as a collection of data, independent of their organizational, social and political context.

It should aim to limit the number of synonyms and overlapping concepts.

BCO is a lightweight ontology (Corcho et al., 2003). Although it can be used to describe a diverse range of BCs, it can only do so because it abstracts from concepts that are very similar. Concepts such as "criterion", "factor", "variable" and "indicator", were all replaced by the single concept "criterion". This way, some of the nuances in semantics between these concepts may have been lost. That is a strength of BCO, because a large and ambiguous ontology would maybe have a higher expressiveness, but not necessarily a higher acceptance in the community. In future work, BCO may be treated as an upper-ontology, to which more specific concepts (from other ontologies) may be related.

It should have a formal description as well as a semi-formal or informal description.

BCO has been described informally using natural language, semi-formally using UML diagrams and formally using Description Logic.

It should be well-accepted in the (IS) business case community.

BCO is only a starting point for further research in this area and is therefore not a well-accepted ontology yet. Still, as mentioned before, it is based on existing literature.

4.6.3 Application of BCO

BCO was first applied during a BCD experiment with 208 participants (anonymized reference). The goal of the experiment was to test whether the usefulness and usability of BCFs can be improved by supporting the reuse of BC components from existing BCs. Therefore 12 existing BCs, consisting of a total of 330 criteria, were structured according to BCO and stored in a database (**Table 4.3**). The criteria were structured hierarchically using the 'hasEffectOn' relation ('relParentID' in **Table 4.3**). I.e., the criterion with ID=16 has an effect on the criterion with ID=15.

Table 4.3: Criteria stored in a relational database table

criterionID	relBusinessCaseID	relParentID	criterionOrder	criterionText
...	...	...	...	...
15	2	14	2	Process Efficiency
16	2	15	1	Time Reduction
...	...	...	...	...

The experiment included different experimental conditions of which the results were compared. In some of the experimental conditions, a recommender algorithm proposed criteria to the participants, who had to develop a BC. The main result of the experiment was that the subjects who used the recommendations were significantly more efficient and had a higher intention to use the system than those who did not get support for reuse. In the context of this paper, this shows that BCO can be applied as a data model in advanced BCF, supporting reuse of BC components.

4.7 Conclusion

Today's BCFs are not based on a standardized model of what a BC is and how it can be developed. As a consequence, most BCFs and BCs are structured rather differently. Using BCO, or another ontology as the basis for BCs has several advantages. First, it allows for the reuse of criteria, methods and values among BCs. Second, it allows decision makers to compare the BCs more easily when they are structured similarly and when calculations are based on similar methods. Third, average values for certain criteria may be calculated for specific industries ('benchmarking'). This allows decision makers to compare their company's performance against others. Fourth, because BC developers use the same criteria and methods more often, they become more knowledgeable about when and how to apply them.

Within larger companies multiple BCFs may be used. As long as those BCF share a common formal model, such as BCO, parts of BCs may be reused. Similarly, partners in the value network may use different BCFs, but if they are based on a common formal model, the partners can easily reuse parts of BCs. It should be noted that reuse is not necessarily a manual activity. When a formal model is used by multiple BCs, reuse may be (partly) automated. When building a new BC, a software algorithm may recommend criteria and methods to be used.

Reuse becomes more complex, when BCs are based on different formal models. A mapping from the respective model to BCO would need to be defined once, after which those BCs could be automatically converted to BCO. As BCO or any other model is never all-encompassing, some information may be lost during translation.

The goal of this work was not to create an all-encompassing ontology. Rather, BCO was limited to a small set of rather generic concepts which can abstract from a relatively large variety of BC-related models. BCO focuses on the BC as an 'artifact', disconnected from its organizational, social and political context. This way, it concentrates on capturing declarative rather than procedural knowledge. In knowledge engineering and decision-support systems, ontologies are often combined with rules. Several scholars (Farbey, Targett, & Land, 1994a; Farbey et al., 1995; Hochstrasser, 1990; Joshi & Pant, 2008; M. Parker & Benson, 1989) defined rules for selecting methods based on the type of IS and the risk of the project under evaluation. This could be an interesting opportunity for extension of BCO.

This work has some limitations. First, an ontology is a model, i.e., a simplification of reality. By necessity it leaves out details and may be based on certain –often implicit– viewpoints. Therefore, researchers are invited to challenge the assumptions and come up with improved versions of BCO. Interesting questions are e.g., if concepts for tangible/intangible benefits, direct/indirect costs, financial/non-financial criteria, strategic/tactic/operational criteria should be included, or if this just makes BCO larger without adding much to its usefulness. Second, the experiment mentioned in **Section 4.6.3** on 'Application of BCO' focused on the reuse of criteria. Thus, BCO has not yet been applied for the reuse of methods or values. Third, the relations between BCO and the existing ontologies and models have not yet been described explicitly. This would enable the conversion of parts of business plans and business models into business cases and vice versa.

Our target is that given further iterations, validation and scientific discussion, BCO may be used as the basis for a standard for describing and realizing future BCs. Developers of BCFs should incorporate BCO in their data models to support the reuse of criteria, methods and values. That may be an important step in alleviating some of the problems that have afflicted IS investment evaluation for so long.

5 Business Case Framework

Bart-Jan van Putten   Humboldt-Universität zu Berlin, SAP Research Dresden

Relevance for this Dissertation

This study aimed to develop a first version of a BCF, based on a generic BCD process, extensible with domain specific components. At this point, those components still had to be pre-defined by domain experts. The BCF was applied to the development of several BCs for the Semantic Product Memory (SemProM) project and evaluated during a field experiment.

Collaborations

- Dr. Barbara Schennerlein, Dr. Carsten Magerkurth and Dr. Theo Dirk Meijler (SAP Research) commented on the manuscript.
- The findings in the paper are partly based on a field experiment with business case development practitioners.

Abstract

Today's business case frameworks (BCF) are either too generic, providing too little support for domain-specific business case development (BCD), or are sufficiently specific but not based on a generic BCD process. Such BCF do not allow for reuse of investment criteria or quantification methods, which hampers the broader applicability of those BCF and limits benchmarking and learning. This research proposes a BCF which is based on a generic BCD process and which can be extended with domain-specific components. The BCF was applied to the development of several BCs for Semantic Product Memory (SemProM) and evaluated during a field experiment. Whereas several components are now available to support BCD for SemProM, more components may be developed to extend the domain-specific support of the BCF to other domains.

5.1 Introduction

The Semantic Product Memory (SemProM) project investigated how meaningful ('semantic') product related information can be stored directly on the products themselves (Kröner, 2010; Wahlster, Kröner, Schneider, & Baus, 2008). For example, in the discrete manufacturing industry, a radio-frequency identification (RFID) tag, including some local memory, i.e., the 'SemProM', can be attached to each part at the beginning of the process. Routing information and production parameters, such as customer-specific finishing requirements, can be stored on this tag. From that point on, the part can find its own way through the factory. RFID readers need to be connected to all machines and routing points. This way, the machines can read the production parameters from the SemProM and configure themselves accordingly. After each production step is completed, the results can be stored on the SemProM. Such a manufacturing process may decrease the dependency on back-end systems, decrease the number of human errors caused by paper-based processes, improve product quality, decrease scrap and increase throughput. However, to make this possible, large investments are needed in e.g., hardware, software, installation, configuration, maintenance, business process reengineering and training of personnel. To justify such investments, a 'business case' (BC) may be developed, describing the benefits, costs and risks of each investment alternative.

BCs commonly appear as spreadsheets, often accompanied by presentations or explanatory documents. They may be presented by the project leader (BC 'owner' or 'champion') to senior management, which is responsible for prioritizing BCs and making investment decisions. This way, the BC can be used to decide about investment before project execution ('ex-ante'), to evaluate progress during project execution and to determine to what extent the proposed value of the investment has been realized after project execution ('ex-post') (J. Ward et al., 1996).

The development of BCs is a complex task. First, collecting, transforming and aggregating the required information demands interdisciplinary teamwork and expertise in a wide range of fields such as business strategy, business operations ('work practice'), information technology, accounting and project management. Second, BCs are based on assumptions concerning the future development of certain variables. Predicting those variables requires accurate data and reliable analysis methods. Third, BCs are subject to a constantly changing business environment, requiring an agile BC development process to adapt to these changes.

Today's business case frameworks (BCF), such as document guidelines and spreadsheet templates, support business case development (BCD) to some extent, but are mostly quite generic. They support the calculation of traditional financial metrics which are not specific to most kinds of investments, or any specific industry or solution domain. The disadvantage of such BCF is that they hardly support the BC developer in developing BCs for specific solutions, such as SemProM. The identification of relevant evaluation criteria, such as benefits, costs and risks and their quantification for specific domains are known to be among the main challenges in BCD (J. Ballantine & Stray, 1998). Thus, BCF are needed which provide domain-specific criteria and quantification methods. However, such BCF run the risk of becoming 'one day flies', being unsuitable for use in future domains which are different than what the BCF was originally intended for. As such BCF can mostly only be used for limited periods of time they do not support benchmarking and learning. Thus, BCF should be based on a generic BCD process to allow for their development, use and improvement over longer periods of time.

In order to overcome the seeming contradiction between the need for generally applicable BCFs which also provide domain-specific support, a BCF will be proposed which is based on a generic BCD process, but which allows to be extended with reusable domain-specific components. At the time of writing, components have been developed for SemProM for the domains of manufacturing, retail and service management.

This text describes the design and evaluation of the BCF and is structured as follows: **Section 5.2** provides a background with respect to business cases, business case development and business case frameworks. **Section 5.3** defines the challenges for BC developers and evaluators and the requirements for the BCF. **Section 5.4** describes the design and process. **Section 5.5** covers the results from the evaluation of the BCF during a field experiment. Finally, **Section 5.6** concludes this text.

5.2 Background

5.2.1 Business Cases

A BC is a recommendation to decision makers to take a particular course of action for the organisation, supported by an analysis of benefits, costs and risks compared to the realistic alternatives, with an explanation of how it can best be implemented (Gambles, 2009). It documents the relevant facts and situational analysis, key metrics, financial analysis, allows different projects with different goals to be compared and contrasted and serves as a communication tool (Gliedman et al., 2004). BCs enable different projects to be compared, act as a mechanism to rank projects in terms of organisational priorities, feed projects planning and resource allocation, act as a control mechanism over expenditure, benefits and the development and implementation of projects and facilitate organisational learning (Ginzberg & Zmud, 1988; Irani & Love, 2002; Smithson & Angell, 1991).

Although most BCs differ in contents and structure, the communality is that they include one or more 'investment criteria'. Criteria are concerned with the financial and non-financial justification used in proposing, evaluating, and deciding upon the project or investment. They answer the question: why was the investment decision made? (Bacon, 1992). In BCs, criteria are commonly categorized under benefits, costs and risks.

The BC can be seen as the successor of cost-benefit analysis (King & Schrems, 1978; Sassone, 1988). Whereas the principles of cost-benefit analysis mainly come from accounting and are thus financially oriented, BCs put additional emphasis on strategic benefits, indirect costs, risks, social and organisational factors, i.e., the 'intangible' criteria.

With some exceptions (Ross & Beath, 2002; J. Ward et al., 2008), the term BC is infrequently used in scientific literature. Rather, in the area of information systems (IS), scientists study 'IS (investment) evaluation' (ISE), e.g., (J. Ballantine & Stray, 1999; Farbey et al., 1999a; Irani, 2002; Renkema & Berghout, 1997; Serafeimidis & Smithson, 1999; Smithson & Hirschheim, 1998; Walter & Spitta, 2004). Farbey et al. (1999b, p. 205) define IS evaluation as a process that takes place at different points in time or continuously, for searching for and making explicit, quantitatively or qualitatively, all impacts of an IS project.

5.2.2 Business Case Development

To the best of the author's knowledge there is no definition of business case development (BCD) in literature. Therefore the following working definition is proposed: *Business case development is the process of realising the business case as an 'artefact', by gathering and analysing data to define and valuate evaluation criteria, presenting it in documents, spreadsheets or presentations. It may take place before project execution for investment appraisal, during project execution for continuous monitoring and control, or after project execution for organizational learning.* This definition is quite similar to the ISE definition of Farbey et al. (1999b, p. 205), but focuses on the creation of the BC as an artefact, rather than the organizational process in which it is used. Moreover, BCD is not limited to the domain of IS. Because ISE is better covered in literature and because this chapter does have an IS focus, the terms BCD and ISE will be used interchangeably.

There are many problems in ISE, such as those identified by Farbey et al. (1993), and most of them are still prevalent today, cf. (J. Ballantine & Stray, 1998; Berghout & Remenyi, 2005; Farbey et al., 1999a; Irani, 2002; Walter & Spitta, 2004; J. Ward et al., 2008). Ward et al. (2008) found in a study among over 100 European companies that 65% of respondents indicated their organizations were not satisfied with their ability to identify all benefits, with 69% reporting that they do not adequately quantify and place a 'value' on the benefits for inclusion in the BC. 38% of the respondents believed their current approach led them to frequently overstate the benefits to obtain funding.

5.2.3 Business Case Frameworks

A BCF is a set of guidelines, methods, templates or tools to support BCD.

Guidelines often come in the form of document or presentation outlines, which loosely describe the required components of a BC, e.g., (Cardin et al., 2007; Gliedman et al., 2004), and what metrics to use, depending on the requirements of the BC evaluators of the organization in which the BCF is used. Although these guidelines can be helpful and hardly limit BC developers in their expressiveness, they mainly concern the 'what', i.e., declarative BCD knowledge, and not the 'how', i.e., procedural BCD knowledge. One of the reasons for this is that most BCF have been designed to ease the life of BC evaluators rather than BC developers. As such, guidelines often do not provide much guidance on how the BC developer should achieve the desired results.

Methods or *techniques* such as listed by Irani et al. (1997, p. 699) or Renkema and Berghout (1997, p. 10) have the potential to support BC developers in the 'how' of BCs, but are sometimes rather generic descriptions, see e.g., (J. Ward et al., 2008), and need to be combined with more specific methods, see e.g., (Love et al., 2004), to identify and quantify the benefits, costs and risks for a project in a specific industry. Moreover, it is a question which method is most suitable in which case (Farbey et al., 1995; Joshi & Pant, 2008).

Like guidelines, *templates* are often developed and kept company internal. Templates are built for specific types of projects, so companies may use multiple templates. Mostly they come in the form of a spreadsheet with a rigid structure and strict content requirements, thus limiting the expressiveness of the developer. However, such templates ensure the homogeneity among BCs and the investment alternatives within them. Homogeneity enables BC evaluators to work more efficiently, as they can then more easily compare and prioritize BCs.

Tools or applications often come in the form of advanced spreadsheets, e.g., with data import and export functionality, or controls that trigger changes between different worksheets of the spreadsheet. Tools mainly aim to increase the efficiency of BCD and are often highly organization and project type-specific. Public templates and tools, e.g., (BusinessCase.com, 2010; SolutionMatrix Ltd., 2010) – commercial or for free – are often generic implementations of traditional financials investment appraisal methods, such as Return-on-Investment (ROI), Net Present Value (NPV) and

Payback Time (Brealey & Myers, 1988), without much support for the real challenges for BC developers: the identification of benefits and the quantification of intangible benefits and indirect costs (J. Ballantine & Stray, 1998; Irani, 2002; J. Ward et al., 2008).

5.3 Requirements

There are several groups of stakeholders of a BC (Mcauley, Doherty, & Keval, 2002). First, there are the BC owners or champions who trigger and lead the BC's development. Second, there are the BC developers, i.e., the people who do the situational analysis, who gather and aggregate information, etc. Third, there are the BC evaluators, who make the final investment decision. Within this group, managerial and financial decision makers may be distinguished. The former determines whether the investment fits the strategy of the company, the latter determines whether the BC is financially feasible, e.g., with respect to its risk as part of the overall investment portfolio. Fourth, there are the BC project leaders, who implement the proposed plan after it has been accepted. Fifth, there are the people whose jobs are affected by the implementation of the BC.

This research takes a user-centred design science approach (Hevner et al., 2004; Norman & Draper, 1986) to improve the efficiency and effectiveness of BCD and the satisfaction of BC developers when working with BCF. For the design of the BCF the most relevant groups of stakeholders are those who actually get to use the framework, i.e., collecting and organizing information, or altering and comparing information. Thus, the requirements were derived from the groups of BC developers and BC evaluators. This was achieved through methodological triangulation (Denzin, 2006): by reviewing literature, participant observation during a BCD case study, semi-structured interviews with BC experts and structured interviews with BCD practitioners (Van Putten et al., 2011).

Next, the main challenges for the BC developers and evaluators will be described. Based on that, a set of requirements for the BCF will be presented.

5.3.1 Challenges for Business Case Developers

"A short list of what it takes to produce a good IT BC holds few surprises: one needs to be thorough (track down all possible impacts, costs, and benefits), clear and logical (articulate the cause and effect chain that leads to each cost/benefit impact), objective (unbiased, including everything that is material, good or bad) and systematic (have good models and rules for finding and summarizing values).

Financial talent also helps as does a solid grasp of the interplay between IT capacity, service levels, user needs, and IT resource requirements" (Schmidt, 2003). But it is not just the skills of the BC developer that count. The development of a thorough, clear, objective, etc. BC costs time and thus money. As Anselstetter puts it: "The collection of accurate and complete data to appraise investment alternatives often causes considerable costs or is impossible at all" (Anselstetter, 1984, p. 10), while "forecasts as a consequence of the future-orientation of ex-ante evaluation are difficult due to the uncertainty involved" (Walter & Spitta, 2004).

Many other challenges have been identified, see e.g., (Walter & Spitta, 2004). The two most often mentioned and toughest challenges seem to be the identification and the quantification of (intangible) benefits and (indirect) costs (Irani, 2002).

Regarding identification, Farbey et al. mention that "the impacts of modern IT are so wide-ranging that organisations are often simply unaware of what the costs, benefits and disbenefits of a system might be". Their research showed that the scope of benefits varied greatly and that a straightforward list of costs and benefits which had been achieved by the organisation concerned or by other organisations would be useful in itself (Farbey, Targett, & Land, 1994b).

Regarding quantification, King and Schrems mentioned that "many analysts consider the quantification of benefits to be the greatest obstacle to a cost-benefit analysis in an information system. This results both from inconsistencies among levels and kinds of outputs from information systems, and from the vague intangible benefits that information systems are said to bring" (King & Schrems, 1978).

5.3.2 Challenges for Business Case Evaluators

A major challenge for BC evaluators is to determine the reliability of the BC. One reason for that is that it is often difficult or too labour-intensive to follow the reasoning and assumptions of the BC developer and to determine the sources of information used (Van Putten et al., 2011). Another reason is that precise quantitative values may actually be rough estimates (Norman, 2009). Finally, BC owners and developers sometimes deliberately 'oversell' their cases to overcome the investment hurdle (J. Ward et al., 1996).

Another major challenge is to determine how to incorporate intangible benefits and indirect costs in the decision, if they have not been quantified reliably or clearly by the BC developer. In general, more criteria will only obfuscate the evaluator's decision making ability (Gladwell, 2005). However, simply leaving out intangibles leads to neglect of important aspects of the investments (Farbey et al., 1999a).

Moreover, companies may question how to compare a strategic investment in IT, which delivers a wide range of intangibles, with other corporate investments whose benefits are more tangible (Gunasekaran, Love, Rahimi, & Miele, 2001).

5.3.3 Requirements for the Business Case Framework

Based on the challenges identified, nine main requirements were defined:

1. The BCF should guide BCD in a gradual and iterative manner. This requirement was derived from the observation that existing BCF are often rather 'evaluator centric' and merely provide a template for the end results. However, the process to get to these end results, i.e., the selection of criteria, the calculation of metrics, also requires support.

2. The BCF should allow for the modelling and valuation of any type of criterion, whether financial, non-financial, tangible, or intangible. This requirement was mainly derived from literature which states that traditional investment appraisal techniques focus too much on financial criteria alone (Irani, 2002).

3. The BCF should allow for the use of different ISE techniques. This requirement was derived from literature stating that "each technique has its own distinctive characteristics which dictate the situations in which it can be used" (Farbey et al., 1999a) and from the observation that strict and inflexible frameworks can only be effective in a limited domain.

4. The BCF should support the reuse of criteria to ease their selection for use in specific BCs. This requirement was derived from the observation that selecting and structuring the relevant criteria for the BC is one of the most labour intensive parts of BCD.

5. The BCF should support the reuse of quantification methods to reduce the number of methods that need to be defined from scratch. This requirement was derived from the observation that developing reliable quantification methods is one of the most labour intensive and difficult parts of BCD. Additionally, the practitioner interviews showed that the 'reuse of structure', such as quantification methods, should be supported by BCF (Van Putten et al., 2011).

6. The BCF should show the reliability of the information used and the quantification methods applied. This requirement was derived from the observation that it is often unclear how the results in a BC were obtained, on which assumptions they are based and thus whether they are reliable. Moreover, this was confirmed by the

practitioner interviews, where 'information quality' was among the most urgent topics for further research (Van Putten et al., 2011).

7. The BCF should support all stakeholders, and BC evaluators in particular, to understand the underlying reasoning and assumptions, as well as the results and their usefulness for decision making. This requirement is based on the observation that BCs developed by others are often difficult to understand and on the practitioner interviews which showed that 'clarifying reasoning' is one of the major challenges (Van Putten et al., 2011).

8. The BCF should support 'market potential estimation'. The practitioner interviews showed that this is one of the biggest challenges for BC developers who make 'provider perspective BCs', i.e., when an organisation needs to decide if it will further develop and market a new product (Van Putten et al., 2011).

5.4 Design & Process

Based on the requirements, a BCF was developed through iterative prototyping in Balsamiq Mockups (Balsamiq, 2010) and Microsoft Excel, a well-known spreadsheet program. This section describes the design of the prototypical software tool, i.e., the spreadsheet template, and the process for using it.

5.4.1 Process

A BCD process was defined on the basis of Requirement 1. The process consists of six steps, each of which corresponds to a worksheet in the spreadsheet template.

1. *Scope:* The BC developer defines the scope of the BC (**Figure 5.1**). This involves defining the challenge and possible solution on a high level of abstraction. The investment alternatives need to be defined, called 'cases'. E.g., in terms of the scenario for decentralized production control as described in the Introduction, the cases could be 'current situation', 'referenced' (the routing information and production parameters are stored in back-end systems; RFID is only used for identification of the part), 'distributed' (some data is stored locally on the part), 'local' (all data is stored locally, no connection to the back-end systems is needed).

2. *Processes:* The BC developer defines the business processes which need to be considered for evaluating the solution (**Figure 5.2**). These processes may or may not be affected by the solution, i.e., it should also be clear when a BC does not affect a certain business process, because BC evaluators may be looking for BCs that do improve specific processes.

65

Solution		
	Solution:	Semantic Product Memory
	Description:	An RFID tag (the 'SemProM') is attached to each part. All routing information and production parameters (such as customer specific finishing requirements) are loaded from the ERP/MES and written on the SemProM at the beginning of the process. From that point on, the part can find its own way through the factory. RFID readers need to be connected to all machines and routing points. This way, the machines can automatically read the production parameters from the SemProM and configure themselves accordingly. After each production step is completed, the results are stored on the SemProM. (This solution is based on SAP's use case 'Decentralized Production Control')
	Assumptions:	We assume that the SemProMs have enough memory, but no processing power. In the current situation all routing information and production parameters are printed or written on paper. This paper has to accompany the part throughout the production process.
	Out of scope:	We only investigate the benefits for the use of SemProM within the factory, but not in the entire supply chain.
Cases		
	Case A:	Current situation: All work instructions and results from process steps are written on paper. Assumption: Work instructions can not be downloaded from the ERP/MES through scanning barcodes. (In that case the time savings of case D will be smaller.)
	Case B:	"Referenced from RFID": Each part can be identified through an RFID tag, after which the production parameters can automatically be downloaded from the ERP/MES to the specific machine.
	Case C:	"Distributed on RFID/server": Each part can be identified through an RFID tag. Some of the production parameters are stored on the part at the beginning of the production process, others have to be downloaded from the ERP/MES to the specific machine when needed.
	Case D:	"Local on RFID memory": The production parameters can directly be read from an RFID tag on the part. No communication with the ERP/MES is needed during the production process.

Figure 5.1: A part of the Scope worksheet of the Decentralized Production Control BC

3. *Criteria:* The BC developer defines the criteria for evaluation (**Figure 5.3**). They can be structured hierarchically for better usability and to depict how criteria may influence each other. E.g., less 'rework' leads to a better 'quality rate', which in turn leads to a shorter 'delivery time' and a higher 'customer satisfaction'. The BC developer should also define valuation methods on a high level of abstraction and shortly explain the potential impact of each of the cases on each of the criteria.

4. *Methods:* The BC developer defines the methods for valuating each of the criteria (**Figure 5.4**). Valuating can mean quantifying, e.g., in financial terms ('material costs'), as a ratio ('quality rate'), time, number of human errors, etc. Valuating can also mean defining a qualitative value for a criterion, such as 'high', 'mid', 'low', or a score.

5. *Results:* The BC developer selects the most interesting results from the methods and structures them to get to an abstraction of the BC which is suitable for presentation to decision makers and other stakeholders. In the example, the BC developer has restructured the criteria along the categories 'performance', 'quality', 'environment', and 'costs', of which the latter is shown in **Figure 5.6**.

6. *Conclusion:* The BC developer concludes on the impact of each of the cases on the criteria and concludes on the BC as a whole, i.e., which case seems to be most suitable or if there is a need to define and investigate additional cases.

In the remainder of this section, three aspects of the design and process will be described in more detail: the definition of criteria, the definition of methods and the demonstration of information quality. Finally, an explanation will be given of how the generic BCD process can be extended with domain-specific support.

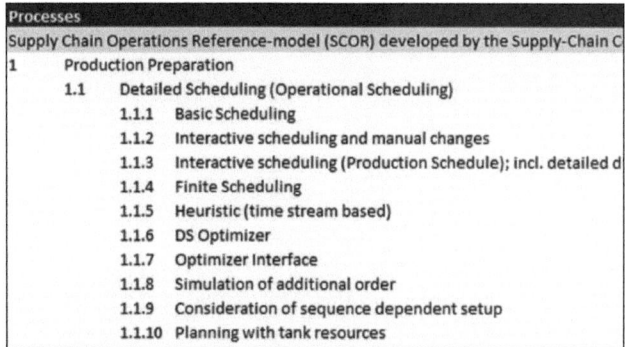

Figure 5.2: The definition of business processes on the Processes worksheet of the Decentralized Production Control BC

5.4.2 Criteria

For several reasons, the BCF supports the modelling and quantification of multiple criteria (Requirement 2). First of all, many BCs are not just needed to evaluate the direct financial impacts of a decision, but also the intangible benefits and indirect costs. Examples of such criteria are 'customer satisfaction' (intangible benefit), 'retraining workers after the change of a business process' (indirect cost). Secondly, the aim was to allow users to choose their own specific ISE techniques, such as 'Information Economics', or the 'Balanced Scorecard' (Requirement 3) (Kaplan & Norton, 1992; M. M. Parker et al., 1988). Although a detailed discussion of these techniques goes beyond the scope of this text, multi-criteria support increases the likelihood that such specific techniques can be used within the generic BCD process, see e.g. (Walter & Spitta, 2004), which classifies several such techniques as multi-criteria techniques.

Criterion					Method	Unit	Goal	Solution Impact
1	2	3	4	5				
Customer satisfaction					? (survey)		max.	
	Delivery time (Manufacturing cycle time)				? = number of days	time	min.	Slight decrease, depending on number of human errors
	Quality rate				? = (all parts - scrap parts - reworked parts) / all parts * 100	%	max.	Slight increase, depending on number of human errors
	Scrap				? = scrap parts / all parts * 100	%	min.	Decreases due to smaller number of human errors
		Process status information			?		max.	Can be loaded directly from and updated on the material.
		Human errors			? = number of errors / 100 parts	int	min.	Number of errors due to executing the wrong work instru
		Quality control			? *see below			
	Rework				? = reworked parts / all parts * 100	%	min.	May decrease due to fewer human errors
		Process status information*			? *see above			
		Human errors*			? *see above			
		Quality control*			? *see below			
	Product quality				?		max.	Can increase due to better quality control
		Quality rate*			? *see above			
		Quality control			? = number of quality checks		max.	Can be increased because results do not need to be stored
	Product recall				? = parts called back / parts delivered * 100	%	min.	May decrease due to better quality control
		Product quality*			? *see above			
		Environmental impact*			? *see below			
Competitive advantage					?		max.	
	Market share				? [market analyst report]	%	max.	May increase due to higher customer satisfaction
	Customer satisfaction				? *see above			
	Time-to-market				?	time	min.	Only decreases if the solution simplifies the planning proc
	Time-to-volume				?	time	min.	No/minor effect
		Quality rate*			? *see above			

Figure 5.3: A part of the Criteria worksheet from the Decentralized Production Control BC

Criteria Hierarchy

For several reasons, the criteria can be structured hierarchically (**Figure 5.3**). First, more generic criteria, i.e., the criteria in the leftward columns, are expected to be impacted by the more specific criteria, i.e., the criteria in the rightward columns. For example, the number of 'human errors' impacts the amount of 'scrap' which in turn impacts the 'quality rate'. Thus, the hierarchy shows dependencies between the criteria. Second, as a high number of criteria may lead to a high cognitive load for the BC developer or evaluator, the hierarchy may also be used to focus on the higher abstraction levels. Third, the structure is an implicit way to model the 'indicator method'. Higher level criteria are often intangible. In that case, the more specific criteria may be used as indicators for the more generic criteria.

The criteria hierarchy is expected to be a flexible model, as a criterion is a broad concept. A criterion can be a goal, key performance indicator (KPI), critical success factor (CSF), variable, parameter, effect, feature, the name of a business process that needs to be improved, etc. In the end, a criterion is nothing more than a 'concept that is evaluated', or 'something that one wants to measure'.

More specific criteria are often related to solutions and processes, while more generic criteria are often related to the industry and organization. Another perspective is that the specific criteria represent features or means, while the generic criteria represent effects or goals. E.g., better 'process status information' is a feature of the SemProM solution, while higher 'customer satisfaction' is the goal (**Figure 5.3**).

Defining and Reusing Criteria

There are two main ways to define the criteria to be used in the BC. The first way is to use common metrics as a starting point. E.g., common metrics in the manufacturing domain are 'product recall' and 'delivery time'. The second way is to reuse criteria from earlier BCs (Requirement 4). The intention of supporting reuse is not just to make it easier to identify relevant criteria, but also to increase the number of BCs that are (partly) using the same criteria, thereby facilitating benchmarking. Benchmarking is useful for BC evaluators who need to prioritize investments prior to project execution and who want to monitor how well running projects are performing.

5.4.3 Methods

The BCF supports the modelling of three different types of valuation methods:

- *Quantification methods:* A quantification method is a simple or complex formula that is mostly used when the data for the parameters used can be obtained relatively easily. **Figure 5.4** shows an example of a quantification method.
- *Indicator methods:* An indicator method uses one or more criteria that are more specific. The criterion that needs to be valuated, but which is too hard to valuate, is represented by another criterion which is more tangible. E.g., if it is too hard to determine 'customer satisfaction' directly, 'delivery time' and 'product quality' may be used as indicators. Subsequently one of the three method types should be applied for each indicator criterion. Thus, an indicator method can be used recursively. E.g., 'delivery time' is an indicator for 'customer satisfaction' and 'quality rate' is an indicator for 'delivery time'.
- *Scoring methods:* A scoring method means assigning a score to a criterion. A score can be qualitative, e.g., 'high/mid/low', or quantitative, e.g., a number between 0 and 1 or between 1 and 5. Scoring methods are mostly applied when it is too hard to find a reliable quantification or indicator method for a criterion, or when multiple stakeholders need to express their opinions (each stakeholder can assign a score and these scores can be combined or compared). In that case it is also possible to first quantify or indicate a criterion and then to use a scoring method additionally. For example, the BC owner may believe that costs of '1 m€ are manageable and apply a score of '3' to the cost criterion, while the financial controller may argue that these costs are much too high when considering the entire IT portfolio and apply a score of '1'.

Example of a Quantification Method: Market Potential Estimation

'Market potential' (or 'sales revenue') is a common criterion in BCs for new products and services. To quantify this criterion, two reusable 'market potential estimation' (MPE) methods were developed (Requirement 8), which both aim at estimating the sum of money that can be earned by selling the proposed product or service.

The first MPE method is a top-down approach. Based on reports from market analyst firms such as Gartner, Forrester and IDC, one starts with a high level financial figure which depicts the total amount of money that is expected to be spent in a certain market. E.g., the market for RFID-based identification of products in retail. Next, one tries to estimate based on several factors such as market share, market saturation and market readiness which 'piece of the cake one can eat'.

Throughput				
Competitive advantage > Time-to-volume > Throughput				
Description: Calculates the increase of production possible due to time savings in reading work instructions and writing process results.				
Conclusion: The production can be increased significantly. Alternatively, the number of quality checks may be increased (not modelled)				
	Current	RFID	Metric	Reliability
Parts produced (p/wk)	1.000		int	guess
Number of workers	30	30	int	guess
Parts produced per worker (p/wk)	33		int	derived
Productive time (p/wk)	2.400	2.400	min	accurate estimate
Time needed per part per worker	72		min	derived
Number of process steps	20	20	int	guess
Time savings due to automatic setting of machine parameters (per part per pro		0,5	min	guess
Time savings due to automatic setting of machine parameters (per part)		10	min	derived
Time savings due to automatic recording of process step results (per part per pr		0,5	min	guess
Time savings due to automatic recording of process step results (per part)		10	min	derived
Time savings per part		20	min	derived
Time needed per part per worker		52	min	derived
Parts produced with same number of workers (p/wk)		1.385	int	derived
Loss of production due to RFID failure		2,4	int	derived
Parts produced with same number of workers (p/wk)		1.382	int	derived

Figure 5.4: The quantification method for 'Throughput' on the Methods worksheet of the Decentralized Production Control BC

The second MPE method is a bottom-up approach. The goal is to gradually estimate the number of potential customers and multiply that with the expected price of the product. The number of customers can e.g., be calculated by looking at existing customers and making assumptions about which of those would be interested in the new product.

Whether one applies the top-down or bottom-up approach to MPE depends on the data that is available. If a reliable market analyst report is available which covers the area of interest, one can save a lot of time. However, a bottom-up approach may be more reliable and understandable. Moreover, it may be easier to adjust when market conditions change.

Defining and Reusing Methods

There are two main ways to define the methods to be used in the BC. The first way is to use common metrics as a starting point. E.g., a common way to quantify 'quality rate' is '(all parts - scrap parts - reworked parts) / all parts * 100'. There are several organizations which try to standardize metrics for certain industries, see e.g., (VDMA, 2009). The second way is to reuse methods from earlier BCs (Requirement 5). It should be noted however that a suitable method is not just dependent on the criterion that one tries to valuate, but also on the data that is available. Reuse of methods is important for BC evaluators who need to be able to rely on the quality of methods without evaluating them in-depth.

5.4.4 Information Quality

The BCF supports users in several ways to determine the reliability of the information used and the quantification methods applied (Requirement 6). First, for each piece of information used in the quantification methods, the developer can specify the reliability, ranging from 'guess', via 'rough estimate' and 'accurate estimate' to 'fact' (**Figure 5.5**). This may help both the evaluator to see the limitations of the BC as well as the developer to know where to improve, e.g., by trying to acquire more accurate information. Second, on the results worksheet, there is a similar field, with a smaller number of values (high/mid/low) to show the reliability of the figure resulting from an entire method (**Figure 5.6**), which is based on the reliability of the underlying data.

The BCF supports users in several ways to understand the underlying reasoning and assumptions, as well as the results and their usefulness for decision making (Requirement 7):

- Assumptions can be added almost anywhere by means of the spreadsheet's native commenting function.
- On the Methods worksheet, the 'Source' field should be used to document the source of the data used and the assumptions on which it is based. Moreover, the recommended separation between 'parameters' and 'derived measures' makes it easier for the evaluator to determine when it is the data itself that needs to be considered and when the focus should be on the calculation.
- The Scope and Conclusion worksheets capture explanations.
- On the Results worksheet it is possible to define the Relevance for each criterion, which expresses the interest of the evaluator in the criterion. Next, it is possible to specify the sensitivity of the value, which depicts the impact of choosing a different case, i.e., solution alternative (**Figure 5.6**).

Current	RFID	Metric	Reliability	Source
1.000	1.000	int	guess	Throughput
0,1	0,5	%	guess	Chance of R
1,0	0	%	guess	th SemP
0,5	0	%	guess	th SemP
0,5	0	%	rough estimate	
20	20	%	accurate estimate	rcentage
			fact	
			derived	

Figure 5.5: Selecting the reliability of the calculation step in the quantification method

Criteria	Current	RFID			Unit	Change	Change	Relevance	Sensitivity	Reliability
		2011	2012	2013	2014		abs.	%			
Costs											
Labor costs (p/wk) reducing workforce	60	43				k€	-17	-28	high	high	low
Material costs (p/wk)	58	79				k€	21	36,5	high	high	low
Acquisition costs		224				k€			high	high	low
Installation & configuration costs		400	85	45	45	k€			high	high	low
Maintenance costs		0,81	0,71	0,62	0,52	k€			mid	low	low

Figure 5.6: The cost criteria, a selection of the Results worksheet from the Decentralized Production Control BC

5.4.5 Domain-Specific Components

The aforementioned design and process are believed to be rather generic and thus do not limit BC developers to a particular domain. However, they do not provide much support for domain-specific BCD either. Therefore, the generic BCD process can be extended with domain-specific components (Requirement 4,5). A component consists of common criteria and related methods in a certain domain. A domain can e.g., be an industry (e.g., manufacturing), solution (e.g., SemProM), or organization.

Components can be defined by using common metrics in the domain as a starting point or by extracting criteria and methods from earlier BCs. For SemProM, components were developed using a combination of these approaches, for the domains of manufacturing, retail and service management.

In the current spreadsheet template the reuse of criteria and methods from these components would come down to manual copying. Future BCF prototypes may support this task in a more convenient manner by offering search functionality to retrieve criteria and methods from a database and by automatically including them in the new BC.

5.5 Evaluation

During a field experiment, the BCF has been applied to the development of several BCs for SemProM solutions. There were several goals for this experiment:

- To develop BCs for SemProM investment decision making;
- To develop reusable components to facilitate future BCD for SemProM;
- To collect feedback to improve the BCF;
- To increase awareness on the availability of the BCF;
- To make people comfortable with using the BCF.

Five large organizations were invited to participate. Two organizations participated actively by developing one or more BCs. Three organizations decided, in view of the effort required to produce a BC, to only provide feedback on the BCF after attending a presentation. Out of the five organizations, a total of ten BC developers participated. Eight of them did not have solid experience with BCD. This sample of users is representative for the target population of the BCF: people who do BCD as a secondary task but who have other primary expertise.

All participants received the materials for the field experiment, i.e., the spreadsheet template, a textual guideline for the BCD process and an exemplary BC made with the BCF. After that, each of the participants got an individual training session, based on a standardized protocol which had been pre-tested. Next, the participants started to develop a BC with the BCF. The goal was to develop a BC for a topic that they found interesting and useful, within the time limit of two months. During the BCD process, the participants were asked to take notes of any particularities they encountered, whether positive or negative. Moreover, they kept track of the time they invested. All participants requested a reviewing session after some initial efforts. During this session notes were taken of the feedback from the developers, questions were answered and some hints were given for further improvement of the BCs. In the end, the following BCs were developed during the field experiment:

- *Decentralized Production Control:* Is it worth to invest in SemProM for storing routing information and production parameters locally on the parts in a manufacturing process?
- *Asset Identification for Maintenance:* Is it worth to invest in SemProM for improving the efficiency of asset identification during maintenance tasks?
- *Remote Service Management:* Is it worth to invest in SemProM for improving the efficiency and effectiveness of servicing assets remotely?
- *Retail Product Recommendation:* Is it worth to invest in SemProM for giving product recommendations to customers in a retail environment?
- *Peer-to-Peer vs. Client-Server:* What are the benefits, costs and risks of using SemProM in a client-server architecture when compared to a peer-to-peer architecture?

Together with the feedback of the participants, received during and at the end of the experiment, these BCs provide insight in the challenges for the participants and ways to improve the BCF. Some observations by the facilitator of the experiment will be presented first. Next, the feedback from the participants will be presented, structured along 'observations', 'likes' and 'opportunities for improvement'. Due to space limitations, not all feedback can be presented here. Therefore a selection has been made, based on the number of participants mentioning a similar issue and on the expected importance of the feedback for the future improvement of the BCF.

5.5.1 Observations by the Facilitator

The possibility to model business processes is infrequently used. On the one hand this may be due to the limited support for this: the only place where the processes from the Processes worksheet are used is on the Criteria worksheet to indicate which criteria have a relation to which processes (**Figure 5.7**). On the other hand it may be explained by the observation that the use of business processes to estimate business improvements requires a lot of process knowledge and thus experience in the respective domain.

The use of Microsoft Excel introduced a threshold for those participants who were inexperienced with the software. Due to the large amount of freedom in the BCF template and the rich functionality of Excel itself, there is a lot that one can 'do wrong'. E.g., when a value in a cell gets to long after a calculation, the cell contents change to '######'. An inexperienced Excel user would not know how to solve this issue.

Most participants were uncertain about how to quantify risks. The participants who did model risks often used a probability (e.g., p=0,2 or 20%), to quantify the risk (**Figure 5.8**). However, the risk event was often insufficiently described. For example, the chance that one RFID tag breaks every day is probably smaller than the chance that one RFID tag breaks once a month.

One participant decided to model two different perspectives of the BC: the provider perspective and the customer perspective, resulting in two spreadsheet documents sharing a considerable amount of criteria. E.g., both perspectives share the criterion 'asset availability', however they are grouped under different more generic criteria (**Figure 5.9**).

One participant added a scoring system to the Results worksheet of the Client-Server vs. Peer-to-Peer BC (**Figure 5.10**). The score was calculated in the following way: first, for each criterion the winner of the two cases was selected. E.g., Peer-to-Peer wins on 'load balancing' and thus gets a 1, the other case gets a 0. This number is then multiplied by the relevance of the criterion. Low=1, Mid=2, High=3. In this case the relevance factor is 2. Next, it is multiplied by the percentual change caused by the winning case, in this case 50%. This leads to the following score for the Peer-to-Peer case: 1 * 2 * 50 = 100 and 0 * 2 * 50 = 0 for the Client-Server case. This approach can be repeated for and summed up over all criteria, leading to an overall score for each case. Although the overall score is a number with little meaning (it has no unit), it can be used to ease decision making.

Defining the quantification methods was the most challenging and labour-intensive job. Most participants tried to minimize their work in this respect, even though they were developing a BC that should be relevant for their work. On the one hand the challenge lies in splitting up the concept that one wants to measure into smaller concepts which one actually can measure. This requires some creativity and trial-and-error. On the other hand the challenge lies in estimating which data will be obtainable to put values on the concepts to be measured.

Some participants developed new quantification methods and tried to estimate the values at the same time, i.e., while developing the quantification formulae. Although one could argue that the BCF should support different working styles, it seems to be more efficient to first roughly develop the method, possibly with some rough figures, before starting to estimate the actual values.

Several participants quantified the criteria by directly recording the expected percentual change between the current situation and the other cases (**Figure 5.11**). Although this may initially save time, it is likely that this approach makes it more difficult to convince stakeholders of the arguments in the BC, as it is unclear how the information was derived. Moreover, when the implicit underlying assumptions change, it is unclear if the estimated percentual change is still accurate.

Criterion					Goal	Solution Impact	Business Process
1	2	3	4	5			
Customer satisfaction					max.		
	Delivery time (Manufacturing cycle time)				min.	Slight decrease, depending on number of human errors	3.1.4 Execute Work Instructions, 3.2 Production Progress Confirmation, 3.3.1 Trigger Site Logistics Request, 7.1 Final production progress confirmation
			Quality rate		max.	Slight increase, depending on number of human errors	4.2.1 Quality Management and Production Documentation for externally processed parts, 5.1 In Process Inspection, 5.2 Post Process Inspection

Figure 5.7: A participant modelled the relation between criteria and business processes on the Criteria worksheet

Instantiation with RFID based infrastructure				
Parameters	2010 Metric	Probability (%)	Source	
CSF: Computer Systems General Failure Rate	7 %	0,80	Gartner Group (2006): Benchmarking P(	
RFR: Failing RFID tags	5 %	0,80	http://www.packagingdigest.com/file/	
NF: Time network not available (downtime)	0,1 %	0,80	http://www.netcraft.com (measureme	
SF: Probability of software failure due to misfunction	0,9 %	0,80	http://en.wikipedia.org/wiki/Software	
Derived Measures				
TFE:Technical Faults and Errors	13 %	0,80	It is plausible that privacy concerns mo	

Figure 5.8: A participant quantified risks using probabilities

Criteria		Criterion	
		1	2
Customer Satisfaction		Maintenance Indicators	
	Retention (Delta)		Asset availability (Delta)
	Asset availability (Delta)		First-time Fix (Delta)
	First Time Fix Rate (Delta)		Mean Time To Repair (MTTR; Delta
	Mean Time To Repair (MTTR, Delta		Mean Time Between Failure (MTBF
	Mean Time Between Failure (MTBF		Percent of calls resolved without t(
	Percent of calls resolved without t(		Total service cost (Delta)
	Contract renewal rate (Delta)	Technical Infrastructure	
	Total service cost (Delta)		Costs per sensor
	Total service revenue (Delta)		
	Service revenue per customer (Del		

Figure 5.9: A participant modelled two perspectives on the same BC, the provider's perspective (left) and the customer's perspective (right)

Criteria	ClientServer	P2P	Unit	Change abs.	Change %	Relevance	CS win?	P2P win?	Factor	CS result	P2P result
Severity of attacks	0,8	0,2	chance	0,6	75	mid	0	1	2	0	150
Load balancing	maybe	yes		0,5	50	mid	0	1	2	0	100
Robustness	0,5	0,9	breakdown chance	-0,4	-80	mid	0	1	2	0	160
Handling of churn	irrelevant	yes		0,5	100	mid	0	0	2	0	0
Deployment of security	no	yes		1	100	mid	1	0	2	200	0
Security standards	5	2	no of standards	3	60	mid	1	0	2	120	0
Privacy of information	0,8	0,3	0...1	0,5	63	mid	1	0	2	125	0
Possibility of attacks	0,8	0,2	chance	0,6	75	mid	1	0	2	150	0
Development costs	2000	10000	EUR f 1st prototype	-8000	-400	low	1	0	1	400	0
Configuration costs	1000	1000	EUR f 1st prototype	0	0	low	1	0	1	0	0
										995	410

Figure 5.10: A participant added a scoring approach to the Results worksheet

Cost reduction due to real-time information		
Parameter: mean achieved process cost reduction for p	Metric	Reliability
X: Telephone or Fax	5,00 %	guess
Y: Pure B2B	10,00 %	guess
A: B2B Platform	10,00 %	guess
Workflow based collaboration platform	13,00 %	rough estimate
TM & SNC in on-demand mode	13,00 %	rough estimate

Figure 5.11: A participant used relative values in his quantification methods

5.5.2 Observations by the Participants

- The success of the BC is not just based on the BC itself, but also on how it can be used for communication with stakeholders and to convince decision makers.
- It should not be the goal to find as many criteria as possible, because that does not necessarily lead to better decisions. However, missing a crucial one can have a big impact.
- The main difficulty is developing the quantification methods.

5.5.3 Likes

- The BCD process helps to approach the task in a systematic manner. It supports the thinking process.
- The BCF helps to determine what the most important criteria are (e.g., through the relevance and sensitivity indicators on the Results worksheet) and thus to explore the 'problem space'. Moreover, it is good that the BCF does not aim to provide a final decision, because that is the task of the BC evaluator.
- Microsoft Excel is the right tool because it is flexible.
- The BCF is useful for comparing different cases.

5.5.4 Suggestions for Improvement

- Although it is good that the reuse of SemProM-specific criteria and methods is supported, traditional financial criteria, such as return-on-investment (ROI), net present value (NPV), internal rate of return (IRR) and payback period should be included as well.
- The BCF alone, i.e., without any reusable components, can be used for anything but therefore does not help much either.
- It should be more clear how the business processes can be used.
- The reliability estimates on the Results worksheet could be determined automatically based on the reliability estimates in the quantification methods.

- The BCF should distinguish between different types of BCs, e.g., new products/business models or just an efficiency improvement and support these types in different ways.
- The dependencies between different worksheets and methods should be clearer. The BCF could be stricter in requiring consistency between the criteria on the Criteria worksheet and those shown on the Results worksheet.
- The BCF should provide more support for how a risk can be modelled.
- The time factor should be more explicit in the BCF so that it can not be overlooked.
- The BCF should support modelling multiple perspectives (e.g., provider and customer) in one spreadsheet document, while currently multiple documents are needed.
- The BCF should provide more support for getting from the results to the final conclusion.
- The opportunity costs, i.e., the option of doing nothing, should be included in the spreadsheet template by default.

5.5.5 Conclusions of the Field Experiment

The field experiment provided better insights into the strengths of the BCF and its opportunities for improvement. The BCD process which it supports is appreciated but needs to be combined with reusable components to support BCD for specific situations. From the BCs developed during the field experiment, components were derived for the domains of manufacturing, retail and service management (Microsoft Excel, available upon request). Just like it does not seem plausible to advice the general manufacturing community to replace all barcodes with RFID tags, it does not seem plausible to draw any general conclusions from the BCs realized with the BCF so far. Rather the author would like to encourage the reader to develop a BC with the BCF for his or her specific situation and to share the included criteria and quantification methods as a component for reuse by others.

5.6 Conclusion

Today's business case frameworks (BCF) are sometimes too generic, providing too little support for business case (BC) developers who need to define domain-specific investment criteria and quantification methods. Other times BCF are sufficiently specific, i.e., include domain-specific criteria and methods, but do not support their reuse for BCs in other domains. This limits the broader applicability of those BCF, hampers benchmarking across domains, e.g., to compare the (expected) performance of the project with other projects. It also makes it less likely that BC developers and evaluators will use the BCF over longer periods of time to get skilled at using it and to integrate it in their work practice.

To overcome these challenges, this study proposes a BCF which is based on a generic BCD process, consisting of six steps: Scope, Processes, Criteria, Methods, Results, Conclusion. During this process, domain-specific components consisting of criteria and methods, may be reused.

The BCF was implemented in Microsoft Excel and evaluated during a field experiment. The main goals of the experiment were to develop BCs for Semantic Product Memory (SemProM) and to collect feedback for improvement of the BCF. The feedback from the participants shows that the generic BCD process works, but "does not help much either". This feedback is not surprising as there were no reusable components available yet during the experiment.

From the BCs which were developed during the experiment, reusable components have been extracted for the domains of manufacturing, retail and service management. These are now available for reuse upon request. Reuse is expected to increase the efficiency of BCD as well as the quality of the resulting BCs, e.g., because reuse supports benchmarking and learning. Although the reuse of methods is probably an even more urgent issue than the reuse of criteria, it is less likely that it will be successful. First, the names and semantics of criteria are relatively more often standardized than methods. Second, methods developed by others may be hard to understand. Third, methods are dependent on the data that is available. Therefore different methods may be used to valuate the same criterion, which results in a wider range of methods than criteria, decreasing the chance that a BC developer can easily find a suitable one for reuse.

In the future, more reusable components could be developed to extend the domain-specific support of the BCF to other domains. Moreover, classification and retrieval approaches should be developed to facilitate the reuse of criteria and methods during BCD, which will become even more important when the number of reusable components increases.

6 Supporting Dynamic Reuse in Business Case Development

Bart-Jan van Putten   Humboldt-Universität zu Berlin, SAP Research Dresden
Thomas Irrenhauser   Technische Universität München
Theo Dirk Meijler   SAP Research Dresden

Published as...

Van Putten, B.-J., Irrenhauser, T., Meijler, T. D. (2012). *Supporting Dynamic Reuse in Business Case Development*. Proceedings of the 20th European Conference on Information Systems (ECIS), June 10-13, Barcelona, Spain.

Relevance for this Dissertation

This study aimed to compare dynamic and static reuse of BC components. In the dynamic approach, the reusable, domain-specific criteria and methods do not need to be pre-defined by experts in templates and taxonomies (like in **Chapter 5**), but can be reused from earlier BCs. A recommender system proposes criteria that fit the new BC under development.

Collaborations

- Sebastian Reuther was a working student at SAP Research Dresden and implemented my early ideas for dynamic reuse in an Excel prototype and in C#. Later on, I reimplemented the functionality myself in the PHP web application that was used for the experiment.
- Prof. Oliver Günther, PhD (HU Berlin), Prof.Dr. Antonio Krüger (Saarland University), Prof.Dr. Jelke Bethlehem (University of Amsterdam) and Philipp Herzig (SAP Research) commented on my experimental set-up and statistical analysis plan.
- Dr. Angelika Salmen, Dr. Bettina Laugwitz, Dr. Jochen Rode and Dr. Sven Horn (all from SAP Research) provided support during the pilot usability tests.
- Thomas Irrenhauser (TU München) provided the 'RAN Nutzenkatalog' which was used in the experiment. He also commented on the manuscript.
- Dr. Theo Dirk Meijler (SAP Research) commented on the manuscript.

Abstract

Business case development (BCD) is a complex activity, which can potentially be improved by supporting the reuse of investment criteria and valuation methods. The goal of this research was to improve the usefulness and usability of business case frameworks (BCFs), while limiting the effort required to develop and maintain static databases of reusable components. Therefore, an approach was proposed for the dynamic reuse of business case components and contrasted with static reuse of business case components. In the dynamic approach, the reusable, domain-specific criteria and methods do not need to be pre-defined by experts in templates and taxonomies, but can be reused from earlier business cases. To test whether support for dynamic reuse improves BCFs, a usability experiment was set up. Three types of support for the reuse of criteria were compared: (1) recommendations, based on collaborative filtering and representative for the dynamic approach, (2) templates, representative for the static approach, and (3) no support. The task represented a simplified BCD activity and was completed by 208 people. The main results show that although the recommendations are as effective as the templates, they are the preferred type of support.

6.1 Introduction

For decades, determining the value and success of information systems (IS) has been high on the agendas of researchers, cf. (King & Schrems, 1978; Davis, 1989; Urbach et al., 2009; Schryen, 2010). Many IS investments are strategic in nature, have long-term, hard to quantify benefits and incur indirect costs (Irani, 2002). 68% of IS projects cope with problems when having to identify the potential benefits of the investment, while 85% have problems with their quantification (J. Ballantine & Stray, 1999). This may lead to investment in the wrong projects, over-investment, under-investment, and makes it attractive to creatively adjust estimates, see e.g. (J. Ward et al., 2008).

To support IS investment evaluation (ISE), in most organisations some kind of business case (BC) is developed. A BC is *"a recommendation to decision makers to take a particular course of action for the organisation, supported by an analysis of benefits, costs and risks"* (Gambles, 2009). Business case development (BCD) is the process of realising the BC as an 'artefact', by gathering and analysing data to define and valuate evaluation *criteria* (Bacon, 1992), presenting it in documents, spreadsheets or presentations. It may take place before project execution for investment appraisal, during project execution for monitoring and control, or after project execution for organizational learning (Van Putten et al., 2011).

When trying to estimate the values of the criteria selected for use in the new BC, a BC developer may spend days on defining *methods*, i.e., ways to put a qualitative, quantitative non-financial, or financial value on these criteria, see e.g., (Renkema & Berghout, 1997). This is especially hard for the intangible benefits and indirect costs (Irani, 2002). Instead, criteria and methods may also come from databases which are specifically designed for the purpose of reuse, e.g., templates and taxonomies of criteria and methods with browse and query functionality for their retrieval (Irani, Ghoneim, et al., 2006).

BCD can be supported by a business case framework (BCF), which often comes in the form of a spreadsheet template with some pre-defined criteria and methods. Today's BCFs are, however, often too generic, providing little support for BC developers who need to define domain-specific criteria and methods, e.g., in the domain of supply chain management, which will be used as an example throughout this paper. Other times, BCFs are sufficiently domain-specific, but are based on templates and taxonomies, which are explicitly defined by domain experts. Such BCFs are expensive to develop and maintain and are therefore often limited to one domain.

This paper proposes a new mechanism applicable in BCFs, namely *dynamic reuse of BC components*. This in contrast to the *static reuse of BC components* as this is known from templates and taxonomies. Dynamic reuse implies that components such as criteria and methods that were developed and used for earlier BCs, when stored in a structured manner, can be reused in later BCs on the basis of a recommender algorithm. This paper focuses on how dynamic criteria reuse could work and describes the result of a large-scale usability experiment, comparing different types of support for reuse, namely no support, templates (static reuse) and recommendations (dynamic reuse).

The following research questions are addressed in this paper:

RQ1: *How can support for reuse improve the usefulness and usability of business case frameworks, while limiting the effort required to develop and maintain static databases of reusable components?*

RQ2: *To what extent does support for the dynamic reuse of criteria (being the focus of this paper), improve the usefulness and usability of business case frameworks?*

This paper is further structured as follows: In **Section 6.2** we describe a scenario from the domain of supply chain management, motivating why it is helpful to be able to dynamically reuse the criteria from an earlier BC in a new BC. In **Section 6.3** we investigate existing BCFs, further substantiating the shortcomings mentioned above. In **Section 6.4** we detail the dynamic reuse concept. **Section 6.5** explains the research method, i.e., the usability experiment, and **Section 6.6** presents the results. Finally, **Section 6.7** concludes this paper.

6.2 Motivation for the Reuse of BC Components

The following scenario illustrates how reuse could take place during BCD:

Imagine an earlier BC on the use of barcodes for tracking items in the supply chain. Due to the use of barcodes, it may become easier for warehouse workers to have fairly precise data on stock levels, which may in turn make it possible to decrease those stock levels and thus decrease warehousing costs. Criteria in this BC may be 'ease of identification', 'stock level' and 'warehousing costs'. Some years later, when developing a BC for the use of radio-frequency identification (RFID), the BC developer would again need to decide which criteria to use. Rather than defining all criteria from scratch, the developer may reuse criteria from earlier BCs. In this case, the criteria 'ease of identification', 'stock level' and 'warehousing costs' would probably also be relevant for the BC for RFID.

Support for reuse has the potential to make life easier for BC developers, by easing the identification of criteria and the development of methods. Estimations in BCs may become more reliable, because the BC developer can build upon the methods developed by others. Moreover, estimations may be compared against benchmarks, e.g., aggregated values from earlier BCs. Reuse also enables longer-term BC development and monitoring and allows BC developers to get skilled at using certain methods. Finally, when BCs are structured similarly, BC *evaluators* may find it easier to compare BCs and decide how to invest.

6.3 Limitations of Business Case Frameworks

For this research, from the perspective of reuse, two classes of BCFs are distinguished (**Table 6.1**):

Traditional BCFs: Mainly support the development of the BC in terms of its cash flow, often accompanied by metrics such as Return-on-Investment (ROI), Net Present Value (NPV), or Internal Rate of Return (IRR). These BCFs are often domain agnostic and have rigid structures. Sometimes, new criteria can be entered, but those then need to be quantified directly in financial terms. These BCFs are often implemented as a stand-alone Microsoft Excel file and do not allow for sharing content with other BCs or BCFs. An example of a BCF in this class is Financial Metrics Lite (SolutionMatrix Ltd., 2010).

Modern BCFs: Support the development of the BC in financial terms and often include specific criteria and methods for one or a few domains, such as RFID in the supply chain (Ivantysynova, 2008, p. 155). The relevant ones then need to be selected from a template or taxonomy, which has been pre-defined by domain experts. It is mostly possible to add new criteria and methods, however those can not be reused in other BCs or BCFs; they would need to be entered/copied manually. These BCFs may be implemented as a stand-alone Microsoft Excel file, but some of them are web applications that ease collaborative BCD, such as the Value Lifecycle Manager (SAP AG, 2011).

The problems with the modern BCFs are still that (1) they are limited to the domains for which criteria and methods have been pre-defined by experts, (2) the criteria and methods need to be assigned explicitly to templates or taxonomies to facilitate their reuse and (3) the criteria, methods and their assignment to templates and taxonomies need to be maintained by the experts to enable the applicability of the BCF to new and changing domains.

Table 6.1: Simplified comparison of traditional and modern BCFs

	Traditional BCFs	Modern BCFs
Example	Financial Metrics Lite	Value Lifecycle Manager
Financial criteria	Included	Included
Domain-specific criteria/methods	Not included	Included, mostly limited to one domain
Selection of criteria/methods	No or little choice	Possible, e.g., select from template or taxonomy
Possible to define own criteria/methods	Sometimes possible, but only in financial terms	Mostly possible
Possible to reuse criteria/methods from other BCs/BCFs	Only manually, reusable components are fixed in the BCF	Only manually, reusable components are fixed in the BCF
Effort to maintain pre-defined criteria/methods	Low (financial methods have not changed much over the years)	High (experts need to develop templates or taxonomies)

6.4 Support for the Dynamic Reuse of Criteria

This paper proposes a new mechanism applicable in BCFs, namely *dynamic reuse of BC components*. It distinguishes itself from the *static reuse of BC components* in modern BCFs in that the reusable, domain-specific criteria and methods do not need to be pre-defined by experts, but can be reused from earlier BCs, possibly developed by other BC developers. It is most likely that this will take place in large organizations with many BCs and limited restrictions for sharing strategic data. But it is not unthinkable that BCs will even be shared across organizational boundaries, possibly in an anonymized or aggregated form. To select criteria and methods (semi-)automatically from earlier BCs to be reused, a mechanism is needed, such as collaborative filtering (Hussein & Ziegler, 2011). Collaborative filtering is common in other domains, such as online stores. For example, when looking at a certain book on Amazon, other books are recommended that were bought by other customers in combination with the book of interest. This principle can be applied to BCD as well. The development of a new BC is supported by means of an algorithm that scores criteria in similar earlier BCs. The algorithm globally works as follows (also see **Figure 6.1**):

1. It identifies the criteria which have been entered into the new BC.

2. It searches the database of earlier BCs, looking for BCs in which some of these criteria appear as well. These will be called the 'matching BCs'. The criteria in these BCs need to be identifiable as such and should be structured hierarchically.

3. Each matching BC contains what will be called 'potentially related criteria'. The strength of this potential relation is scored as follows. Criteria that are closer in the hierarchy to the place where the new and the earlier BC matched get more points.

4. For each of the potentially related criteria the scores are summed up over all the matching BCs. A limited set of the highest scoring criteria can then be recommended to the BC developer.

The scoring algorithm works as follows:

- siblings get 4 points (a sibling is on the same level *and* in the same branch of the hierarchy)
- parents and children get 3 points
- grandparents and grandchildren get 2 points
- all other criteria get 1 point

When a criterion occurs multiple times in the new BC (it is possible to repeat criteria in the criteria hierarchy), all matching BCs are scored only once with respect to that criterion. However, when an earlier BC matches to multiple different criteria in the new BC, all criteria in that earlier BC are scored for each matching criterion. Finally, when a matching criterion occurs multiple times in the earlier BC, that criterion will get scored multiple times, depending on its different positions in the hierarchy. For example, if 'Turnover time' would also occur below 'Benefit ob3' in **Figure 6.1**, it would receive 4+1=5 points.

New business case: RFID	Earlier business case: barcode	
Criteria	Points	Criteria
Impacts	1	Benefits
Benefit nb1	1	Benefit ob1
Benefit nb2	1	Benefit ob2
Warehouse search time	1	Benefit ob3
Stock levels	2	Costs
Cost nc1	3	Warehousing costs
Contingencies	match	Stock levels
Risk nr1	4	Turnover time
Risk nr2	1	Cost oc1
	1	Risks
	1	Risk or1
	1	Risk or2

Figure 6.1: Scoring criteria in the earlier BC based on matching criteria in the new BC

Compared to *static reuse of BC components*, the advantages of *dynamic reuse of BC components* are that it is not limited to a certain domain, the dimensions for reusability do not need to be defined explicitly, i.e., no formalization of the domain is needed. Moreover, there is little or no need for maintenance, the recommendations are always up-to-date and the recommendations may get better the more the system is used. This approach however also has some disadvantages: the quality of the recommendations may sometimes be insufficient and the recommender algorithm needs a starting point, i.e., it can only start looking for similar BCs as soon as some criteria have been entered in the new BC.

An important limitation of the algorithm used for the usability experiment presented in this paper, is that it only identifies similar BCs when they include criteria that are literally similar to the criteria in the new BC. This was not a problem during the usability experiment, because a rather homogeneous set of earlier BCs was used (see **Section 6.5.2**). However, in the real world, BCs may be more heterogeneous, because they will include typos and other nuances that are common in natural language. Therefore, future versions of the algorithm should include natural language processing to enable more intelligent matching of new BCs to earlier BCs.

6.5 Method

6.5.1 Research Model

A usability experiment was set-up to compare different types of possible support for the reuse of criteria. **Figure 6.2** shows the research model, which is based on the Technology Acceptance Model (Davis, 1989; Venkatesh, Morris, Davis, & Davis, 2003). It consists of the following dependent variables:

- *Actual Efficiency:* The time or effort the BC developer needs to develop a BC.
- *Actual Effectiveness:* The quality of the resulting BC, e.g., in terms of its reliability or acceptance by decision makers.
- *Perceived Ease of Use:* How easy to use the BCF is according to the BC developer.
- *Perceived Usefulness:* How useful the BCF is according to the BC developer.
- *Intention to Use:* How likely it is that the BC developer will use the BCF in his/her daily work (assuming that the BCF would be available and use would be voluntarily).

And the following independent variables:

- *BCD Task:* The type of BC that needs to be developed, e.g., determined by its size, domain, or complexity.
- *BCD Experience:* The experience of the BC developer in executing tasks similar to the BCD Task. Experience may concern BCD in general, but also the specific domain, e.g., industry or business processes affected.
- *BCD Support:* The information and tools that are available to the BC developer for completing the BCD Task.

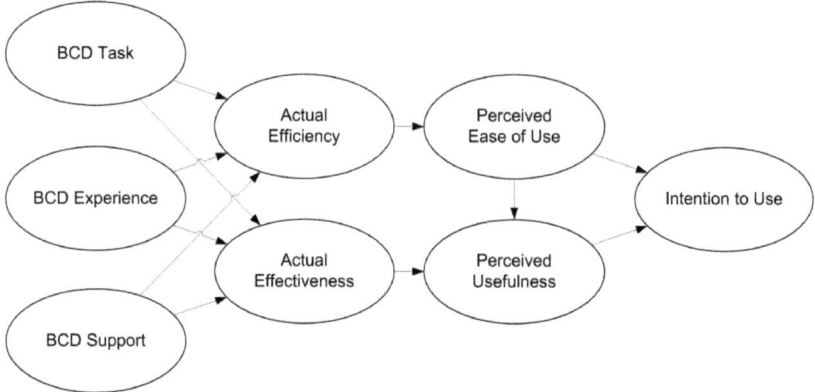

Figure 6.2: The research model

6.5.2 Experimental Design

The usability experiment consisted of the following main phases:

- *Pre-test:* A questionnaire to investigate the BCD Experience variable;
- *Introduction:* A text explaining what needed to be done during the task;
- *Benefit Definition Task:* A simplified BCD task to compare different types of support for the reuse of criteria;
- *Post-test:* A questionnaire to investigate the perceptions of the participant;

The task was to define five benefit criteria for a certain domain, in this case the use of Radio-Frequency Identification (RFID) in the automotive supply chain. Normally, a BC would also consist of cost and risk criteria, but to keep it simple, the task was limited to the identification of benefits. There were three experimental conditions (variations of the independent variable ‚BCD Support'):

Recommendations (**Figure E.4 to Figure E.8**): Five benefits were recommended for reuse, based on the collaborative filtering principle presented in **Section 6.4**. Each time a participant included a recommended benefit or came up with a benefit him/herself, the list of recommendations was updated automatically. This condition represents dynamic reuse of BC components.

Templates (**Figure E.9 to Figure E.12**): All benefits in the benefit database were listed, structured along the business processes to which they are related. Participants could enter benefits manually or include them from the templates. This condition represents static reuse of BC components, as common in modern BCFs such as the Value Lifecycle Manager (see **Section 6.3**).

No support (control-condition) (**Figure E.13**): All benefits needed to be invented and entered manually. This condition represents traditional BCFs, such as Financial Metrics Lite (see **Section 6.3**).

In all conditions, one exemplary benefit criterion was provided, to help the participant get started. For the recommender system it was necessary to have at least one benefit criterion entered in the new BC, so that it could directly start identifying related earlier BCs.

The database of benefit criteria was developed through action research with domain experts in the RFID-based Automotive Network research project (Project RAN, 2011; Reinhart et al., 2011). It consists of 330 benefits (criteria) for the use of RFID in the automotive supply chain. The benefits are structured hierarchically and divided over 12 BCs. Each BC represents the use of RFID to improve a certain business process in the automotive supply chain, e.g., 'Goods Receipt', 'Transportation' and 'Storage'. In the recommendations-condition, benefits are recommended from this database. In the templates-condition, all benefits are drawn from this database and presented as hierarchically structured lists. Using such an expert validated dataset allowed for the reliable evaluation of the Actual Effectiveness. Moreover, by using it for both of the conditions where support was provided, the results became comparable.

A between subjects design was applied; each new participant was assigned automatically to the next experimental condition. Because not every participant completed the experiment, in the end the three groups did not have exactly the same size.

The *independent* variable 'BCD Experience' was measured with several questions during the pre-test (**Figure E.1**, **Figure E.2**). The *dependent* variables were measured as follows:

- *Actual Efficiency:* The time in seconds was automatically measured from the start of the task until the participant continued to the next phase of the experiment.

- *Actual Effectiveness:* Benefits entered by participants were compared to the benefit database. For each exact match to the right category of Transportation benefits one point was assigned. For each exact match to another category half a point was assigned. For each benefit that was highly/somewhat similar (judged manually) to one in the Transportation category: one or half a point. All other benefits received zero points. The overall Actual Effectiveness for the participant was calculated as the mean of these points.

- *Perceived Ease of Use:* Some questions after the task had been completed (**Figure E.14**).
- *Perceived Usefulness:* Some questions after the task had been completed (**Figure E.14**).
- *Intention to Use:* Some questions after the task had been completed (**Figure E.14**).

The main hypotheses were that participants in the recommendations-condition would be the most efficient and those in the control-condition would be the least efficient. Participants in the templates-condition would be slightly more effective than those in the recommendations-condition, but those in the recommendations-condition would score higher on ease of use, usefulness and intention to use. For a more comprehensive list of the hypotheses please refer to **Table 6.5**.

6.5.3 Pilot

For the execution of the usability experiment, a custom web application was developed (**Figure E.1** to **Figure E.14**), to be used by the participants from their office desks or wherever and whenever they would want to participate. A pilot was done with two usability experts and two people who were representative for the target group of participants (see **Section 6.5.4**). They were observed to see where they experienced trouble and after completing the experiment their experiences were discussed. Based on the pilot, several changes were made. The main change was the reduction of the number of criteria from 10 to 5, making the task easier for participants and reducing the overall time needed.

6.5.4 Sampling

Participants were invited among three types of people, who are representative for the target users of BCFs:

- *Value Engineers:* People who develop BCs for customers to support the sales of e.g., software solutions. These people are highly experienced in BC development and execution.
- *Business Developers:* People who develop BCs for improving the performance of the company internally, or its relations to partners. Although BC development is not necessarily part of their daily work, there is a high likelihood that there are many BCD experts among this group.

- *Others:* All other people who may have to develop a BC one day, e.g., to get an idea across to senior management. Most of these people have very little experience developing BCs.

The experiment was carried out within SAP, a global business software company. Invitations were sent by e-mail. Value Engineers were invited when they had the keyword ‚value engineer(ing)' in their profiles in the corporate address book. Business Developers were invited when they had the keyword ‚business develop(er/ment)' in their profiles. For the ‚Others' category, all employees of the research department were invited.

6.6 Results

6.6.1 Demographics

The participants were mainly male (77%) and highly educated (20% Bachelor, 53% Master, 17% PhD, or equivalent). The mean age was 33. Most participants usually work in Germany (46%), but several other countries were also well represented: France (11%), USA (8%), Great Britain (6%). 25% of the participants used the German language version of the experimental system; all others used the English version. The time was measured for every phase of the experiment. The phase requiring most time was the benefit definition task itself, with a median time of 2min 57sec. **Table 6.2** shows the three types of participants, how many were invited, how many started with the experiment and how many completed it.

Table 6.2: Different types of participants and their completion rates

	Invited	Started	Completed	Completion Rate: Completed/Started	Response Rate: Completed/Invited
Value Engineer	115	52	29	56%	25%
Business Developer	335	90	49	54%	15%
Others	710	228	130	57%	18%
TOTAL	1160	370	208	56%	18%

6.6.2 Hypotheses Testing

The recommendations-, templates- and control-conditions were compared on the five dependent variables. An analysis of variance (ANOVA) was conducted, with post-hoc tests using the Tukey correction (**Table 6.3**). In several cases, Levene's test of equality of error variances was significant and Welch's F is reported (Field, 2005, p. 350). The results show that people using the recommendations are more efficient (lower time value) than those using templates (hypothesis H1a, **Table 6.3**) or those without support (hypothesis H1b). People using recommendations or templates are more effective than those without support (H2b, H2c), but the templates are not more effective than the recommendations (H2a). The recommendations are perceived to be easier to use than the templates and the control-condition (H3a, H3b). The recommendations are more useful than the control-condition (H4b), however they are not perceived to be more useful than the templates (H4a). The intention to use the recommendations is higher than that for the templates (H5a) or the control-condition (H5b). To conclude, the recommendations are preferred over the other conditions, but do not differ from the templates in terms of effectiveness.

In addition to the ANOVAs, bivariate correlations were computed between the independent variable 'Experience' and the dependent variables, as well as among the dependent variables (**Table 6.4**). The results show that more experience leads to a higher effectiveness (H6b), ease (H6c), usefulness (H6d), intention (H6e), but not to more efficiency, i.e., a lower time value (H6a). Less efficient people (higher time value) actually perform better (higher effectiveness) (H7a). A higher effectiveness leads to a higher ease of use (H8a), usefulness (H8b) and usage intention (H8c). A higher ease of use leads to a higher usefulness (H9a) and usage intention (H9b). By itself, a higher usefulness also leads to a higher usage intention (H10). These findings are conform the relations in the Technology Acceptance Model (Davis, 1989; Venkatesh et al., 2003). However, it needs to be noted that only the last three correlations that were described are strong ($r > .40$).

	N			M			SD			ANOVA	Pairwise Comparisons		
	R	T	C	R	T	C	R	T	C	F, Sig.	R vs T	R vs C	T vs C
Efficiency	76	64	75	163	256	245	111	163	127	$H1_0$ $F^*(2,133)=12, p<.001$	H1a p<.001	H1b p<.01	H1c p=.89
Effectiveness	377	318	341	0.91	0.89	0.74	0.19	0.21	0.29	$H2_0$ $F^*(2,657)=45, p<.001$	H2a p=.39	H2b p<.001	H2c p<.001
Ease of Use	71	61	57	4.1	3.7	3.6	0.87	0.67	0.86	$H3_0$ $F(2,186)=6.6, p<.01$	H3a p<.05	H3b p<.01	H3c p=.72
Usefulness	70	60	54	3.8	3.5	3.2	0.81	0.99	1.3	$H4_0$ $F^*(2,109)=4.8, p<.05$	H4a p=.26	H4b p<.01	H4c p=.25
Intention	72	61	61	3.7	3.2	2.9	0.96	1.0	1.3	$H5_0$ $F^*(2,122)=9.0, p<.001$	H5a p<.05	H5b p<.001	H5c p=.46

Table 6.3: Analysis of variance. R=Recommendations, T=Templates, C=Control-condition, F*=Welch's F. Hypotheses are indicated as Hx_y

	Efficiency	Effectiveness	Ease of Use	Usefulness	Intention to Use
Experience	H6a r(215)=.089, p=.19	H6b r(1036)=.07, p<.05	H6c r(189)=.16, p<.05	H6d r(184)=.24, p<.001	H6e r(194)=-.32, p<.001
Efficiency		H7a r(1036)=-.11, p<.001	H7b r(189)=-.02, p=.77	H7c r(184)=.14, p=.064	H7d r(194)=.082, p=.27
Effectiveness			H8a r(921)=.08, p<.05	H8b r(902)=.085, p<.05	H8c r(947)=.17, p<.001
Ease of Use				H9a r(179)=.47, p<.001	H9b r(187)=.45, p<.001
Usefulness					H10 r(182)=.66, p<.001

Table 6.4: Bivariate correlations for Task 1 (Reuse of Criteria). Hypotheses are indicated as Hx_y

Table 6.5: The hypotheses and results (***p<.001; **p<.01, *p<.05)

H1$_0$	There is no difference in *Actual Efficiency* among the experimental conditions.	reject***
H1a	The *Actual Efficiency* of Recommendations is better than Templates.	accept***
H1b	The *Actual Efficiency* of Recommendations is better than Control group.	accept**
H1c	The *Actual Efficiency* of Templates is better than Control group.	reject
H2$_0$	There is no difference in *Actual Effectiveness* among the experimental conditions.	reject***
H2a	The *Actual Effectiveness* of Recommendations is lower than Templates.	reject
H2b	The *Actual Effectiveness* of Recommendations is higher than Control-condition.	accept***
H2c	The *Actual Effectiveness* of Templates is higher than Control-condition.	accept***
H3$_0$	There is no difference in *Perceived Ease of Use* among the experimental conditions.	reject**
H3a	The *Perceived Ease of Use* of Recommendations is higher than Templates.	accept*
H3b	The *Perceived Ease of Use* of Recommendations is higher than Control-condition.	accept**
H3c	The *Perceived Ease of Use* of Templates is higher than Control-condition.	reject
H4$_0$	There is no difference in *Perceived Usefulness* among the experimental conditions.	reject*
H4a	The *Perceived Usefulness* of Recommendations is higher than Templates.	reject
H4b	The *Perceived Usefulness* of Recommendations is higher than Control-condition.	accept**
H4c	The *Perceived Usefulness* of Templates is higher than Control-condition.	reject
H5$_0$	There is no difference in *Intention to Use* among the experimental conditions.	reject***
H5a	The *Intention to Use* of Recommendations is higher than Templates.	accept*
H5b	The *Intention to Use* of Recommendations is higher than Control-condition.	accept***
H5c	The *Intention to Use* of Templates is higher than Control-condition.	reject
H6a	*BCD Expertise* is positively correlated with *Actual Efficiency*.	reject
H6b	*BCD Expertise* is positively correlated with *Actual Effectiveness*.	accept*
H6c	*BCD Expertise* is positively correlated with *Perceived Ease of Use*.	accept*
H6d	*BCD Expertise* is positively correlated with *Perceived Usefulness*.	accept***
H6e	*BCD Expertise* is positively correlated with *Intention to Use*.	accept***

H7a	*Actual Efficiency* is positively correlated with *Actual Effectiveness*.	accept***
H7b	*Actual Efficiency* is positively correlated with *Perceived Ease of Use*.	reject
H7c	*Actual Efficiency* is positively correlated with *Perceived Usefulness*.	reject
H7d	*Actual Efficiency* is positively correlated with *Intention to Use*.	reject
H8a	*Actual Effectiveness* is positively correlated with *Perceived Ease of Use*.	accept*
H8b	*Actual Effectiveness* is positively correlated with *Perceived Usefulness*.	accept*
H8c	*Actual Effectiveness* is positively correlated with *Intention to Use*.	accept***
H9a	*Perceived Ease of Use* is positively correlated with *Perceived Usefulness*.	accept***
H9b	*Perceived Ease of Use* is positively correlated with *Intention to Use*.	accept***
H10	*Perceived Usefulness* is positively correlated with *Intention to Use*.	accept***

Table 6.5 shows all hypotheses and whether they can be accepted or should be rejected. The hypotheses for Actual Efficiency should be read carefully, because a higher Actual Efficiency means more time, which is worse. Thus, when there is a positive correlation between Actual Efficiency and e.g. Actual Effectiveness, this means that people spending more time are more effective.

6.6.3 Qualitative Results

The participants had the possibility to enter comments in an open text field, after each set of questions throughout the experiment. Those comments were clustered manually and some of the most noteworthy ones will now be presented.

With respect to *Usefulness*, the main comment (mentioned 18 times) was that the recommendations and templates reduce the participant's creativity. In the recommendations-condition, only 83% of the benefits entered were reused, while in the templates-condition 88% of the benefits were reused. This may imply that the recommendations-condition allows for more creativity than the templates-condition. Several participants (13x) who were assigned to the control-condition (no support) expressed some confusion when having to answer the ease of use, usefulness and intention to use questions for a system that did not provide any support at all. Four participants in the templates-condition mentioned that they found the list of benefits too long. With respect to *Ease of Use*, there were similar comments. Additionally, three participants mentioned that they found it confusing that the list of recommendations was updated after each benefit selection. Two participants in the templates-condition found it confusing that the list also contained non-relevant benefits. With respect to *Intention to Use*, six participants found it hard to answer the question, because they did not know what to compare the system to.

6.7 Conclusion

Business case development (BCD) is a complex activity, which can potentially be improved by supporting the reuse of investment criteria and valuation methods. The goal of this research was to improve the usefulness and usability of business case frameworks (BCFs) (Research Question 1), while limiting the effort required to develop and maintain static databases of reusable components. Therefore, an approach was proposed for the *dynamic reuse of BC components* and contrasted with *static reuse of BC components*. In the dynamic approach, the reusable, domain-specific criteria and methods do not need to be pre-defined by experts in templates and taxonomies, but can be reused from earlier BCs. To test whether support for dynamic reuse improves the usefulness and usability of BCFs (Research Question 2), a usability experiment was set up. Three types of support for the reuse of criteria were compared: (1) recommendations, based on collaborative filtering and representative for the dynamic approach, (2) templates, representative for the static approach common in the class of modern BCFs and (3) no support, representative for the class of traditional BCFs. For each type of support, the 'Actual Effectiveness', 'Actual Efficiency', 'Perceived Ease of Use', 'Perceived Usefulness' and 'Perceived Intention to Use' were measured. The task represented a simplified BCD activity, i.e., to define five benefit criteria for the use of RFID in the automotive supply chain, and was completed by 208 people. The results show that although the recommendations are as effective as the templates, they are preferred over the other conditions. Thus, to make BCD more convenient and to save costs in developing databases with reusable BC components, we recommend to apply the recommendations, or another type of support for dynamic reuse, in future research and future BCFs. The dynamic approach does not need to replace pre-defined templates and taxonomies, but could also be used as an extension to the static approach, to facilitate reuse in those cases where the new BC does not match a domain that has been described by experts.

Some limitations of this work are: (1) that all participants of the experiment work for the same company. However, the participants represented ages 20 to 60, work in 24 different countries and range from complete novices to BCD experts. (2) As the different types of support for reuse were integrated in an experimental system, the support was not perceived through the use of the original BCFs that were represented by the experimental conditions. Therefore, when answering the questions in the post-test, it may have been difficult for the participants to distinguish between the functionality being tested, and the experimental system. The integration of the BCFs' functionality in one experimental system was unavoidable to minimize the time needed per participant and to minimize the unintended effect of other variables. (3) The scoring algorithm used for the recommendations-condition, could only identify similar BCs when they included criteria that were literally similar to the criteria in the new BC. In future work, natural language processing techniques should be applied to increase the capability of the algorithm to deal with the heterogeneity of real world BCs.

In spite of these and some other limitations, we believe that this paper makes several significant contributions, because it (1) focuses on BCD as a human activity, with the related human-computer interaction issues, which is new, (2) presents a new approach to facilitate dynamic reuse, and (3) evaluates the approach in a large scale, empirical study, which is uncommon in the field of IS investment evaluation. Some good exceptions are (J. Ballantine & Stray, 1998; Hochstrasser, 1990; Serafeimidis & Smithson, 2000; J. Ward et al., 2008; L. Willcocks & Lester, 1991).

In future work, the dynamic approach should be integrated in a more comprehensive BCF, after which the BCF should be tested with BC developers, working on more comprehensive BCD tasks. One effect that should receive particular attention is the possibility of loss of creativity due to the recommendations. With respect to that, questions are to what extent 'serendipity', i.e., the possibility to use unexpected criteria, may compensate for a loss of creativity and to what extent the loss of creativity may be worth the improvement in terms of efficiency. Additionally, the dynamic approach may be applied to support the reuse of methods. For each criterion in the new BC, the algorithm could select methods that have been applied most often to valuate the respective criterion in earlier BCs.

7 Exploring the Usability of Valuation Methods in Business Cases

Bart-Jan van Putten   Humboldt-Universität zu Berlin, SAP Research Dresden

Relevance for this Dissertation

According to the literature review (**Chapter 3**), one of the challenges for (re)using a valuation method is its 'usability'. This study explores how the 'Perceived Ease of Use' and the 'Perceived Usefulness' affect the intention of BC developers to (re)use certain methods. This knowledge can be used to improve systems that recommend methods for reuse.

Collaborations

- Prof. Oliver Günther, PhD (HU Berlin), Prof.Dr. Antonio Krüger (Saarland University), Prof.Dr. Jelke Bethlehem (University of Amsterdam) and Philipp Herzig (SAP Research) commented on my experimental set-up and statistical analysis plan.
- Dr. Angelika Salmen, Dr. Bettina Laugwitz, Dr. Jochen Rode and Dr. Sven Horn (all from SAP Research) provided support during the pilot usability tests.
- Dr. Theo Dirk Meijler (SAP Research) commented on the manuscript.

Abstract

Business case development (BCD) is a complex activity, which can be improved by supporting the reuse of investment criteria (benefits, costs, risks) and valuation methods. The aim of this paper was to find out why certain methods are more likely to be reused than others, from the perspective of usability. Therefore a usability experiment was set up in which 199 people compared several methods, drawn from different types of business case frameworks (BCF) and for different types of criteria. The results of the experiment led to the definition of several guidelines which can be used to decide which existing methods are most usable, or how methods should be designed to make them more usable.

7.1 Introduction

For decades, determining the value and success of information systems (IS) has been high on the agendas of researchers, cf. (King & Schrems, 1978; Davis, 1989; Urbach et al., 2009; Schryen, 2010). Many IS investments are strategic in nature, have long-term, hard to quantify benefits and incur indirect costs (Irani, 2002). 68% of IS projects cope with problems when having to identify the potential benefits of the investment, while 85% have problems with their quantification (J. Ballantine & Stray, 1999). This may lead to over-investment, under-investment, and makes it attractive to creatively adjust estimates (J. Ward et al., 2008).

To support IS investment evaluation (ISE), in most organizations some kind of business case (BC) is developed. A BC is *"a recommendation to decision makers to take a particular course of action for the organization, supported by an analysis of benefits, costs and risks"* (Gambles, 2009). Business case development (BCD) is the process of realizing the BC as an 'artifact', by gathering and analyzing data to define and valuate evaluation *criteria* (Bacon, 1992), presenting it in documents, spreadsheets or presentations. Examples of criteria are 'Return-on-Investment', 'Time Reduction' and 'Customer Satisfaction'. BCD may take place before project execution for investment appraisal, during project execution for monitoring and control, or after project execution for organizational learning (Van Putten et al., 2011).

When trying to estimate the values of the criteria selected for use in a new BC, a BC developer may spend days on defining *methods*, i.e., ways to put a qualitative, quantitative non-financial, or financial value on these criteria, see e.g., (Renkema & Berghout, 1997). This is especially challenging for the 'intangible' benefits and indirect costs (Irani, 2002). Instead, criteria and methods may also be *reused* from templates and taxonomies with browse and query functionality for their retrieval (Irani, Ghoneim, et al., 2006). Another way to support reuse is by selecting the components directly from the BCs in which they were used, e.g., through collaborative filtering (Van Putten, Irrenhauser, & Meijler, 2012). Supporting reuse has the potential to significantly improve the efficiency and effectiveness of BCD.

Because there may be multiple methods to valuate a certain criterion, it is necessary to understand why BC developers prefer to reuse certain methods over others. Milis and Mercken (2004) for example explain why the less sophisticated and less accurate financial methods are used more frequently: *"Companies tend to choose for the payback period and ROI because these techniques are perceived as being 'more easy' than IRR and NPV. Consequently, it is very doubtful that techniques with adjusted cost/benefit estimates or risk sensitivity will become popular"*. There are different factors which are known to influence the reuse decision (anonymized reference) and 'usability' is one of them. Usability is the extent to which a product can be used by specified users to achieve specified goals with effectiveness, efficiency and satisfaction in a specified context of use (ISO, 1998). In the context of BCD, we may consider the (re)usability of criteria and methods as the ease with which relevant criteria and methods can be identified and applied, the reliability of the resulting estimations and the satisfaction of the BC developer when applying them.

The goal of this paper is to identify usability reasons for why certain methods are more likely to be reused than others. This is investigated for three types of criteria: financial criteria, tangible non-financial criteria and intangible criteria. With this knowledge one can on the one hand develop a business case framework (BCF) that recommends methods for reuse based on their usability properties. On the other hand, when a BC developer decides to develop a new method, the BCF can provide support to develop the method in such a way that it is likely to be (re)usable by other BC developers.

This paper is further structured as follows: In **Section 7.2**, two types of Business Case Frameworks will be described. **Section 7.3** introduces potential aspects influencing the usability of valuation methods. **Section 7.4** explains the methods that were compared. In **Section 7.5**, the research method, a laboratory experiment, is described. **Section 7.6** presents the results. The paper ends with a discussion (**Section 7.7**) and a conclusion (**Section 7.8**).

7.2 Business Case Frameworks

A BCF is a set of guidelines, methods, templates or tools to support BCD. In this paper, methods from different BCFs will be compared. In the context of this paper we distinguish between two classes of BCFs, which are not mutually exclusive:

- *Financial BCFs:* Support the development of the BC in terms of its cash flow, often accompanied by metrics such as Return-on-Investment (ROI), Net Present Value (NPV), or Internal Rate of Return (IRR). These BCFs are often domain agnostic and have rigid structures. Sometimes, new criteria can be entered, but those then need to be quantified directly in financial terms. These BCFs are often implemented as a Microsoft Excel spreadsheet. An example of a BCF in this class is Financial Metrics Lite (FML) (SolutionMatrix Ltd., 2010). FML is freely available from the website of a company which focuses on BC consulting.

- *Domain-specific BCFs:* Support the development of the BC in terms of criteria that are specific to a domain, such as RFID in the supply chain (Ivantysynova, 2008, p. 155). The relevant ones then need to be selected from a template or taxonomy, which has been pre-defined by domain experts. These BCFs may be implemented as a Microsoft Excel spreadsheet, but some of them are web applications that ease collaborative BCD, such as the Value Lifecycle Manager (VLM) (SAP AG, 2011). As employees of the company, the authors had access to some of the contents in VLM.

A major difference between BCFs is thus which types of criteria are supported. Three classes of criteria are generally distinguished: financial, tangible non-financial and intangible criteria (Irani, Gunasekaran, & Love, 2006). Financial criteria, such as Return-on-Investment, are supported by almost every BCF and especially by the Financial BCFs. Tangible non-financial criteria, such as Time Reduction, are less common but often needed to derive the financial figures. They are frequently supported by domain-specific BCFs. Such BCFs then offer a domain-specific way of putting a value on that criterion. Some domain-specific BCFs also offer support to convert the tangible non-financial value to a financial value. Intangible criteria, such as Customer Satisfaction, are least common because they are hard to measure and quantify (anonymized reference).

7.3 Usability Aspects of Valuation Methods

The usability of a method may be affected by many factors, ranging from functional to aesthetical aspects (Nielsen, 1993). In this paper several methods will be compared in terms of usability. We identified some of the aspects that have the potential to contribute to the observed differences in usability between those methods. In this section, those aspects will be introduced:

- *Type of criterion that is valuated:* Financial criteria, such as revenue, profit, or costs, are generally perceived to be easier to valuate than less tangible criteria such as customer satisfaction (Farbey et al., 1992). However, from our point of view, this also depends on the data that is available and the person whom is developing the BC. E.g., for people who are financially trained it is likely to be easier to apply a financial method than for a domain expert.

- *Unit of estimation:* Some methods require the estimation of financial values, others require the estimation of non-financial values, e.g., in terms of time or number of pieces. In some cases non-financial values are estimated at first, before they are converted to financial values. Another way of estimation which is sometimes used, is scoring: BC developers add a number on a scale of e.g., 1 to 5, to estimate the likelihood that a certain benefit will occur (Chou et al., 2006).

- *Absolute vs. relative:* Some methods require values to be estimated in absolute terms. E.g., when estimating the future inventory costs, one would first estimate the future average number of days in inventory and slowly work towards a cost figure. Other methods may require the estimation of values relative to a figure that is already known, e.g., a 2% decrease in inventory costs. We expect that relative estimations are easier to do, while absolute estimations may be more reliable.

- *Present value:* Within the category of financial methods, discounted methods, such as NPV, take the present value of the money into account and are generally perceived to be more difficult to understand and use (Milis & Mercken, 2004).
- *Size:* In general, methods that are composed of fewer steps are more efficient and thus perceived to be easier to use (Nielsen, 1993).
- *Visual appearance:* The appearance of methods may differ in terms of color, structure, and more. Although it is hard to predict which design will be best perceived by the users of the method, it is at least likely that this factor affects the method's usability (Green & Petre, 1996). A related issue is whether the internal complexity of the method is shown at the user interface level, e.g., when formulae are shown. Although this may make the method more usable, it can also give it a more complex appearance.
- *Multiple viewpoints:* Some methods allow the capturing of multiple viewpoints, e.g., alternative cases (worst case, likely case, best case) or alternative opinions from different stakeholders. This may make a method more usable because it shows the potential success of implementation of the BC (Campbell & Brown, 2005). Multiple viewpoints may also prevent the necessity to calculate one 'perfect' value.

7.4 Comparing Valuation Methods

In this paper, an experiment will be described where different methods were compared. This was done on the basis of three criteria: ROI (financial), Time Reduction (tangible non-financial), Customer Satisfaction (intangible). These three criteria were chosen because they are common and representative for their classes of criteria (Milis & Mercken, 2004). For each of these exemplary criteria, three methods will be compared with respect to their usability. For each criterion, one method was drawn from FML, one method was selected from VLM and the third method for each criterion was specifically developed for the purpose of the experiment, with the aim to change some of the properties of the method and see if that would improve its usability. For each of the three criteria we will now shortly explain each of the selected/developed methods. An overview can be found in **Table 7.1**.

	Return-on-Investment			Time Reduction			Customer Satisfaction		
	FML	VLM	New	FML	VLM	New	FML	VLM	New
Figure in Appendix	Figure E.15	Figure E.16	Figure E.17	Figure E.18	Figure E.19	Figure E.20	Figure E.21	Figure E.22	Figure E.23
Unit	Financial	Financial	Financial	Financial	Financial	Time (non-financial)	Financial	Percentage	Score
Abs. / rel.	Absolute	Absolute	Absolute	Absolute	Relative	Absolute	Absolute	Relative	N/A
Present value	no	yes	no	N/A	N/A	N/A	N/A	N/A	N/A
Size	small	small	small	medium	small	medium	medium	small	large
Appearance	complex formulae are shown	no comments	no comments	no comments	looks very complex	shows reliability	no comments	looks complex	no comments
Viewpoints	no	no	no	no	no	no	no	no	yes

Table 7.1: An overview of the methods that were compared and some of their properties

7.4.1 Return-on-Investment (financial criterion)

The method that was selected from FML is a 'Simple ROI' calculation, i.e., a non-discounted cash flow method (**Figure E.15**). It shows the formulae that are used. The method that was selected from VLM is a discounted cash flow method (**Figure E.16**). The newly developed method is a non-discounted cash flow method (**Figure E.17**), with a simpler visual appearance than the FML method.

7.4.2 Time Reduction (tangible non-financial criterion)

The most suitable method for valuating this criterion which is available in FML is a cash flow method, in which it is possible to enter specific benefit/cost items that are caused by the time savings. However, the time savings themselves can not be estimated (**Figure E.18**), rather they need to be entered directly in financial terms. The method selected from VLM is a domain-specific method for the estimation of productivity improvement in the transportation domain. The productivity improvement is estimated as a percentual value which translates into a cost reduction (**Figure E.19**). In our opinion, the method is visually cluttered. The newly developed method is also domain-specific, but the result is a time value, rather than a financial value (**Figure E.20**).

7.4.3 Customer Satisfaction (intangible criterion)

When selecting a method from FML, the one that seemed to be the most suitable was again the cash flow method with the possibility to enter specific benefit/cost items (**Figure E.21**). From VLM, a generic method for estimating customer satisfaction was selected (**Figure E.22**). The criterion needs to be estimated directly as a percentual value. The method that was newly developed for the purpose of the experiment does three things differently. First, the criterion is estimated on a unitless scale from 1 to 5 (1 = bad, 5 = good). Second, the opinions of multiple stakeholders are captured and a weighted average is calculated. Third, different alternatives are compared, e.g., barcode vs. RFID (**Figure E.23**).

7.5 Research Method

7.5.1 Research Model

A *laboratory* experiment was set-up to compare the usability of the different methods. The experimental set-up allowed to control for several factors, such as the BCD task. In earlier research we had done a *field* experiment, but found it hard to control the task (anonymized reference). **Figure 7.1** shows the research model, which is based on the Technology Acceptance Model (TAM) (Davis, 1989; Venkatesh & Bala, 2008). This model was applied because it is the most widely employed model of IT adoption and use and because it has shown to be highly predictive (Venkatesh & Davis, 2000). We used the following dependent variables:

- *Perceived Ease of Use:* "The degree to which a person believes that using a system would be free of effort." (Davis, 1989)

- *Perceived Usefulness:* "The degree to which a person believes that using a particular system would enhance his or her job performance." (Davis, 1989)
- *Intention to Use:* "An individual's positive or negative feelings about performing the target behavior." (Davis, 1989)

In addition, we used the following independent variables:

- *BCD Task:* The type of criterion that needs to be valuated, i.e., financial, tangible non-financial, or intangible. This variable was added, because in terms of TAM3 (Venkatesh & Bala, 2008), depending on the task ('job'), the BCF ('information technology') may have a lower or higher 'job relevance'.
- *BCD Experience:* The experience of the BC developer. Experience may concern BCD in general, but also the specific domain. Experience is known to moderate several relationships in TAM3.
- *BCD Support:* The valuation method provided to support the BC developer in valuating the criterion. This variable was added because there were different experimental conditions in which different types of support were offered.

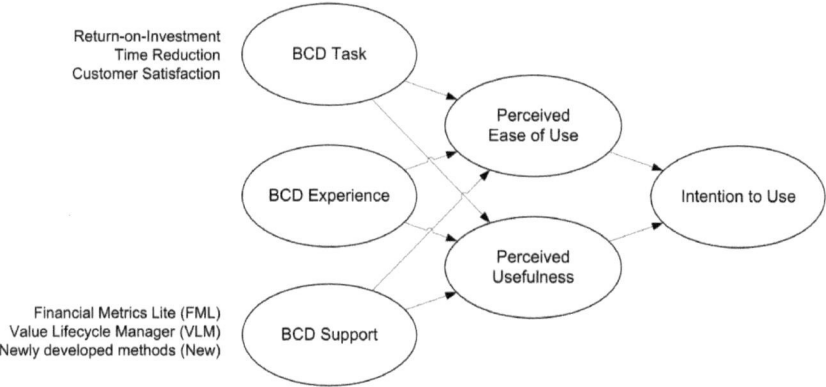

Figure 7.1: The research model

7.5.2 Experimental Design

Each participant in the experiment evaluated the three methods (variations of the independent variable 'BCD Support'), for one of the three criteria. Thus, there were three experimental conditions, the criterion being a variation of the independent variable 'BCD Task' (**Figure 7.2**). Participants were assigned randomly to one of the three conditions, but the algorithm made sure that the group sizes would not differ

107

more than 10%. For each method a screenshot was included in the experimental system (**Figure E.15** to **Figure E.23**) and the participant was asked to judge the Perceived Ease of Use, Perceived Usefulness and Intention to Use on a five-point Likert-scale.

	1/3 participants ROI		1/3 participants Time Reduction		1/3 participants Customer Satisfaction		
FML	Ease Usefulness Intention	FML	Ease Usefulness Intention	FML	Ease Usefulness Intention	within-subjects	For each criterion: which method is most usable?
VLM	Ease Usefulness Intention	VLM	Ease Usefulness Intention	VLM	Ease Usefulness Intention		
New	Ease Usefulness Intention	New	Ease Usefulness Intention	New	Ease Usefulness Intention		

Figure 7.2: Overview of the experimental design.

7.5.3 Hypotheses

The hypotheses can be found in **Table 7.4**. We have assumed that VLM is better (more useful, easier to use, higher intention to use) than FML because it includes domain-specific methods. Such methods generally give BC developers more support to gradually come up with financial figures, rather than requiring financial figures in the first place. For one hypothesis we made an exception, H4a: "For Time Reduction, the Ease of Use of the FML method is higher than the VLM method." This was hypothesized because the VLM method for Time Reduction has a high degree of visual clutter (**Figure E.19**). With respect to the new methods, we have assumed that they were better than the methods from FML and VLM. This because the new methods were designed to deal with the limitations of the other methods.

7.5.4 Sampling

Participants were invited among three types of people, who are representative for the target users of BCFs:

- *Value Engineers:* People who develop BCs for customers to support the sales of e.g., software solutions. These people are highly experienced in BC development and execution.

- *Business Developers:* People who develop BCs for improving the performance of the company internally, or its relations to partners. Although BC development is not necessarily part of their daily work, there is a high likelihood that there are many BCD experts among this group.

- *Others:* All other people who may have to develop a BC one day, e.g., to get an idea across to senior management. Most of these people have very little experience developing BCs.

The experiment was carried out within a global business software company. In the company, there are BCs that support the decision whether new product ideas should be commercialized, there are BCs that support specific customers how to invest in certain products, and there are BCs that propose improvements to organizational processes. Thus, there is a large number and variety of BCs developed each year. Therefore it could be expected that a relatively large number of employees had experience with BCD. This was relevant, because we wanted to test if experience had an influence on the preferences of BC developers. Other more practical reasons for choosing the company were that the authors could get senior management support for the survey and that the results could benefit the company in the long term. Thus, there was an incentive for employees to participate.

Invitations were sent by e-mail. Value Engineers were invited when they had the keyword ‚value engineer(ing)' in their profiles in the corporate address book. Business Developers were invited when they had the keyword ‚business develop(er/ment)' in their profiles. For the ‚Others' category, all employees of the research department were invited.

7.6 Results

7.6.1 Demographics

The participants were mainly male (77%) and highly educated (20% Bachelor, 53% Master, 17% PhD, or equivalent). The mean age was 33. Most participants usually work in Germany (46%), but several other countries were also well represented: France (11%), USA (8%), Great Britain (6%). 25% of the participants used the German language version of the experimental system; all others used the English version. The time was measured for every phase of the experiment. The phase requiring most time was the method evaluation task itself, with a median time of 3min 40sec. **Table 7.2** shows the three types of participants, how many were invited, how many started with the experiment and how many completed it. We believe that the 54% completion rate is not as bad as it may seem. The task reported in this paper was actually the second task in a larger experiment (anonymized reference). On the other task a median time of 8min 22sec was spent. Thus, some participants may have quit for time reasons. Another possible explanation is that the task that is presented in this paper may not have appealed to all participants, especially to those who do not do BCD in their daily jobs.

Table 7.2: Different types of participants and their completion rates

	Invited	Started	Completed	Completion Rate: Completed/Started	Response Rate: Completed/Invited
Value Engineer	115	52	29	56%	25%
Business Developer	335	90	44	49%	13%
Others	710	228	126	55%	17%
TOTAL	1160	370	199	54%	17%

7.6.2 Hypotheses Testing

Paired samples T-tests were conducted to compare the within-subjects results for Ease of Use, Usefulness, Intention to Use among the methods for each of the conditions (**Table 7.3**). The only significant result for *ROI* is that there is a higher intention to use the VLM method than the FML method (hypothesis H3a, **Table 7.3**, **Table 7.4**). With respect to *Time Reduction*, the FML method and the new method are easier to use than the VLM method (H4a, H4c). The new method is more useful than FML (H5b) and VLM (H5c), which is also reflected by the intention to use (H6b, H6c). With respect to *Customer Satisfaction*, the new method is easier to use than FML (H7b) and VLM (H7c). VLM and the new method are more useful than FLM (H8a, H8b) and the new method is more useful than VLM (H8c). This is also reflected by the intention to use (H9a, H9b, H9c).

	N			M			T-Tests		
	V vs F	N vs F	N vs V	V vs F	N vs F	N vs V	V vs F	N vs F	N vs V
Return-on-Investment									
Ease	61	60	61	3.5/3.5	4.0/3.5	3.9/3.5	H1a t(60)=-.17, p=.87	H1b t(59)=2.1, p=.043	H1c t(60)=1.8, p=.073
Usefulness	57	57	57	3.8/3.3	3.3/3.4	3.3/3.8	H2a t(56)=2.0, p=.054	H2b t(56)=-.63, p=.53	H2c t(56)=-2.1, p=.046
Intention	56	56	56	3.6/3.0	3.1/3.1	3.1/3.6	H3a t(55)=2.5, p<.025	H3b t(55)=.073, p=.94	H3c t(55)=-1.7, p=.092
Time Reduction									
Ease	62	62	63	2.9/3.7	3.7/3.7	3.7/2.8	H4a t(61)=-3.0, p<.01	H4b t(61)=.073, p=.94	H4c t(61)=3.8, p<.001
Usefulness	52	55	57	2.9/2.8	3.8/2.8	3.8/3.0	H5a t(51)=.54, p=.59	H5b t(54)=3.5, p<.01	H5c t(56)=3.2, p<.01
Intention	53	55	60	2.8/2.7	3.7/2.7	3.7/2.8	H6a t(52)=.41, p=.68	H6b t(54)=3.5, p<.01	H6c t(59)=3.4, p<.01
Customer Satisfaction									
Ease	71	71	70	3.5/3.8	4.3/3.8	4.3/3.5	H7a t(70)=-1.6, p=.12	H7b t(70)=3.1, p<.01	H7c t(69)=4.4, p<.001
Usefulness	67	69	68	3.5/2.5	4.0/2.6	4.0/3.5	H8a t(66)=4.5, p<.001	H8b t(68)=7.1, p<.001	H8c t(67)=3.1, p<.01
Intention	69	69	70	3.2/2.3	3.8/2.3	3.8/3.2	H9a t(68)=4.4, p<.001	H9b t(68)=6.9, p<.001	H9c t(69)=3.1, p<.01

Table 7.3: Paired samples T-tests. F=FML, V=VLM, N=New

Table 7.4: The hypotheses and results (***p<.001 one-tailed; **p<.01 one-tailed, *p<.025 one-tailed)

H1$_0$	For ROI, there is no difference in Ease of Use among the methods.	accept
H1a	For ROI, the Ease of Use of the VLM method is higher than the FML method.	reject
H1b	For ROI, the Ease of Use of the new method is higher than the FML method.	reject
H1c	For ROI, the Ease of Use of the new method is higher than the VLM method.	reject
H2$_0$	For ROI, there is no difference in Usefulness among the methods.	reject
H2a	For ROI, the Usefulness of the VLM method is higher than the FML method.	reject
H2b	For ROI, the Usefulness of the new method is higher than the FML method.	reject
H2c	For ROI, the Usefulness of the new method is higher than the VLM method.	reject
H3$_0$	For ROI, there is no difference in Intention to Use among the methods.	reject
H3a	For ROI, the Intention to Use the VLM method is higher than the FML method.	accept*
H3b	For ROI, the Intention to Use the new method is higher than the FML method.	reject
H3c	For ROI, the Intention to Use the new method is higher than the VLM method.	reject
H4$_0$	For Time Reduction, there is no difference in Ease of Use among the methods.	reject
H4a	For Time Reduction, the Ease of Use of the FML method is higher than the VLM method.	accept**
H4b	For Time Reduction, the Ease of Use of the new method is higher than the FML method.	reject
H4c	For Time Reduction, the Ease of Use of the new method is higher than the VLM method.	accept***
H5$_0$	For Time Reduction, there is no difference in Usefulness among the methods.	reject
H5a	For Time Reduction, the Usefulness of the VLM method is higher than the FML method.	reject
H5b	For Time Reduction, the Usefulness of the new method is higher than the FML method.	accept**
H5c	For Time Reduction, the Usefulness of the new method is higher than the VLM method.	accept**
H6$_0$	For Time Reduction, there is no difference in Intention to Use among	reject

	the methods.	
H6a	For Time Reduction, the Intention to Use the VLM method is higher than the FML method.	reject
H6b	For Time Reduction, the Intention to Use the new method is higher than the FML method.	accept**
H6c	For Time Reduction, the Intention to Use the new method is higher than the VLM method.	accept**
$H7_0$	For Customer Satisfaction, there is no difference in Ease of Use among the methods.	reject
H7a	For Customer Satisfaction, the Ease of Use of the VLM method is higher than the FML method.	reject
H7b	For Customer Satisfaction, the Ease of Use of the new method is higher than the FML method.	accept**
H7c	For Customer Satisfaction, the Ease of Use of the new method is higher than the VLM method.	accept***
$H8_0$	For Customer Satisfaction, there is no difference in Usefulness among the methods.	reject
H8a	For Customer Satisfaction, the Usefulness of the VLM method is higher than the FML method.	accept***
H8b	For Customer Satisfaction, the Usefulness of the new method is higher than the FML method.	accept***
H8c	For Customer Satisfaction, the Usefulness of the new method is higher than the VLM method.	accept**
$H9_0$	For Customer Satisfaction, there is no difference in Intention to Use among the methods.	reject
H9a	For Customer Satisfaction, the Intention to Use the VLM method is higher than the FML method.	accept***
H9b	For Customer Satisfaction, the Intention to Use the new method is higher than the FML method.	accept***
H9c	For Customer Satisfaction, the Intention to Use the new method is higher than the VLM method.	accept**

Bivariate correlations were computed between the independent variable BCD Experience and the dependent variables, as well as among the dependent variables (**Table 7.5**). The results show that experience has no effect on the FML methods or the new methods, that experience has a positive effect on the VLM methods for ROI and Customer Satisfaction, but not for Time Reduction. All other correlations are in accordance with the Technology Acceptance Model (Davis, 1989; Venkatesh et al., 2003), i.e., ease correlates positively with usefulness and intention, usefulness correlates positively with intention. One exception is that for Customer Satisfaction, FML's ease does not correlate with usefulness and intention.

Table 7.5: Bivariate correlations

		Ease	Usefulness	Intention
Return-on-Investment				
FML	Experience	r(61)=.23, p=.078	r(59)=.10, p=.45	r(57)=-.020, p=.88
	Ease		r(58)=.57, p<.001	r(56)=.51, p<.001
	Usefulness			r(56)=.82, p<.001
VLM	Experience	r(62)=.46, p<.001	r(58)=.38, p<.01	r(57)=.39, p<.01
	Ease		r(58)=.69, p<.001	r(57)=.77, p<.001
	Usefulness			r(57)=.92, p<.001
New	Experience	r(61)=-.22, p=.085	r(58)=-2.1, p=.11	r(57)=-.31, p<.05
	Ease		r(58)=.69, p<.001	r(57)=.64, p<.001
	Usefulness			r(57)=.90, p<.001
Time Reduction				
FML	Experience	r(62)=.20, p=.12	r(55)=.007, p=.96	r(55)=.022, p=.88
	Ease		r(55)=.34, p<.05	r(55)=.36, p<.01
	Usefulness			r(55)=.97, p<.001
VLM	Experience	r(63)=.28, p<.05	r(57)=.16, p=.25	r(60)=.16, p=.23
	Ease		r(57)=.75, p<.001	r(60)=.77, p<.001
	Usefulness			r(57)=.89, p<.001
New	Experience	r(63)=.007, p=.95	r(62)=.024, p=.85	r(62)=.040, p=.76
	Ease		r(62)=.71, p<.001	r(62)=.76, p<.001
	Usefulness			r(62)=.89, p<.001
Customer Satisfaction				
FML	Experience	r(72)=.007, p=.96	r(70)=-.028, p=.82	r(69)=-.009, p=.94
	Ease		r(70)=.22, p=.068	r(69)=.20, p=.096
	Usefulness			r(68)=.84, p<.001
VLM	Experience	r(71)=.29, p<.05	r(69)=.29, p<.05	r(70)=.36, p<.01
	Ease		r(69)=.48, p<.001	r(70)=.57, p<.001
	Usefulness			r(68)=.86, p<.001
New	Experience	r(71)=-.019, p=.87	r(71)=-.17, p=.15	r(71)=-.033, p=.79
	Ease		r(71)=.62, p<.001	r(71)=.65, p<.001
	Usefulness			r(71)=.83, p<.001

7.7 Discussion

The results of the experiment show that, especially for the tangible non-financial and intangible criteria, the newly developed methods are significantly easier to use and more useful than the other methods, which also leads to a higher intention to use the new methods. Unfortunately, the number of qualitative comments received through the survey was disappointing. It is therefore not easy to derive why certain methods were preferred over others. The following findings should thus be treated as preliminary results which could be re-examined in future work.

The FML method and the new method for Time Reduction are easier to use than the VLM method. The latter requires direct estimation of the percentual effective improvement. This may imply that asking the user to input improvement as a percentual value is too difficult. Although this seems to be common practice in many BCFs, it is ineffective because there is no support for figuring out which percentual value is realistic. Simply assuming that the improvement of any business process in any industry always lies between 5 and 10 percent is dangerous. Better valuation methods therefore support the BC developer in determining the actual values (with a unit of measurement), e.g., the time spend in minutes. When comparing the current time and the expected future time, the percentual value may then be *derived*.

The new method for Time Reduction is more useful than both the FML and the VLM methods. This may imply that people prefer to quantify the future situation in the original unit of measurement (in this case time in minutes), rather than requiring the BC developer to input financial values directly.

The new method for Customer Satisfaction is easier to use than both the FML and the VLM methods. This again shows that requiring the user to directly input a percentual value, without any support for quantifying the 'as-is' and 'to-be' situations, may not be acceptable for BC developers.

The VLM method for Customer Satisfaction is more useful than the FML method. This shows that financial cash flow methods are (obviously) not suitable for the estimation of intangible criteria.

The new method for Customer Satisfaction is more useful than both the FML and the VLM methods. This implies that especially for intangible criteria, methods become more useful when a scoring method is used or when the opinions of multiple stakeholders are taken into account.

7.8 Conclusion

When trying to estimate the values of the criteria selected for use in a new business case (BC), a BC developer may spend days on defining *methods*, i.e., ways to put a qualitative, quantitative non-financial, or financial value on these criteria. To ease the life of BC developers, our general research aim is to investigate how the reuse of methods can be supported. The more specific aim of this paper was to find out why certain methods are more likely to be reused than others, from the perspective of usability. This was investigated for three types of criteria: financial criteria, tangible non-financial criteria and intangible criteria. 199 SAP employees participated in an experiment. Each participant evaluated three methods. Those methods were drawn from a traditional financial business case framework (BCF), from a modern domain-specific BCF which is also suitable for estimating non-financial and intangible criteria, or were specifically developed for the experiment. The results of the experiment show that, especially for the tangible non-financial and intangible criteria, the newly developed methods are significantly easier to use and more useful than the other methods, which also leads to a higher intention to use the new methods. The experience of the BC developer has no direct effect on ease of use, usefulness or intention to use. Based on these findings, the following preliminary guidelines could be derived:

- Methods should support the BC developer in estimating the original values of the as-is and to-be situations, from which a percentual improvement may be derived, rather than requiring the percentual improvement in the first place.

- Methods should support the BC developer in estimating with the original unit of measurement, from which a financial value may be derived, rather than requiring the financial value in the first place.

- Methods that are used to estimate intangible criteria should support the inclusion and comparison of the opinions from multiple stakeholders and may use scores rather than absolute or relative values.

This research has several limitations. In some cases the methods that were compared differed in more than one property. We had hoped for more qualitative feedback, which would explain why a certain method was preferred over another. As such feedback was very limited we can only guess which property has caused the measured differences in terms of usefulness, ease of use and intention to use. Another limitation is that the subjects did not use the methods, but merely looked at the screenshots. This was done to keep the complexity and duration of the experiment low and thus to be able to do quantitative analysis. However, with hindsight we would have taken a different approach. We would have done a more qualitative study, where the subjects have to use the methods and only minor differences between the methods are tested. This would however require a much larger number of experiments, to uncover all the possible usability factors and their effects. Another limitation of this research is that compared to the large number of methods available in today's BCFs, only a small number of methods could be evaluated. Those were therefore selected to represent different classes of criteria and drawn from different types of BCFs.

Future work could aim to extend and refine the model of method properties, based on existing theories. This would make it easier to speak of classes of methods, rather than of specific instances which will always be slightly different among BCFs. Moreover, further experiments could investigate smaller differences between the methods to dig deeper into which properties contribute to the observed differences in usability. This may finally lead to knowledge that can be used to build BCFs that support BC developers in reusing the most usable methods, and when developing new methods, to design them in such a way that they are more (re)usable.

8 The Relation Between Dynamic Business Models and Business Cases

Bart-Jan van Putten   Humboldt-Universität zu Berlin, SAP Research Dresden
Markus Schief   TU Darmstadt, SAP Research Darmstadt

Published as...

Van Putten, B.-J., Schief, M. (2011). *The Relation Between Dynamic Business Models and Business Cases.* Proceedings of the 5th European Conference on Information Management and Evaluation (ECIME), September 8-9, Como, Italy. *Best PhD Paper Award.*

Van Putten, B.-J., Schief, M. (2012). *The Relation Between Dynamic Business Models and Business Cases.* The Electronic Journal of Information Systems Evaluation, Volume 15, Issue 1, Pages 138-148.

Relevance for this Dissertation

This study aimed to clarify how business models, as an implementation of a company's strategy, can be aligned with BCs, as an abstraction of a company's operations. This knowledge may help companies to decide more efficiently and effectively which BCs need to approved (before their execution) or changed (during execution).

Collaborations

- Markus Schief (SAP Research) made a significant contribution, e.g., with his ideas on mergers & acquisitions, he commented several times on the manuscript and he wrote several parts, among which the contents of **Table 8.3** and **Table 8.4**.

Abstract

This paper analyses the relation between two well-known business concepts. It clarifies how business models, as an implementation of a company's strategy, can be aligned with business cases, as an abstraction of a company's operations. The relations are analyzed from a static as well as a dynamic point of view by means of inductive reasoning and literature review. Based on the understanding of the relations, a continuous business model-business case alignment approach is proposed. Further, managerial guidelines are presented supporting the approach. Finally, two software tools, business case framework and business model composer, are presented indicating how the proposed conceptual alignment could be implemented. This paper contributes to research and practice. Both can benefit from the conceptual relation between two well-known concepts that have hardly been linked so far. Practitioners can apply the proposed alignment approach and the managerial guidelines to review their business. For research, we contribute to the body of knowledge of business model concepts. Researchers can build upon this fruitful ground by validating the proposed concept in empirical settings or by implementing software solutions supporting this approach. Consequently, the agility of companies can be increased when implementing merged or changed business models in the organization and when using business cases to determine if it is time to change the business model.

8.1 Introduction

Companies are continuously striving for more agility. One of the challenges is the rapid translation of changes in a company's strategy to its operations and vice versa. For example, after the acquisition of Sun by Oracle, Oracle cut former Sun partners, without notice, from their hardware maintenance renewals business (Kovar, 2010). For many of those partners, maintenance renewals were an essential part of economic survival. Therefore, these companies needed a very high degree of agility to be able to adapt their strategy and implement it in changed operations before they would go out of business.

Unfortunately, there is a gap between business strategy and business operations, hampering companies' agility (Al-Debei & Avison, 2010, p. 370). Al-Debei & Avison propose to fill this gap with the 'business model' (BM), which can be used to "translate the broad strategy into more specific business architectural, co-operational, value propositional, and financial arrangements needed to achieve the strategic goals and objectives of the business". This study builds upon that claim and aims to show that ‚business cases' (BC), i.e., the (documented) rationale for executing a project or investment in accordance with the strategy, complement the business model in closing the gap between strategy and operations. The mutual relationships between BM and BC may be taken into account in today's business practice implicitly, but with some exceptions, e.g., (Casadesus-Masanell & Ricart, 2010), they did not receive much attention in the literature. Therefore, this study aims to clarify the relation between BM and BC, based on literature review and inductive reasoning. Moreover, this study aims to provide a starting point for incorporating this more explicit understanding in organizational processes and software tools supporting those processes. Throughout the study, mergers & acquisitions (M&A) will be used as an example because they often cause disruptive changes in the strategy and operations of companies.

The structure of this paper is as follows. **Section 8.2** provides a background on the BM and BC concepts and the factors causing BMs and BCs to change over time. **Section 8.3** analyzes static similarities between BMs and BCs and dynamic influences of a BM on BCs and vice versa. **Section 8.4** identifies managerial and technical implications for companies and **Section 8.5** concludes this paper.

8.2 Background

8.2.1 Business Models

While several definitions of business models can be found (Morris, Schindehutte, & Allen, 2005), Osterwalder et al. (2005) provide the following definition: "A business model is a conceptual tool that contains a set of elements and their relationships and allows expressing the business logic of a specific firm. It is a description of the value a company offers to one or several segments of customers and of the architecture of the firm and its network of partners for creating, marketing, and delivering this value and relationship capital, to generate profitable and sustainable revenue streams."

According to Gordijn et al. (2005), in literature, the notion of 'business model' is interpreted in the following ways: (1) as a taxonomy (such as e-shops, malls, auctions) and (2) as a conceptual model of the way we do business. Taxonomies enumerate a finite number of BM types, e.g. (Bambury, 1998; Timmers, 1998; Weill & Vitale, 2002), while a conceptualization of 'business model' describes a reference model, allowing to describe an infinite number of BMs, e.g., (Amit & Zott, 2001; Gordijn & Akkermans, 2003; Mahadevan, 2000; Weill & Vitale, 2002).

Examples of BM conceptualizations, or 'ontologies' (Gruber, 1993), are REA, e3-value, and BMO (Andersson et al., 2006), of which BMO is the ontology that is proposed by Osterwalder et al. (2005). Andersson et al. (2006) state that BMO has the widest scope. For that reason, the BMO ontology will be used in this study as an exemplary conceptualization, to be able to relate the BM concept to the BC concept. **Table 8.1** shows the nine BM building blocks (2005).

Table 8.1: Nine business model building blocks, adopted from (Alexander Osterwalder et al., 2005)

Business Model Building Block	Description
Value Proposition	Gives an overall view of a company's bundle of products and services.
Target Customer	Describes the segments of customers a company wants to offer value to.
Distribution Channel	Describes the various means of the company to get in touch with its customers.
Relationship	Explains the kind of links a company establishes between itself and its different customer segments.
Value Configuration	Describes the arrangement of activities and resources.
Core Competency	Outlines the competencies necessary to execute the company's business model.
Partner Network	Portrays the network of cooperative agreements with other companies necessary to efficiently offer and commercialize value.
Cost Structure	Sums up the monetary consequences of the means employed in the business model.
Revenue Model	Describes the way a company makes money through a variety of revenue flows.

8.2.2 Business Cases

A BC is a recommendation to decision makers to take a particular course of action for the organisation, supported by an analysis of benefits, costs and risks (...), with an explanation of how it can best be implemented (Gambles, 2009). It documents the relevant facts and situational analysis, key metrics, financial analysis, allows different projects with different goals to be compared and contrasted, and serves as a communication tool (Gliedman et al., 2004). BCs can be developed for any type of investment or project, including the investment in the extension of a company's product and service portfolio. Such BCs may be termed 'provider perspective BCs' as the resulting products are then sold to customers who may use 'customer perspective BCs' to evaluate their investment. BCs commonly appear as spreadsheets, sometimes accompanied by presentations or explanatory documents. They may be presented by the project leader (BC 'owner' or 'champion') to senior management, which is responsible for prioritizing BCs and making investment decisions. This way, the BC can be used to decide about investment before project execution ('ex-ante'), to evaluate progress during project execution, and to determine to which extent the proposed value of the investment has been realized after project execution ('ex-post') (J. Ward et al., 1996).

There are many authors who describe the components of a BC, e.g., (Cardin et al., 2007; Gliedman et al., 2004). Although a large variety of components can be included, the common denominator is a set of criteria to evaluate the proposed investment. Those criteria are generally classified as benefits, costs, and risks. To support decision making, a value needs to be assigned to each criterion. The value expresses the estimated future situation, in an absolute manner, or relative to the status quo. The value can be qualitative, quantitative, financial, or non-financial. To estimate the value, a wide range of methods can be applied, such as benchmarking and pilot projects (J. Ward et al., 2008). With some exceptions (Ross & Beath, 2002; J. Ward et al., 2008), the term BC is infrequently used in literature. Rather, scientists study 'information systems (investment) evaluation'. Farbey et al. (1999b, p. 205) define that "as a process that takes place at different points in time or continuously, for searching for and making explicit, quantitatively or qualitatively, all impacts of an IS project".

8.2.3 Business Model/Case Dynamics

With a few exceptions (Al-Debei & Avison, 2010; MacInnes, 2005; Vaccaro & Cohn, 2004), most literature has taken a static perspective on business models (Lindner, Vaquero, Rodero-Merino, & Caceres, 2010). They are used to describe the value-creating logic of organizations at a certain moment in time. Hereby the implicit assumption is that business models remain steady over time, and that choices are rarely adjusted. However, in reality business models do not persist forever. Organizations often have to review their business models in order to keep in line with changing environments (Afuah & Tucci, 2003). As a result, de Reuver et al. (2007) argue that business models have to keep up with external changes during all phases from development to exploitation.

Johnson et al. (2008) describe 'business model innovation' and five strategic circumstances that often require business model change:

- The opportunity to address through disruptive innovation the needs of large groups of potential customers who are shut out of a market entirely because existing solutions are too expensive or complicated for them.
- The opportunity to capitalize on a brand new technology by wrapping a new business model around it, or the opportunity to leverage a tested technology by bringing it to a whole new market.

- The opportunity to bring a 'job-to-be-done' focus where one does not yet exist.
- The need to fend off low-end disrupters.
- The need to respond to a shifting basis of competition.

In a similar way, Weiner et al. (2010) mention strategy, market, technology and regulatory influences on the BM. Moreover, the 'hype cycle phase' can be considered as an influencing factor (Fenn & Raskino, 2008).

As it takes a tremendous amount of time and effort to realize a BM, it is common sense that a BM, although never completely static, is used for a longer period of time (Demil & Lecocq, 2010). This understanding is not as common in the area of BCs, where many companies only use BCs prior to investment (J. Ward et al., 2008), rather than using them as a project realization and evaluation tool. However, some authors understand that a BC can also be useful after the initial investment decision and argue for long time use and organizational learning (Farbey et al., 1999a; J. Ward et al., 1996).

When a BC is used over a longer period of time, the BC (i.e., the project which the BC represents) becomes subject to similar influences like BMs. E.g., due to changes on the market, the expected revenue for a certain product for which the BC was developed, may start to decline. In addition to such external influences, BCs are subject to company internal factors, among which user involvement, project management, implementation, communication and corporate understanding (Farbey et al., 1993).

An illustrative example for BM/BC dynamics can be drawn from mergers and acquisitions (M&A), where heterogeneous BMs and BCs need to be aligned. Thus, this study will present concepts in that context.

8.3 Relations

8.3.1 Similarities Between Business Models and Business Cases

According to Brews and Tucci (2003), BM implementation and management include the "translation" of the BM as a plan into more concrete elements, such as a business structure (e.g., departments, units, human resources), business processes (e.g., workflows, responsibilities), and infrastructure and systems (e.g., buildings, ICT). This study assumes that a BC can be seen as a BM implementation, which raises the question what they have in common. To provide an initial answer, the BM and BC concepts need to be decomposed. Conceptualizations as described in **Sections 8.2.1** and **8.2.2** may be used. The BM concept can be decomposed in its nine building blocks, and the BC concept can be seen as a set of criteria for evaluation, possibly classified as benefits, costs, risks. In **Table 8.2**, for each of the BM building blocks, some examples of common BC evaluation criteria from the domain of information systems (Chou et al., 2006) are presented.

As a BC can theoretically contain any criterion, a BC does not necessarily contain implementations of all BM building blocks. However, on the basis of **Table 8.2** one could argue that there are many overlaps between the BM and BC concepts. In addition to the similarities between BM and BC, there are differences. For example, BCs often aim to improve 'competitive advantage', while Osterwalder et al. (2005) make the following claim about the BM concept: "We excluded all elements related to competition and to business model implementation, which we understand as related to the business model but not as internal part of it." Other common BC criteria that may not be considered as a part of the BM are strategic alignment, flexibility, and risk. Rather than being explicitly part of the BM, these criteria may be seen as properties of the BM as a whole, or as meta-properties of each of the BM building blocks.

8.3.2 Business Models Affecting Business Cases

The similarities between BM and BC constitute a static view on the relation between the two concepts. This static view can be extended with a dynamic view, by analyzing the influence of a change in the BM on BCs and vice versa. Assuming that an M&A usually affects many or all properties of a BM, the challenge is to identify how these changes impact the various BCs of the participating companies. Though the impact heavily depends on the nature and purpose of each BC, **Table 8.3** presents a fictional example of change of each BM building block, as well as the associated impacts on the BCs. To ease the understanding of the relations, they are discussed for each BM building block, every time assuming a change of that building block only while keeping all other building blocks fixed (*ceteris paribus*). The examples apply to fictional companies A and B, which are merged into company C, thereby also merging their BMs. Thus, the properties of company C's BM building blocks have transformed compared to the previous BM building blocks of company A and B.

Table 8.2: BM building blocks and related IS-specific BC evaluation criteria

Business Model	Business Case
Value Proposition	A BC can be developed and maintained for each of the company's products and services. The value proposition then defines the set and scope of BCs. A BC may also be developed to change or extend the company's value proposition. A portfolio approach may be used to help management evaluate the relative importance of BCs (J. M. Ward, 1990). Examples of related IS evaluation criteria are: 'Improved product quality' (Irani, 2002) 'Provides better products or services to customers' (Mirani & Lederer, 1998)
Target Customer	Provider perspective BCs describe market segments and customer needs. 'Improved market share' (Irani, 2002) 'Provides new products or services to customers' (Mirani & Lederer, 1998)
Distribution Channel	BCs describe means to realize the foreseen benefits. Provider perspective BCs may therefore describe distribution channels. Each channel may incur certain cost and revenue streams. 'Reduced delivery lead times', 'Improved product traceability' (Irani, 2002)
Relationship	A provider perspective BC could describe this, often as part of the intangible/strategic benefits. 'Improved customer loyalty' (Chou et al., 2006) 'Improves customer relations' (Mirani & Lederer, 1998)
Value Configuration	The BC describes activities and resources as part of the benefits realization plan. The investment in one specific activity or resource could also be the goal of the BC. BCs may be infeasible due to a lack of resources. 'Labour savings' (Ryan & Harrison, 2000) 'Reduced inventory' (Jones & Beatty, 1998) 'Enhances employee productivity or business efficiency' (Mirani & Lederer, 1998)

Core Competency	Responsible persons or required competencies may be described in the BC as part of the benefits realization plan. 'Whether the CEO has IT knowledge', 'Experience in using IS', 'Skill of IT staff' (Chou et al., 2006) 'Probability of project completion' (Bacon, 1992; Escobar-Perez, 1998) 'Leader in new technology' (Irani, 2002) 'Enables focus on core in-house operations' (Mcauley et al., 2002)
Partner Network	May be described as part of the realization plan. Can be described for the make/buy/partner decision. 'Ally with partner', 'Improved trading partner relations' (Chou et al., 2006) 'Helps establish useful linkages with other organizations' (Mirani & Lederer, 1998)
Cost Structure	A BC contains a cost structure or 'cash flow analysis'. The cost structure in the BM may define upper and lower bounds for the cash flow analysis in the BC. The cost structure may get less attention when it is already certain that the investment needs to be made (Joshi & Pant, 2008). 'Hardware cost', 'Software cost', 'Implementation cost', 'Maintenance cost', 'Consultant cost', 'Reduced inventory' (Chou et al., 2006) 'Save money by reducing...' (Mirani & Lederer, 1998)
Revenue Model	A cash flow analysis is part of a provider perspective BC. The BM may set benchmarks for BCs, e.g., the minimum level of ROI (Return on Investment). 'Improved cash flow' (Jones & Beatty, 1998) 'Net present value' (Bacon, 1992; Escobar-Perez, 1998) 'Internal rate of return' (Bacon, 1992; Escobar-Perez, 1998)

Table 8.3: Examples of BM change affecting BCs

Business Model Building Block (Examples for Change)	Potential Impacts on Business Cases
Value Proposition: Company A has a BC for the development of a new product, which is already part of company B's portfolio. Thus, company C's product portfolio contains a redundant product.	*Benefits:* Decrease if one product attracts the revenues of the other one (cannibalization effects). *Costs:* Decrease due to company B's experience in this area (e.g., some mistakes in development can be avoided).
Target Customer: Company A has a BC for a product that is supposed to address a customer segment which so far has only been focused on by company B. Company C can exploit this customer segment with products from both former companies.	*Benefits:* Increase due to additional target customers for company A. *Costs:* Decrease due to existing target customer awareness of company B (e.g., investments in promotion for this target group can be shared by the different products).
Distribution Channel: Company A has a distribution channel that B does not yet have, but it makes sense to use it for a specific product. In company C, A's distribution channel can also be used for B's products.	*Benefits:* Increase due to additional distribution channels available for company B. *Costs:* Increase due to additional costs for the usage of the additional distribution channel (e.g., logistics costs).
Relationship: Company A has a BC for a product that customers are not loyal to. In company C, B's strong branding, relationship strategy, and customer loyalty can be applied to company A's product.	*Benefits:* Increase of company A's sales as customer loyalty rises with the help of company B. *Costs:* Increase as company A needs to implement B's strategy. For instance, they might spend additional time with customers to build trust.

Value Configuration: Company A has a BC for product development. Company B has resources which could be used for that development. In company C those resources can be used.	*Benefits:* Increase of company A's product development efficiency as capabilities of company B's resources can be used. *Costs:* Increase due to costs for additional resources (e.g., more alignments needed with all stakeholders).
Core Competency: Company A and company B have different core competencies. In company C B's core competencies may be applied to company A's BCs, if applicable.	*Benefits:* Increase of company A's BCs due to positive impact of additional core competencies. *Costs:* Increase as firm A's employees need to be trained in B's core competencies.
Partner Network: Company A has a BC for a product that does not reflect company B's partner network. In company C, B's partner network can be used for company A's product.	*Benefits:* Increase of company A's BC due to strengths of company B's partner network. *Costs:* Increase due to costs for interacting with more partners (e.g., communication efforts).
Cost Structure: Company A has a BC for a product that is based on off-shoring. In company C the strategy is changed from off-shoring to near-shoring. The associated cost model in company C is hence different.	*Benefits:* n/a *Costs:* Change due to changing cost structures (e.g., changes in the wage level and the exchange rates will impact the cost structure of the BC).
Revenue Model: Company A has a BC for a product that is based on upfront license fees. In company C the revenue model is changed from license fees to 'pay per usage'.	*Benefits:* Change in cash flows due to changing revenue structures (e.g., switch from license-based payment to pay per usage results in short-term revenue losses and contributes to more regular cash flows in the long-run). *Costs:* n/a

8.3.3 Business Cases Affecting Business Models

Similar to a BM change affecting BCs, BCs may affect the BM. There are at least two ways in which this is possible. First, the analysis of existing BCs can provide insight in the better performing parts of the business. When merging two companies, the goal is to combine the best of both businesses, but potential synergies are hard to predict and achieve. However, BCs can be used as a basis for synergy analysis on a more operational level. By comparing BCs from both companies, benchmarks and performance rankings can be derived. Based on those rankings, further analyses can be started. While the well performing BCs can identify best practices, the lesser ones can identify those practices that should not be continued. The conclusions from the BC analyses may then trigger an adaptation of the BM.

The second type of effect of BCs on a BM occurs when using BCs to simulate the effects of a certain BM before the BM is implemented in the organization. As Osterwalder et al. (2005) put it: "Simulating and testing business models is a manager's dream." For example, in the post-M&A phase the resulting BM is usually subject to analyses and discussions. Often some alternatives are proposed and a decision needs to be made. E.g., if redundant products exist in terms of the BM value configuration, a decision needs to be made if one product should be dropped for the sake of the other or if both products will remain in the portfolio. For example, in PeopleSoft's takeover by Oracle, the redundant PeopleSoft products remained in the portfolio (Buxmann, Diefenbach, & Hess, 2008). Table 8.4 presents some exemplary conclusions that may be derived from BC analysis and may trigger BM adaptation.

Table 8.4: Examples of BC analysis affecting the BM

Business Model Building Blocks	Exemplary Conclusions Due to BC Analysis
Value Proposition	A certain product area offers high ROIs.
Target Customer	A particular target customer segment creates strong revenues.
Distribution Channel	Some distribution channels are more efficient, i.e. create the same revenue with less costs.
Relationship	A particular way how to deal with customers is superior to others.
Value Configuration	Certain activities and resources outperform other ones in the internal value chain.
Core Competency	A specific competency of involved colleagues (such as very intensive relationship to the customers) drives performance.
Partner Network	One dedicated partnership supports a strong performance of a BC.
Cost Structure	Offshoring parts of product development increases overall costs.
Revenue Model	Pay-per-use contracts yield better returns on the long run than initial license-based fees.

8.4 Implications

A better understanding of the static and dynamic relations between BM and BC will allow companies to become more agile, if they are able to continuously align BM and BCs. This section describes some managerial and technical implications of this understanding, and explains an approach for continuous alignment, which is visualized in **Figure 8.1**.

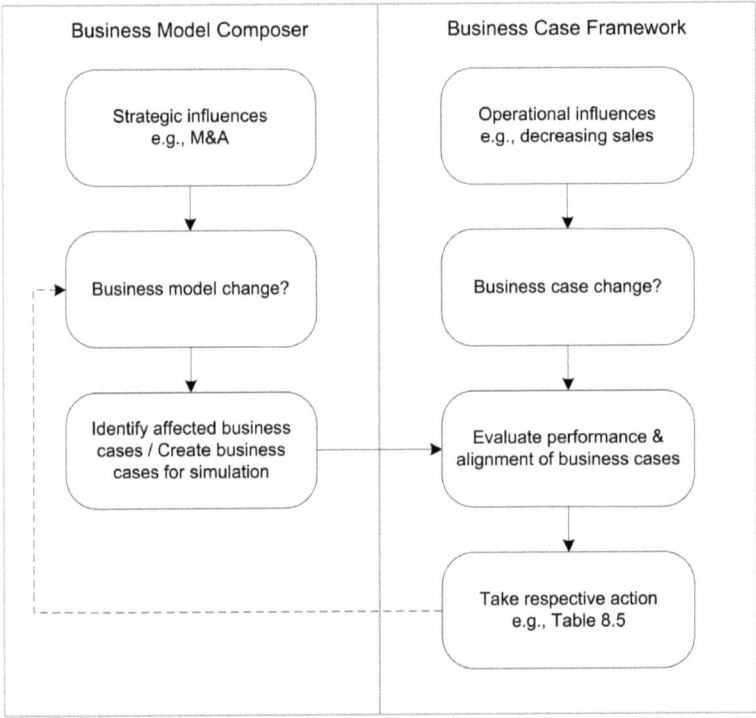

Figure 8.1: Approach for the alignment of BM and BCs

8.4.1 Managerial Implications

There are at least three different triggers for the BM-BC alignment process. The first is a strategic influence, such as an M&A. Most likely, the M&A will cause a change of the BM. If so, the BCs that are affected by the changed BM need to be identified. Therefore, BCs could be 'tagged' with the related BM building blocks. For instance, while BCs for product development are strongly related to all BM building blocks, BCs for internal projects may not be related to BM building blocks such as the distribution channel. Next, the performance of the affected BCs and the alignment of the BCs with the BM need to be evaluated. **Table 8.5** provides four high level recommendations on possible actions that could be taken: (1) When the performance of the BC is high and it is well-aligned with the changed BM, the BC (i.e., the projects associated with the BC) should be maintained. (2) When the performance of the BC is low, but it is well-aligned with the changed BM, it should be determined whether the BC may be altered to improve performance. (3) When the performance of the BC is high but it is not aligned with the changed BM, the question arises whether it will be possible to maintain the BC's performance under the new BM. (4) Finally, when the BC is not performing well and is not aligned with the BM, the BC (and the projects associated with the BC) should probably be stopped.

Table 8.5: Possible actions after a BM or BC change

	Good Alignment	Bad Alignment
High Performance	Keep/expand BC	After BM change: will performance remain? After BC change: redesign BM to focus on this area?
Low Performance	Can we improve the performance of the BC?	Kill projects associated with BC

The second trigger for BM-BC alignment is when management wants to simulate a proposed BM. Existing affected BCs need to be identified and re-evaluated, but new BCs may also be developed. As it is a simulation and not an implementation of a BM, the actions in **Table 8.5** only need to be considered theoretically.

The third trigger occurs when management notices that a BC has reached a critical level. E.g., due to unexpected declining sales revenue, the ROI (return on investment) has reached the level of 150%, which is the minimum allowed by senior management. In such a case, critical BCs need to be re-evaluated on their performance and alignment with the BM. The conclusions are similar to those from when a BM change caused the BC re-evaluation, apart from the case of a high performing BC which is not aligned with the BM. In that case, the question needs to be asked whether the BM should be adapted to focus more on such BCs. If so, the dotted arrow in **Figure 8.1** may be followed and the BM will be changed based on the lessons learned from the changed BCs. The changed BM may in turn affect other BCs, which would then need to be re-evaluated, etc. This iterative process continues until management is satisfied with the BM and BCs no longer change in critical ways.

The presented relationships between BM and BC offer many opportunities. By integrating these two concepts, the chasm between strategic management and tactical/operational implementation can be crossed. For instance, the presented concept can support the business-IT alignment of a post-M&A company (A Osterwalder & Pigneur, 2003). Osterwalder et al. (2005) already 'speculated' that the BM could play an important role in deciding which IT investments are needed for future strategic agility. They propose to cross the nine BM building blocks with Weill and Vitale's (2002) conceptualization of IT infrastructure services. Similarly, the BM building blocks may be crossed with the BC model, as many IT investments are anyway reflected in BCs. Using the BM-BC relationship as a basis for analysis it could be possible to achieve a better post-M&A alignment between the BM of a company and the IT services provided by the IS department.

8.4.2 Technical implications

In addition to management support and an organizational implementation, the continuous alignment of BM and BC can benefit from two complementary software tools: a business case framework (BCF) and a business model composer (BMC).

The BCF is used to develop and monitor BCs. First of all, it is a collection of BCs, which should use similar structures and evaluation criteria, in order to make the BCs comparable and their contents suitable for aggregation. Second, the BCF may be connected to business systems, such as an enterprise resource planning system (ERP), receiving up-to-date information, and keeping track of critical levels on selected indicators, e.g., ROI, costs, number of customers, average processing time, etc. When a critical level is reached, i.e., the BC is under- or overperforming, management will be notified.

The BMC is used as a strategic decision support tool to (re)design, monitor and simulate BMs, based on a BM conceptualization, such as BMO (Alexander Osterwalder et al., 2005). It supports the visualization of the business model and the relationships among the various BM building blocks. It allows for the monitoring of key performance indicators and the adaptation of the BM based on those. Finally, the BMC can support the dissemination of the BM (changes) and the cascading of the BM to more operational levels, e.g., by (semi-)automatically configuring IT systems and service compositions managing and controlling business processes.

In spite of these more or less common and useful features of BCFs and BMCs, their full potential will only be reached when they are connected and benefit from each other. For example, when considering a BM adaptation, one over- or under-performing BC will most likely not be sufficient evidence. Rather, the entire portfolio of BCs needs to be considered. Unless a software tool can provide adequate aggregates of values in the BCs, decisions will be hard to make. Another example of complementary use of the tools is when the effects of BM changes on BCs are measured and recorded. When considering future BM changes, past effects on BCs may be taken into account.

8.5 Conclusion

The agility of companies can be increased when implementing merged or changed business models in the organization and when using business cases to determine if it is time to change the business model. This study clarifies the relation between business models, as an implementation of a company's strategy, and business cases, as an abstraction of a company's operations. The relations are analyzed from a static as well as a dynamic point of view by means of inductive reasoning and literature review. The main contribution of this paper is the relation of two common concepts, which are often implicitly used and related in practice, but which' relations had not been described explicitly in literature. Future work should test the validity of the proposed relations in practice, e.g., in specific industries and in the context of different influencing factors such as M&A. Moreover, it may go into more depth on how managers can implement a continuous BM-BC alignment process in their companies and how software tools can be designed to support this process.

9 Decision Support By Automatic Analysis of Business Process Models

Bart-Jan van Putten	Humboldt-Universität zu Berlin, SAP Research Dresden
Clarissa Romeiro	Federal University of the State of Rio de Janeiro, NP2Tec
Leonardo Azevedo	Federal University of the State of Rio de Janeiro, NP2Tec

Published as...

Van Putten, B.-J., Romeiro, C., Azevedo, L.G. (2011). *Decision Support by Automatic Analysis of Business Process Models*. Proceedings of the 19th European Conference on Information Systems (ECIS), June 9-11, 2011, Helsinki, Finland.

Relevance for this Dissertation

This study shows how information can be extracted automatically from business process models to support decision making in a certain domain. The original idea behind the work was to use business process models to automatically compare the 'as-is' and 'to-be' states of a BC and quantify the difference, e.g., in terms of a reduced number of processes. This study is the first step to make that possible.

Collaborations

- Clarissa Romeiro was an intern at SAP Research Dresden. Under my supervision she developed the analysis method, implemented the software prototype and executed the user test.
- Dr. Leonardo Azevedo (Uni Rio) was Mrs. Romeiro's academic supervisor. He commented several times on the manuscript and wrote major parts of the related work section.

Abstract

It is advantageous for companies to have an in-depth understanding of their business processes. To support companies in decision making, based on the properties of their business processes, a method was developed for the automatic analysis of business process models. A machine-readable representation of the model is parsed to extract several features. Based on a set of domain-specific business rules, a recommendation is generated. The method was validated by implementing it in a software program and applying it to the domain of product data storage. Several experts in that domain participated in a survey. From the three features tested in this study, the 'data access frequency' seems to be most useful. This feature could thus be reused in future applications of the method. The method could be helpful for companies that have many large, complex, dynamic business processes, and which would like to (dynamically) optimize product data storage. In addition, by replacing a set of domain-specific rules, the method may be applied to other domains where business process models need to be analyzed to support decision making.

9.1 Introduction

Many companies want to store more information directly on the 'smart' products that they produce and sell, e.g., with RFID technologies (Chui, Löffler, & Roberts, 2010). For example, in the domain of manufacturing, companies want to store production process related information, such as the product's customized finishing, desired delivery time, and results from quality checks, directly on the product (Günther, Kletti, & Kubach, 2008). In the domain of retail, companies want to provide customers with more information so that the customer can make more informed buying decisions (Klein & Permenter, 2010; Schmitz, Baus, & Dörr, 2008). E.g., 'local' information on a bottle of wine could provide details on the taste of the wine, while information on perishable products such as milk, meat, and vegetables, could show if the product was not exposed to an extreme temperature.

It is however questionable if local storage is always the best solution. For example, when information often needs to be updated by the product manufacturer, it may be better to keep the information centralized and have the products connect to a central server where the information is stored ('referenced'). In some cases, the best solution may be to store information partly decentralized and partly centralized ('distributed'). Such different 'data storage types' may incur different costs and benefits for different business processes (Jaenen, Tummel, & Henning, 2010). Unfortunately, deciding which data storage type is most beneficial is difficult, as many properties of the business process need to be taken into account.

This study investigates how business process models could be used to support making the data storage type decision. More specifically, a method was developed for the *automatic analysis* of business process models. This method could be helpful for companies that have many large, complex, dynamic business processes, and which would like to (dynamically) optimize product data storage. In addition, by replacing a set of domain-specific rules, the method may be applied to other domains where business process models need to be analyzed to support decision making.

The remainder of this paper is structured as follows: **Section 9.2** describes the proposed method. **Section 9.3** describes how the method was applied to the product data storage type case. In **Section 9.4** the validation of the method is described. Related work is covered by **Section 9.5**. **Section 9.6** concludes this paper and provides directions for future work.

9.2 Method Design

The method is intended to be used as part of a decision support system. Although the authors believe that after some adaptations the method may be used for a wide range of decision support situations, the decision was made to 'start small' and focus on one specific case, namely the data storage decision. Therefore, the required output of the method is a recommendation for a certain data storage type (local, referenced, or distributed). The input for the method is a business process model describing how the product is expected to be used and which data intensive tasks will occur. Business process models describe, in a structured way, the logical order and dependence of activities within an enterprise whose objective is to produce a desired result (Aguilar-Savén, 2004). They help the organization to understand the information flow and serve as a strong base for many tasks in different research areas.

To get from the input to the output, five steps need to be executed (**Figure 9.1**). The first step is to make sure that the business process model is available in a machine-readable format, e.g., BPMN 2.0 XML (OMG, 2010), so that it can be parsed by a software program. The second step is to extract features from the model, such as 'data access frequency', which may in turn be based on lower level indicators, such as 'the number of tasks accessing a data store object' and the 'total number of tasks'. The third step is to execute business rules which specify the most suitable data storage type, depending on the value of the feature. For example, the rule may be that when the data access frequency is low, the recommended data storage type is 'referenced'. Thresholds for the levels, i.e., what is high and what is low, need to be set by the user of the method. The fourth step is to resolve any conflicts that may occur between rules. E.g., based on the data access frequency rule, referenced storage should be recommended, but based on the network availability rule, local storage may be recommended. To resolve this conflict, rules need to be weighted by the user of the method. Based on the number of times a certain recommendation occurs and the weight of the specific recommendation, one recommendation can then be generated and presented to the user.

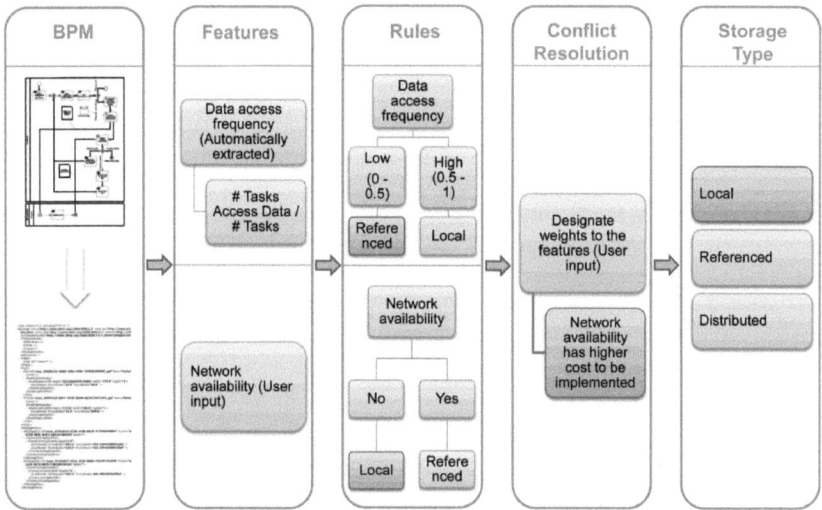

Figure 9.1: Overview of the analysis method

9.3 Method Implementation

To enable the validation of the concept, the method was implemented in a software program, for the specific case of the data storage type decision. The development and working of this algorithm will now be explained in more detail.

9.3.1 Selecting the Modelling Language

The first step was to select a suitable business process modelling language. Therefore, some requirements were defined:

- It should have a graphical representation;
- It should have a machine-readable representation;
- It should support the modelling of communication and data in- and output (this is especially useful for modelling business processes in the context of the data storage type decision);
- It should be well-adopted or have the potential to become well-adopted by the BPM community.

Ko *et al.* (2009) provide an overview of several BPM languages, classified as graphical standards, interchange standards, execution standards, and diagnosis standards. As it does not lie within the scope of this research to simulate and execute business process models, the languages of interest were selected from the graphical and interchange classes. From those, five of the most stable and popular ones have been selected for comparison against the requirements. Finally, BPMN 2.0 (OMG, 2010), was selected after a rather extensive analysis process which is beyond the scope of this paper.

9.3.2 Selecting the Modelling Environment

The second step was to select the modelling environment. The requirements were that it should support visual modelling of BPMN 2.0 and the automatic conversion of such a visual model to a BPMN 2.0 XML document. Two tools were selected: Gravity, originally a BPM plug-in for Google Wave for collaborative business process modelling (Elliott, 2009), and Oryx (Hasso Plattner Institute, 2010), an academic open source framework. Both tools are web-based and support BPMN 2.0. The support of Oryx for BPMN 2.0 was more comprehensive and therefore Oryx was selected for use in the study at hand.

9.3.3 Defining the Business Rules

The third step was to define the business rules in collaboration with domain experts. **Table 9.1** shows the business rules in tabular form. E.g., when the data storage duration is short, the recommended storage type is local. Such rules are domain specific. This means that depending on the domain where the proposed method is applied, different business rules will need to be defined. For this study's case 30 rules were defined. The three rules that will be evaluated as an example in this paper concern the storage duration of product data, the collaboration and interaction among 'smart products' (Wahlster et al., 2008), and the frequency in which product data needs to be accessed.

Table 9.1: Examples of business rules

Feature	Value	Local	Distrb.	Ref.
Data storage duration	short term	x		
	long term			x
Collaboration / interaction	necessary		x	x
	not necessary	x		
Data access frequency	high	x		
	low			x

9.3.4 Defining the Features and Indicators

The fourth step was to define the features and indicators that need to be extracted from business process models in order to be able to evaluate the business rules. The left column in **Table 9.1** shows the features. The three features for which a feature extraction algorithm was implemented are: data storage duration, collaboration/interaction, and data access frequency. These features were selected from a larger set, based on the researchers' expectations regarding the feasibility of automatically extracting them. Each feature is calculated based on one or more indicators. Each of the features and the associated indicators will now be explained.

Data storage duration concerns the time the data is needed. Short-lived information may be stored locally since storage space will be cleared before it is needed again for other data. However, long-lived information is often better stored referenced. There are several indicators for this feature:

- *Number of tasks:* The number of tasks gives a direct notion of the size of the model and the bigger its size, the more likely it is that the process has a high duration.

- *Relative incoming message flows:* The number of incoming messages may influence the duration of a process as tasks may only be executed after the message has arrived. This indicator is calculated relatively to the size of the model.

- *Relative delay events in normal flow:* Intermediate catch events, more specifically the timer, message, signal, and condition events that appear in the normal flow indicate that the process has to wait for a message, a certain time, a condition to become true, or a signal to happen. This indicator is calculated relatively to the size of the model.

- *Sequentiality:* A sequence in a model indicates that an activity has to wait for the predecessor node to finish, making the process less efficient compared to parallelized processes. This effect is calculated based on Mendling's metric of sequentiality (Mendling, 2008). If sequentiality is 1, then the model is a complete sequence of tasks and events.

- *Relative loops:* A loop means repetition, increasing the time as long as the loop's condition is true. This indicator is calculated relatively to the size of the model.

- *Collaboration/interaction* concerns products that need to communicate or interact with other products. For example, a product could check if another product is available and if so, recommend itself for a lower price. Such interactions require more complex logic, which is often stored in a distributed or referenced manner. Indicators that can be used for this feature are:

- *Relative message flows:* The number of messages (incoming and outgoing), relative to the size of the model.
- *Relative handover sequence flows:* The number of message flows and sequence flows between different pools and lanes, relative to the size of the model.
- *Data access frequency* concerns the number of tasks accessing a data store object (retrieve and/or store operations). There is only one indicator for this feature, which has the same name and which is calculated relative to the size of the model.

9.3.5 Defining the Thresholds and Weights

The fifth step was to define thresholds for the 'fuzzy values' as described in the business rules. I.e., it needs to be clear when the data access frequency is 'high' and when it is 'low'. Moreover, the weights of the features and indicators need to be defined to enable conflict resolution as described in **Section 9.2**. For validation of the method, some default thresholds and weights were used. However, ideally, the thresholds and weights are determined by experts and tuned by the users of the method.

9.3.6 Selecting the Business Process Model

The sixth step was to select a business process model for analysis. For this study, three business process models were selected. They all represented use cases for smart products, they were relatively small in size, and they covered different domains (maintenance, retail, and logistics). As an example, the maintenance model (**Figure 9.2**) concerns the failure and repair of a dishwasher:

"A customer places the tableware into his dishwasher and selects the appropriate washing program. Unfortunately, the rotary program selector knob breaks off. Normally, this would mean the customer would have to wash his dishes by hand for a few days or even weeks. In the future, the dishwasher could be equipped with a 'digital product memory' (the 'DPG' in **Figure 9.2**). With an enabled smartphone, the customer can identify his broken equipment. With support of the data stored in the DPG, the customer can contact the manufacturer through his smartphone. The manufacturer's service department may ship a spare part directly to the customer, or provide him with a CAD drawing to be printed on a 3D printer in a nearby copy shop.

This reduces storage and transportation costs for the manufacturer and improves the speed of the solution process considerably."

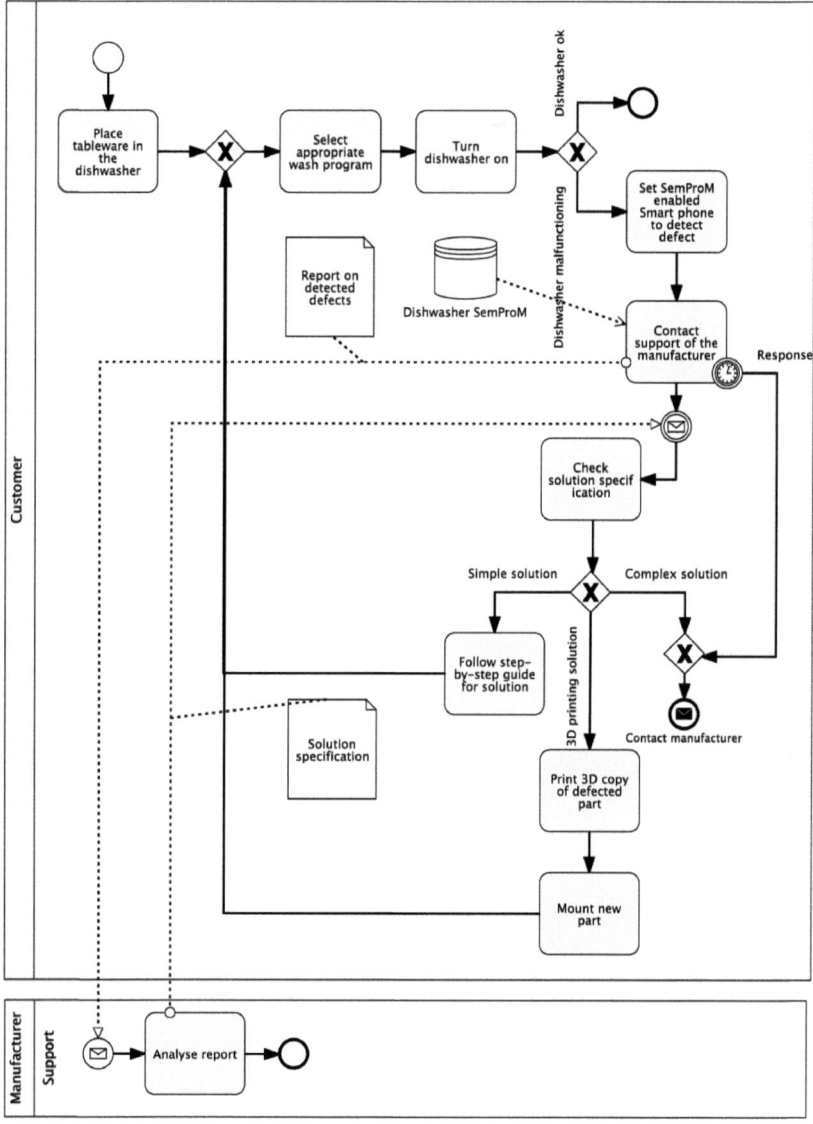

Figure 9.2: Business process model of a smart dishwasher (DPG is the dishwasher's digital product memory). The automatic analysis result is shown in **Figure 9.3**

9.3.7 Executing the Software Program

The seventh step was to execute the feature extraction algorithm, which was implemented as a C# software program. Oryx was used to convert the graphical business process model to a BPMN 2.0 XML document. The program parses the document, calculates the indicators and presents the results to the user, as shown in **Figure 9.3**. The user may then decide to change some thresholds and weights and regenerate the recommendation.

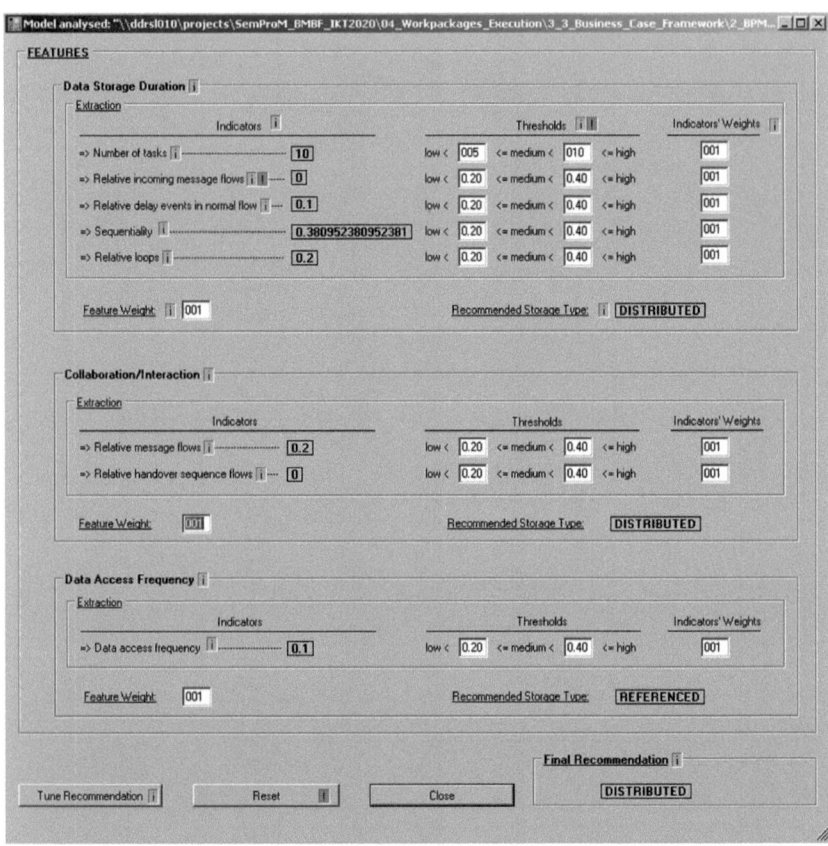

Figure 9.3: Screenshot of the software program's user interface after parsing the business process model in **Figure 9.2**

9.4 Validation

9.4.1 Method

The goal of the validation was to determine whether the method's recommendation would fit with recommendations provided by domain experts. 17 experts were selected among researchers in a research project investigating (among other things) the local storage of data during production processes. Six experts took part in the online survey. The experts' recommendations were investigated in several stages: first, a graphical business process model was presented and they were asked which data storage type they would recommend. Second, the experts were asked to judge the levels (high, mid, low) of the features and indicators in the business process model, in order to be able to tune the algorithm's pre-defined thresholds for the indicator levels. Third, the experts were again asked to indicate which data storage type they would recommend, to see if they had changed their minds based on the features and indicators. Fourth, the experts rated the usefulness of the features and indicators for making the data storage type decision. This sequence of questions was repeated for the three selected business process models. Finally, there were some open questions:

- To what extent do you believe it is possible to determine the right storage type based on a business process model?
- Do you believe a software tool extracting features from business process models could assist you in determining the right storage type for a certain business process?
- Should we consider another feature?
- Should we consider another indicator?

For the test to work, the experts needed to be able to understand the business process models. Therefore, three use cases of product data, which were known to the experts, were selected. Whereas the algorithm could only 'see' the syntax of the models, the experts could also see the semantics, i.e., the names of the model's elements, and read an additional description. This way the experts could imagine the business processes described by the models.

9.4.2 Results

Directly comparing the experts' recommendations with the algorithm's recommendations is possible, but would be based on the pre-defined thresholds for the indicator levels, which may not be in correspondence with the thresholds that were determined through the survey questions. For example, the algorithm initially uses a threshold of five, to determine whether the 'number of tasks' indicator is low or mid. However, the experts may believe that a 'mid' level of tasks is only reached above 20 tasks. Therefore, the experts' recommendations were evaluated by comparing their perceived feature levels with the business rules. For example, for the first business process model, expert 2 recommended the referenced data storage type. In the next question, expert 2 stated that the data storage duration was high. Thus expert 2 implicitly associated (moderated by any other impressions the expert may have had of the model) that a high storage duration requires referenced storage. This is in conformance with the business rule in **Table 9.1**. This way, all 20 answers (which only include the high and low levels and not the mid levels) were checked with the business rules. 70% of the answers (14 out of 20) were in conformance (**Table 9.2**).

Table 9.2: Conformance of expert recommendations with business rules

Feature	Answers	Conform	%
Data storage duration	7	4	57
Collaboration / interaction	6	4	67
Data access frequency	7	6	86
Total	20	14	70

The difference between the experts' recommendations directly after having seen the graphical business process models and later after answering the questions regarding the features and the indicators were compared as well. Out of the 13 recommendations in total (by all experts over all models), six experts changed their minds. Although it is hard to draw any reliable conclusions from this, it is most likely that this effect is attributable to either a better understanding of the models by the experts after studying the features and the indicators, or to chance.

The usefulness of the features was questioned explicitly in the survey and is shown in **Table 9.3**. N represents the number of answers received, Mean is the mean of the scores, where a score of 1 was assigned to the 'useless' category and a score of 5 to the 'useful' category. SD is the standard deviation, to give an indication of the range of answers received. Among these three features, only the 'data access frequency' feature seems to be useful enough.

Table 9.3: Usefulness of the features

Feature	N	Mean	SD
Data storage duration	13	3,3	1,3
Collaboration / interaction	11	3,3	1,6
Data access frequency	13	4,0	1,1

In a similar way, the usefulness of the indicators was calculated (**Table 9.4**). If the minimal usefulness of 4,0 is applied again, the features 'relative message flows', 'relative handover sequence flows', and 'data access frequency indicator' seem to be useful enough to be used in future versions of the recommender system. However, the 'relative message flows' and 'relative handover sequence flows' indicators are used to calculate the 'collaboration/interaction' feature, which was not perceived to be useful enough by itself. Only 'data access frequency' is an indicator for a feature which is also perceived to be useful by itself. Thus, out of the features and indicators tested in this study, only data access frequency seems to be useful for a recommender system as proposed in this paper. The open questions were answered by only three of the experts and did not lead to any noticeable insights.

Table 9.4: Usefulness of the indicators for indicating the features

Feature	Indicator	N	Mean	SD
Data storage duration	Number of tasks	10	3,6	1,5
	Relative incoming message flows	10	3	0,9
	Relative delay catch events in normal flow	10	3,9	1,5
	Sequentiality	10	3,4	1,0
	Relative loops	10	3,9	1,2
Collaboration / interaction	Relative message flows	7	4,4	0,5
	Relative handover sequence flows	7	4,6	0,5
Data access frequency	Data Access Frequency indicator	8	4,4	1,4

9.5 Related Work

In this section, some work will be presented which aims to derive information from business process models, in order to handle aspects of business or IT.

Fiorini *et al.* (1996) and Weston *et al.* (2004) propose the use of business processes for software requirements elicitation. Fiorini *et al.* propose a method to represent business processes in a conceptual model, aimed at making the relationships between pieces of process information explicit. The first step of the method is the construction of the model. In the second step, elements of the model are linked. In the third step, the analyst navigates on the linked data to locate requirements. Fiorini *et al.* also argue that other techniques, such as interviews and surveys can be used to elicit requirements. However, their experience shows that by using process models it becomes simpler to define concrete business actions.

Weston *et al.* (2004) define 'process thinking', i.e., thinking about current and possible future ways in which organised sets of value added activities can realise business goals by transforming inputs (such as material, sub-products, information and knowledge) into outputs (such as products and services) required by customers. Becker *et al.* (2000) state that modelling languages and tools can be used to enable process thinking for a broad range of purposes, such as business process reengineering, workflow specification, team systems design, and knowledge management. The study at hand proposes decision making as another purpose.

Klose *et al.* (2007), Papazoglou and Heuvel (2006) take a business process model as a starting point and aim to identify services (in a Service Oriented Architecture approach) from certain parts of the process. Azevedo *et al.* (2009) present a method that considers syntactical (structural) and semantic analysis of a process model towards service identification. Services are identified directly from business process elements without considering their value for business decision making. Moreover, the business process models used as input are often exclusively comprised of automatable tasks, while the study at hand proposes a method that also works with business process models consisting of human tasks.

Riehle and Züllighoven (1996) define a pattern as 'the abstraction from a concrete form which keeps recurring in specific non-arbitrary contexts'. Van der Aalst *et al.* (2003) define several types of 'workflow patterns' of which at least two are interesting for this work: control flow and data flow. Control flows represent the flow of execution control, e.g., sequence, choice, parallelism and join synchronization. Data flow patterns aim to capture the various ways in which data is represented and used in workflows. These patterns consider e.g., data visibility, data interaction, data transfer and data-based routing. Russel *et al.* (2005) extended the work of Van der Aalst *et al.* to the data perspective and propose thirty nine data flow patterns. Future work may investigate if and how workflow patterns could be used as indicators in the method proposed in this study.

Dijkman *et al.* (2008) define metrics for business process models, which are somewhat similar to the features and indicators, but mainly focus on semantic analysis, while the proposed method strives for a purely syntactic analysis. The work by Mendling (2008) also identifies metrics for business process models, but aims to identify syntactic errors in those models, rather than to create new knowledge that can support decision making.

In the area of 'process mining', information is extracted from information systems (such as Enterprise Resource Planning or Business Process Management Systems) event logs to discover the process model (Alvarez, 2002; Van der Aalst & Weijters, 2005). Decisions may be made on the basis of such models, but for their construction only the output of information systems is used. Human activities are not considered, since they normally do not appear in the event logs. Thus, using only this approach to identify relevant information for decision making may discard important information regarding human activities.

9.6 Conclusion

In this work a method for automatic analysis of business process models to facilitate human decision making is proposed. The method describes how features can be extracted from business process models stored in a machine-readable representation, and how those features can be used to evaluate business rules in the respective decision making domain. The method may make decision making more informed and efficient, which could be useful for companies that have many large, complex or dynamic business processes.

The method was evaluated by applying it to the domain of product data storage. Deciding how and where to store product-related data during the different phases of a product's lifecycle, (e.g., production, logistics, retail, usage, maintenance, recycling) can be a difficult issue as many properties of the business process need to be taken into account. Examples of such properties are how long the data is needed and how often it needs to be accessed. Those properties are the 'features' which are extracted and used to decide on the right data storage type: local, distributed, or referenced.

For the purpose of validation, three business process models related to the usage of product data were selected from the areas of maintenance, retail and logistics. The method was implemented in a software program and executed for each of the models. Next, the recommendations generated by the software program were compared with those of human decision makers. Therefore, several experts in the product data storage domain were asked to express which data storage type they would choose and how useful they would find the features and indicators for supporting their decision. The conformance between the experts and the program ranged from 57%-86% depending on the features of interest. Overall, with the current set of features implemented in the program, a conformance was reached of 70%. From the three features tested in this study, the 'data access frequency' seems to be most useful. This feature could thus be reused in future applications of the method.

Although the results provide some early signals regarding the usefulness of the features and indicators, their internal validity is limited due to the rather small number of participants in the survey (6). This can be explained by the relatively small number of people who were invited to take part (17), but also because several participants quit the survey before finishing it, most likely because it required more time than expected. In future work, the experiment could be repeated with a larger number of participants, but the different business process models under review should be distributed over the participants, to shorten the time needed for one person to complete the survey.

In future work, business process models could be analyzed by simulating or executing them. Especially for features that consider time and durations and for models that include repetitive tasks, this could provide more reliable information. Process mining techniques (Alvarez, 2002; Van der Aalst & Weijters, 2005) could be used to analyse logs resulting from process executions. Besides, new features and indicators could be identified by considering the workflow patterns from Van der Aalst *et al.* (2003) and Russel *et al.* (2005). Another way to obtain more reliable features could be to involve the semantics of the business process model elements, as used by Fiorini *et al.* (1996) in the third step of their method to identify requirements. A simpler approach would be to investigate the use of other features. Human experts probably use many more and other 'features' than just those three evaluated in this study. Examples of such features in the domain of product data could be 'data size' and 'data security'.

To extend the external validity of this research, the method could be applied to the analysis of business process models in other domains. The adaptation to other domains would require the definition of business rules for that respective domain and the definition of features and indicators to be extracted. In domains with a similar focus on the data-centric parts of the business process, features and indicators from this study could be reused. As features are based on indicators, indicators can be more domain agnostic than features. By developing a more extensive library of indicators, features may be composed more easily, to efficiently apply the method to other domains.

10 Conclusion

Business case development (BCD) can be supported by a business case framework (BCF), which often comes in the form of a spreadsheet template with some pre-defined criteria and methods. Today's BCFs are, however, often too generic, providing little support for business case (BC) developers who need to define domain-specific criteria and methods. Other times, BCFs are sufficiently domain-specific, but are based on templates and taxonomies, which are explicitly defined by domain experts. Such BCFs are expensive to develop and maintain and have a limited applicability to the domain for which they were designed, which hampers cross-domain reuse.

This dissertation aimed to develop the knowledge for making a BCF that is generic enough to apply it to multiple domains, but at the same time specific enough to provide useful support for BCD in a specific domain, while reducing the effort to develop and maintain templates and taxonomies. An approach for the reuse of domain-specific BC components, on top of a generic BC basis, was developed and evaluated from the perspective of the BC developer.

This way, the following general research questions, which abstract from the more specific research questions in the individual chapters, were addressed in this dissertation:

RQ1: *What is the effect of different kinds of BCF-support for reuse on the efficiency and effectiveness of BCD?*

RQ2: *What is the effect of different kinds of BCF-support for reuse on the ease of use and usefulness of BCFs and the intention of BC developers to use such BCFs?*

Supporting reuse was identified as an opportunity to improve BCFs in **Chapter 2**. The groundwork for defining and answering the general research questions was then laid in **Chapters 3 to 5**. The literature review in **Chapter 3** showed that reuse is an inventive topic in the domain of IS investment evaluation. There are several arguments for supporting reuse, but also challenges to be overcome. To enable software-supported reuse, the common components of a BC, among which *criteria* and *methods,* were identified and then defined in an ontology in **Chapter 4**. In **Chapter 5**, a BCF was developed, based on a domain-agnostic BCD process. The qualitative feedback obtained through the field experiment showed that the BCD process is easy to follow, but the BCF is not very useful without domain-specific components. Therefore, some templates with domain-specific content were developed, based on the BCs that were developed during the field experiment. However, such templates are difficult and costly to develop, especially for the domain experts who often have little BCD experience. Therefore, another approach for reuse was developed in **Chapter 6**. In the *dynamic* approach, the reusable, domain-specific criteria do not need to be pre-defined by experts in templates or taxonomies, but can be reused directly from earlier business cases. To test whether support for dynamic reuse improves BCFs, a laboratory experiment was set up. Three types of support for the reuse of criteria were compared: (1) recommendations, based on collaborative filtering and representative for the dynamic approach, (2) templates, representative for the static approach, and (3) no support. The quantitative results show that the BC developers using the recommendations are most efficient, while still being as effective as those using the templates. Moreover, the recommendations are the preferred type of support because the intention to use them is the highest. The work in **Chapter 6** focused on the reuse of *criteria*. The work in **Chapter 7** then continued to support the reuse of *methods*. Several guidelines were defined which can be used to decide which existing methods are the easiest to use. **Chapters 8 and 9** focused on another opportunity for improvement of BCFs, as defined in **Chapter 2**, namely 'adaptation'. **Chapter 8** showed how BCs can be made adaptive to business models. Finally, **Chapter 9** showed how business process models can be used as a source of information for improved decision making.

10.1 Summaries of the Individual Papers

In the individual papers, that are part of this cumulative dissertation, several specific research questions were addressed:

Chapter 2. Challenges in Business Case Development and Requirements for Business Case Frameworks

What are the challenges in business case development?
What are the opportunities to improve business case frameworks?

The results of a case study and several interviews show that the main challenges are estimating the market potential of new information systems, judging and guaranteeing the quality of information in the BC and clarifying the reasoning underlying the BC. The reuse of BC structure is also identified as a topic with high relevance for BC developers. Moreover, three areas for the improvement of BCFs were identified: supporting reuse, adaptation and collaboration.

Chapter 3. Reuse in Business Case Development: Arguments, Challenges and Guidelines

Which business case components are considered for reuse in the literature?
Which arguments for reuse can be found in the domain of IS evaluation?
Which challenges may hinder reuse in the domain of IS evaluation?

The findings of a review of over 100 scientific articles show that the common components of BCs are the investment criteria and the valuation methods. Those components are candidates for reuse. The main derived *arguments* for reuse are (1) to improve the efficiency and effectiveness of BCD, (2) to facilitate the comparison of BCs and benchmarking of values, (3) 'ritualistic' use and more deliberate use to achieve acceptance of the BC by decision makers, (4) that some criteria and methods are easier to understand and because reuse may facilitate learning. The *challenges* that may hinder reuse are: (1) a lack of formal evaluation procedures and a lack of easily accessible BC archives, (2) unclarity of the reliability of the methods used in earlier BCs, (3) a lack of familiarity with certain criteria and methods, (4) a low usability of certain criteria and methods, and (5) a limited applicability of certain criteria and methods.

Chapter 4. Business Case Ontology

How can a model of business case components be defined, in order to support their reuse?

After defining requirements and analyzing related work, an initial business case ontology was defined in UML and Description Logic. It describes the common components of business cases and the relations between them. BCO was applied as a data model for the Business Case Framework (**Chapter 5**) and for the recommender system (**Chapter 6**).

Chapter 5. Business Case Framework

How can a business case framework be generic enough to be applicable to multiple domains and at the same time support the development of business cases for specific domains?

A domain-agnostic business case development process was defined and a prototypical tool was implemented to support that process. A field experiment showed that the tool provides enough flexibility to apply it to multiple domains, but does not provide much support either. Therefore reusable, domain-specific components were created based on the business cases that were built during the field experiment.

Chapter 6. Supporting Dynamic Reuse in Business Case Development

How can support for reuse improve the usefulness and usability of business case frameworks, while limiting the effort required to develop and maintain static databases of reusable components?

To what extent does support for the dynamic reuse of criteria, improve the usefulness and usability of business case frameworks?

An approach was proposed for the *dynamic reuse of BC components* and contrasted with *static reuse of BC components*. In the dynamic approach, the reusable, domain-specific criteria and methods do not need to be pre-defined by experts in templates and taxonomies, but can be reused from earlier BCs. In a laboratory experiment with 208 participants, three types of support for the reuse of criteria were compared: (1) recommendations, based on collaborative filtering and representative for the dynamic approach, (2) templates, representative for the static approach common in the class of modern BCFs and (3) no support, representative for the class of traditional BCFs. The results show that although the recommendations are as effective as the templates, they are preferred over the other conditions. Thus, to make BCD more convenient and to save costs in developing databases with reusable BC components, the application of recommendations, or another type of support for dynamic reuse in BCFs, is encouraged.

Chapter 7. Exploring the Usability of Valuation Methods in Business Cases

Why are certain valuation methods more likely to be reused than others, from the perspective of usability?

To answer this question, an experiment was done in which 199 people compared several methods, drawn from different types of business case frameworks and for different types of criteria. The results of the experiment led to the definition of several guidelines which can be used to decide which existing methods are most usable, or how methods should be designed to make them more usable.

Chapter 8. The Relation Between Dynamic Business Models and Business Cases

What is the relation between business models and business cases?

How can this understanding be incorporated in organizational processes and software tools supporting those processes?

This chapter clarifies how business models, as an implementation of a company's strategy, can be aligned with business cases, as an abstraction of a company's operations. The relations are analyzed from a static as well as a dynamic point of view by means of inductive reasoning and literature review. Based on the understanding of the relations, a continuous business model-business case alignment approach is proposed. Further, managerial guidelines are presented supporting the approach. Finally, two software tools, business case framework and business model composer, are presented indicating how the proposed conceptual alignment could be implemented.

Chapter 9. Decision Support by Automatic Analysis of Business Process Models

How can business process models be analyzed automatically, in order to support decision making in a specific domain?

A method was developed for the automatic analysis of business process models. A machine-readable representation of the model is parsed to extract several features. Based on a set of domain-specific business rules, a recommendation is generated. The method was validated by implementing it in a software program and applying it to the domain of product data storage. Several experts in that domain participated in a survey. From the three features tested in this study, the 'data access frequency' seems to be most useful. This feature could thus be reused in future applications of the method. The method could be helpful for companies that have many large, complex, dynamic business processes, and which would like to (dynamically) optimize product data storage. In addition, by replacing a set of domain-specific rules, the method may be applied to other domains where business process models need to be analyzed to support decision making.

10.2 Design Artifacts

In addition to the knowledge that was developed through the studies that were summarized in the previous section, the 'design artifacts' form the tangible contributions of this dissertation:

- A business case ontology, defined in UML and Description Logic (**Chapter 4**).
- A business case framework, implemented in Microsoft Excel, based on a domain-agnostic business case development process. It is extensible with domain-specific components, for the domains of manufacturing, retail and service management (**Chapter 5**).

- A recommender system (PHP, MySQL) that supports the reuse of criteria (**Chapter 6**).
- Improved valuation methods for the criteria 'Return-on-Investment', 'Time Reduction' and 'Customer Satisfaction' (**Chapter 7**).
- A model that depicts the interdependencies between business cases and business models (**Chapter 8**).
- A method and software program, implemented in C#, for extracting information from business process models (**Chapter 9**).

10.3 Contributions

If we abstract from the specific contributions of the studies presented in this dissertation, this dissertation contributes to science by providing a better understanding of BCD from the perspective of the individual BC developer. Or, as two of the paper reviewers formulated:

- "The research is important, and the general research approach – qualitatively studying business case development – is an excellent idea." (**Chapter 2** reviewer for AMCIS'10)
- "What is really interesting and inspiring is the application of user-centered design approaches to describe the challenges when performing business case analysis (I have not read about doing this in the area of business case analysis before)." (**Chapter 2** reviewer for WI'11)

This way, the aim was not just to improve the effectiveness of the resulting BCs, i.e., the traditional organizational perspective on IS evaluation, but also to improve the efficiency of the development process and the satisfaction of individual BC developers with the BCFs.

Finally, this work has already contributed to practice in the following ways:

- The BCF (**Chapter 5**) was applied to the development of several BCs in the Semantic Product Memory project (SemProM, 2010).
- The findings from the laboratory experiment (**Chapter 6, Chapter 7**) were used for the improvement of the BCF that was developed in the context of the RFID-based Automotive Networks project (Project RAN, 2011).

- The findings from the laboratory experiment (**Chapter 6, Chapter 7**) were used for the improvement of the SAP Value Management Center, a BCF used by the (pre-)sales department in SAP to develop value propositions for customers.
- Four patent proposals were filed:
    - "Supporting Reuse in Business Case Development through Collaborative Filtering" (based on **Chapter 6**)
    - "Process-Aware Business Case Framework"
    - "Enabling Multiple Viewpoints in Business Case Frameworks"
    - "From Business Process Model to Data Storage Location" (based on **Chapter 9**)

10.4 Limitations

If we abstract from the specific limitations of the studies presented in this dissertation, some general limitations can be identified:

- First, from the literature review (**Chapter 3**) it appeared that the topics of reuse in BCD and the user-centered evaluation of BCD and BCFs are hardly explored. This made it more difficult to connect to existing work, leading to the relatively explorative, but probably also inventive, focus of this dissertation.
- Second, some of the findings, especially those from the laboratory experiment, still need to be integrated into real and comprehensive BCFs to prove that dynamic reuse is feasible with heterogeneous real-world BCs.
- Third, this research has been done in the context of two publicly-funded projects (Project RAN, 2011; SemProM, 2010) and the SAP Research organization. This may have influenced the research questions, the selection of scientific research methods, and the perspective of the author when interpreting the results.
- Fourth, all BCs, BCD and BCFs have been studied in the context of corporate information systems and/or information technology. It needs to be investigated if the findings from this dissertation also apply to other types of investments, such as those for consumer goods, financial services or real estate.

10.5 Recommendations & Future Work

If we abstract from the specific recommendations for future work as presented in the studies in this dissertation, some general recommendations can be identified:

- The approach for dynamic reuse should be included in a real and comprehensive BCF and tested during real BCD. This way, it can be tested if an archive of more heterogeneous BCs, i.e., in terms of structure, contents, quality, is still suitable to enable dynamic reuse. More specifically, the question is how large such an archive should be, to obtain useful recommendations for reuse. If it shows that the required size of the archive is larger than what is common in most organizations, the recommender algorithm could be extended with natural language processing (NLP) techniques.

- The current recommender algorithm can only identify similarities between BCs when they share identical text strings. In the future, natural language processing (NLP) techniques could be used to improve the identification of (dis)similarities between BCs and thus give the recommender algorithm a better basis for recommendation. This could lead to more useful recommendations and/or to a smaller minimum size of the BC archive from which the recommendations are drawn.

- To facilitate the *reuse of methods*, the principles that were identified to support the *reuse of criteria* might be re-applied. For example, once a criterion has been selected for which a method needs to be defined, the recommender algorithm could search the BC archive and identify the methods that were used to valuate the criterion of interest. When some earlier BCs apply a similar method to that criterion, that could imply that that method is more useful than other methods which occur less often in the database. This would however lead to the next challenge: how to identify the similarity between methods. Moreover, in addition to how frequent certain methods occur in the archive, there may be other aspects that influence the usefulness and usability of a method (**Chapter 7**). Those aspects need to be investigated further.

- In addition to the reuse of criteria and methods, the reuse of values could improve the efficiency and effectiveness of BCD. In some cases, individual values may be reused. It is however more likely that values could be reused in the form of aggregates, or 'benchmarks'. An example of a benchmark is 'average throughput time in manufacturing in the automotive industry'. It can be determined by taking the average value of all the BCs in the archive that were built for the automotive industry, in the last years, and which include the throughput time criterion. Next, when estimating the value of the throughput time criterion in a new BC, the benchmark could be used to either derive the new value, e.g., "we want to be 3% better than the industry's average", or to check how big the discrepancy is between the estimated value and the benchmark.

- This dissertation focused on BCD for information systems. According to several authors, information systems investment projects have specific properties, when compared to for example investments in real estate. It is however likely that findings from this dissertation will also apply to BCD in other domains, such as real estate, consumer goods and financial services. Future work could show if, when and how that is the case.

- BCD could potentially be further improved by supporting the adaptation of BCs (**Chapter 2**). For example, BCs frequently include values that are derived from an information system in the organization. BC developers generally copy such values manually into the BC. If the BC would however be adaptive to the information system, the BC could be updated automatically as soon as the original value changes. This would lead to more accurate BCs and allow BCs to be used over longer periods of time.

- BCD could also be further improved by enabling better collaboration between and among BC developers and stakeholders (**Chapter 2**). For example, BC evaluators, and BC developers who try to reuse, often have trouble judging the quality of the information in the BC. Clarifying information sources, determining information reliability and showing the underlying assumptions might enhance the shared understanding of the BC. Moreover, it should be investigated what makes a high quality BC from the perspective of the BC evaluator. Is that e.g., mainly the reliability of the information, or also how the BC is structured and presented? Are there specific criteria that need to be included, or stakeholders that need to be involved? BCFs should support BC developers to focus on those aspects. In the end, the goal should be to develop BCs that include precisely that information that is relevant for BC evaluators, no more and no less.

10.6 Closing Remarks

BC *development* can be 'looking into a crystal ball', BC *evaluation* is often subject to political power play and BCs that are *executed* are frequently affected by external factors that are hard to predict and control. Therefore it would be naive to claim that this dissertation solves all of these challenges. Rather, it aimed to make the life of BC developers a bit easier, by investigating opportunities for the improvement of BCFs in general and for how BC components can be reused in particular. The findings have shown that the dynamic reuse approach especially has the potential for improving the ease of use of BCFs, when compared to modern BCFs that support reuse from templates or taxonomies („static reuse"). Reuse in general, static or dynamic, improves the effectiveness of BCD. When dynamic reuse is developed further to support the reuse of methods, BCs may become even more reliable and BC developers may be less tempted to creatively adjust estimates. But we are not there yet. Therefore other researchers are encouraged to join and turn this vision into reality.

References

ADiWa. (2010). Retrieved from http://www.adiwa.net

Afuah, A., & Tucci, C. (2003). *Internet Business Models and Strategies*. Boston, MA, USA: McGraw-Hill.

Aguilar-Savén, R. S. (2004). Business Process Modelling: Review and Framework. *International Journal of Production Economics*, *90*(1), 129–149.

Al-Debei, M. M., & Avison, D. (2010). Developing a Unified Framework of the Business Model Concept. *European Journal of Information Systems*, *19*, 359–376.

Aletheia. (2010). Retrieved from http://www.aletheia-projekt.de

Alvarez, R. (2002). Discourse Analysis of Requirements and Knowledge Elicitation Interviews. *35th Hawaii International Conference on System Sciences (HICSS)*. January 7, Hilton Waikoloa Village, Hawaii.

Amit, R., & Zott, C. (2001). Value Creation in e-Business. *Strategic Management Journal*, *22*(6-7), 493–520.

Andersson, B., Bergholtz, M., Edirisuriya, A., Ilayperuma, T., Johannesson, P., Gordijn, J., Grégoire, B., et al. (2006). Towards a Reference Ontology for Business Models. *25th International Conference on Conceptual Modeling*. November 6, Tucson, AZ, USA.

Anselstetter, R. (1984). *Betriebswirtschaftliche Nutzeffekte der Datenverarbeitung: Anhaltspunkte für Nutzen-Kosten-Schätzungen*. Berlin: Springer.

Azevedo, L. G., Santoro, F., Baião, F., Souza, J., Revoredo, K., Pereira, V., & Herlain, I. (2009). A Method for Service Identification from Business Process Models in a SOA Approach. In T. Halpin, J. Krogstie, S. Nurcan, E. Proper, R. Schmidt, P. Soffer, & R. Ukor (Eds.), *Enterprise, Business-Process and Information Systems Modeling* (pp. 99–112).

Bacon, J. (1992). The Use of Decision Criteria in Selecting Information Systems/Technology Investments. *MIS Quarterly*, *16*(3), 335–353.

Ballantine, J. A., Galliers, R. D., & Stray, S. J. (1996). Information Systems/Technology Evaluation Practices: Evidence from UK Organizations. *Journal of Information Technology*, *11*, 129–141.

Ballantine, J., & Stray, S. (1998). Financial Appraisal and the IS/IT Investment Decision Making Process. *Journal of Information Technology*, *13*(1), 3–14.

Ballantine, J., & Stray, S. (1999). Information Systems and Other Capital Investments: Evaluation Practices Compared. *Logistics Information Management*, *12*(1/2), 78–93.

Balsamiq. (2010). Rapid Wireframing Tool. Retrieved from http://balsamiq.com

Bambury, P. (1998). A Taxonomy of Internet Commerce. *First Monday*, *3*(10).

Becker, J., Rosemann, M., & Von Uthmann, C. (2000). Guidelines of Business Process Modeling. In W. M. P. Van der Aalst, J. Desel, & A. Oberweis (Eds.), *Business Process Management: Models, Techniques, and Empirical Studies*, LNCS (Vol. 1806, pp. 30–49). Berlin Heidelberg: Springer-Verlag.

Berghout, E. W., & Remenyi, D. (2005). The Eleven Years of the European Conference on IT Evaluation: Retrospectives and Perspectives for Possible Future Research. *The Electronic Journal Information Systems Evaluation*, *8*(2), 81–98.

Borst, W. N., & Akkermans, J. M. (1997). Engineering Ontologies. *International Journal of Human-Computer Studies*, *46*(2/3), 365–406.

Brealey, R. A., & Myers, S. C. (1988). *Principles of Corporate Finance*. New York: McGraw-Hill.

Brews, P. J., & Tucci, C. (2003). Building Internet Generation Companies: Lessons from the Front Lines of the Old Economy. *Academy of Management Executive*, *17*(4).

Brugger, R. (2009). *Der IT Business Case - Kosten Erfassen und Analysieren, Nutzen Erkennen und Quantifizieren, Wirtschaftlichkeit Nachweisen un Realisieren*. Berlin Heidelberg: Springer-Verlag.

Brynjolfsson, E., & Hitt, L. (1996). Paradox Lost? Firm Level Evidence on the Returns of IS Spending. *Management Science*, *42*(4), 541–558.

BusinessCase.com. (2010). CaseBuilder(TM) for IT Initiatives. Retrieved from http://www.businesscase.com/itcasebuilder.html

Butler, J. S., & Schacter, B. (1989). The Investment Decision: Estimation Risk and Risk Adjusted Discount Rates. *Financial Management*, *18*(4), 13–19.

Buxmann, P., Diefenbach, H., & Hess, T. (2008). *Die Softwareindustrie: Ökonomische Prinzipien, Strategien, Perspektiven*. Berlin Heidelberg: Springer-Verlag.

Campbell, H. F., & Brown, R. (2005). A Multiple Account Framework for Cost-Benefit Analysis. *Evaluation and Program Planning*, *28*(1), 23–32.

Cardin, L., Cullen, A., Symons, C., & Belanger, B. (2007). *The Components of a Quality Business Case*. Forrester Research, Inc. Retrieved from http://www.forrester.com/go?docid=42164

Casadesus-Masanell, R., & Ricart, J. E. (2010). From Strategy to Business Models and onto Tactics. *Long Range Planning*, *43*, 195–215.

Chandler, J. S. (1982). A Multiple Criteria Approach for Evaluating Information Systems. *MIS Quarterly*, *6*, 61–75.

Chou, T.-Y., Chou, S. T., & Tzeng, G.-H. (2006). Evaluating IT/IS Investments: A Fuzzy Multi-Criteria Decision Model Approach. *European Journal of Operational Research*, *173*(3), 1026–1046.

Chui, M., Löffler, M., & Roberts, R. (2010). The Internet of Things. *McKinsey Quarterly*, (2).

Corcho, O., Fernandez-Lopez, M., & Gomez-Perez, A. (2003). Methodologies, Tools and Languages for Building Ontologies. Where is Their Meeting Point? *Data & Knowledge Engineering*, *46*, 41–64.

Davis, F. D. (1989). Perceived Usefulness, Perceived Ease of Use, and User Acceptance of Information Technology. *MIS Quarterly*, *13*(3), 319–339.

de Reuver, M., Bouwman, H., & MacInnes, I. (2007). What Drives Business Model Dynamics? A Case Survey. *8th World Congress on the Management of eBusiness (WCMeB)*. July 11, Toronto, Ontario, Canada.

Demil, B., & Lecocq, X. (2010). Business Model Evolution: In Search of Dynamic Consistency. *Long Range Planning*, *43*, 227–246.

Denzin, N. K. (2006). *Sociological Methods: A Sourcebook*. New Brunswick, NJ, USA: Aldine Transaction.

DeWalt, K. M., DeWalt, B. R., & Wayland, C. B. (1998). Participant Observation. In H. R. Bernard (Ed.), *Handbook of Methods in Cultural Anthropology*. Walnut Creek, CA: AltaMira Press.

Dijkman, R. M., Dumas, M., & Ouyang, C. (2008). Semantics and Analysis of Business Process Models in BPMN. *Information and Software Technology*, *50*(12), 1281–1294.

Douglas, J. D. (1976). *Investigative Social Research*. Beverly Hills, CA: Sage Publications.

Elliott, T. (2009, October 15). SAP's Gravity Prototype: Business Collaboration Using Google Wave. October 15. Retrieved November 24, 2010, from http://www.sapweb20.com/blog/2009/10/sap%E2%80%99s-gravity-prototype-business-collaboration-using-google-wave/

Escobar-Perez, B. (1998). Information Systems Investment Decisions in Business Practice: The Spanish Case. *European Journal of Information Systems, 7*(3), 202–209.

Farbey, B., Land, F., & Targett, D. (1992). Evaluating Investments in IT. *Journal of Information Technology, 7,* 109–122.

Farbey, B., Land, F., & Targett, D. (1993). *How to Assess Your IT Investment: a Study of Methods and Practice.* Oxford: Butterworth-Heinemann.

Farbey, B., Land, F., & Targett, D. (1995). A Taxonomy of Information Systems Applications: The Benefits' Evaluation Ladder. *European Journal of Information Systems, 4,* 41–50.

Farbey, B., Land, F., & Targett, D. (1999a). Moving IS Evaluation Forward: Learning Themes and Research Issues. *The Journal of Strategic Information Systems, 8*(2), 189–207.

Farbey, B., Land, F., & Targett, D. (1999b). IS Evaluation: A Process for Bringing Together Benefits, Costs and Risks. In W. Currie & B. Galliers (Eds.), *Rethinking Management Information Systems: An Interdisciplinary Perspective* (pp. 204–228). Oxford, UK: Oxford University Press.

Farbey, B., Targett, D., & Land, F. (1994a). Matching an IT Project with an Appropriate Method of Evaluation: A Research Note on "Evaluating Investments in IT." *Journal of Information Technology, 9,* 239–243.

Farbey, B., Targett, D., & Land, F. (1994b). The Great IT Benefit Hunt. *European Management Journal, 12*(3), 270 – 279.

Fenn, J., & Raskino, M. (2008). *Mastering the Hype Cycle.* Harvard Business Press.

Field, A. (2005). *Discovering Statistics Using SPSS.* London, UK: SAGE Publications Inc.

Fiorini, S., Leite, J. C. S. P., & Soares, T. (1996). Integrating Business Processes with Requirements Elicitation. *5th International Workshop on Enabling Technologies: Infrastructure for Collaborative Enterprises.* June 19, Stanford, CA, USA.

Frakes, W., & Terry, C. (1996). Software Reuse: Metrics and Models. *ACM Computing Surveys (CSUR), 28*(2), 415–435.

Gambles, I. (2009). *Making the Business Case - Proposals that Succeed for Projects that Work.* Farnham: Gower.

Ginzberg, M. J., & Zmud, R. W. (1988). Evolving Criteria for Information Systems Assessment. In N. Bjorn-Anderson & G. B. Davis (Eds.), *Information Systems*

Assessment: Issues and Challenges (pp. 41–52). Noordwijkerhout: North Holland.

Gladwell, M. (2005). *Blink - The Power of Thinking Without Thinking*. New York, NY: Little, Brown and Company.

Gliedman, C., Leganza, G., Visitacion, M., Cecere, M., & Brown, A. (2004). *Key Elements in an IT Business Case*. Forrester Research, Inc. Retrieved from http://www.forrester.com/go?docid=34046

Gordijn, J., & Akkermans, H. (2003). Value Based Requirements Engineering: Exploring Innovative e-Commerce Ideas. *Requirements Engineering Journal, 8*(2), 114–134.

Gordijn, J., Osterwalder, A., & Pigneur, Y. (2005). Comparing Two Business Model Ontologies for Designing e-Business Models and Value Constellations. *18th Bled eConference eIntegration in Action*. June 6, Bled, Slovenia.

Green, T. R. G., & Petre, M. (1996). Usability Analysis of Visual Programming Environments: A "Cognitive Dimensions" Framework. *Journal of Visual Languages & Computing, 7*(2), 131–174.

Gruber, T. R. (1993). A Translation Approach to Portable Ontology Specifications. *Knowledge Acquisition, 5*(2), 199–220.

Gunasekaran, A., Love, P. E. D., Rahimi, F., & Miele, R. (2001). A Model for Investment Justification in Information Technology Projects. *International Journal of Information Management, 21*(5), 349 – 364.

Günther, O., Kletti, W., & Kubach, U. (2008). *RFID in Manufacturing*. Berlin Heidelberg: Springer-Verlag.

Hasso Plattner Institute. (2010). Oryx. Retrieved from http://bpt.hpi.uni-potsdam.de/Oryx

Hevner, A. R. (2007). A Three Cycle View of Design Science Research. *Scandinavian Journal of Information Systems, 19*(2), 87–92.

Hevner, A. R., March, S. T., Park, J., & Ram, S. (2004). Design Science in Information Systems Research. *MIS Quarterly, 28*(1), 75–105.

Hochstrasser, B. (1990). Evaluating IT Investments – Matching Techniques to Projects. *Journal of Information Technology, 5*, 215–221.

Hochstrasser, B., & Griffiths, C. (1991). *Controlling IT Investment; Strategy and Management*. London, UK: Chapman and Hall.

Hussein, T., & Ziegler, J. (2011). Situationsgerechtes Recommending. *Informatik-Spektrum, 34*(2), 143–152.

Irani, Z. (2002). Information Systems Evaluation: Navigating Through the Problem Domain. *Information & Management, 40*(1), 11 – 24.

Irani, Z., Ezingeard, J.-N., & Grieve, R. J. (1997). Integrating the Costs of a Manufacturing IT/IS Infrastructure into the Investment Decision-making Process. *Technovation, 17*(11-12), 695–706.

Irani, Z., Ghoneim, A., & Love, P. E. D. (2006). Evaluating Cost Taxonomies for Information Systems Management. *European Journal of Operational Research, 173*(3), 1103 – 1122.

Irani, Z., Gunasekaran, A., & Love, P. E. D. (2006). Quantitative and Qualitative Approaches to Information Systems Evaluation. *European Journal of Operational Research, 173*(3), 951 – 956.

Irani, Z., & Love, P. E. D. (2000). The Propagation of Technology Management Taxonomies for Evaluating Investments in Information Systems. *Journal of Management Information Systems, 17*(3), 161–177.

Irani, Z., & Love, P. E. D. (2002). Developing a Frame of Reference for Ex-Ante IT/IS Investment Evaluation. *European Journal of Information Systems, 11*(1), 74–82.

Irani, Z., & Love, P. E. D. (2008). Information Systems Evaluation: A Crisis of Understanding. *Evaluating Information Systems* (p. xix – xxxvi). Oxford: Butterworth-Heinemann.

ISACA. (2010). *The Business Case Guide: Using Val IT 2.0*. ISACA. Retrieved from http://www.isaca.org/Knowledge-Center/Research/ResearchDeliverables/Pages/Val-IT-Framework-2.0.aspx

ISO. (1998). *Ergonomic requirements for office work with visual display terminals (VDTs) -- Part 11: Guidance on usability* (No. ISO 9241-11:1998). Retrieved from http://www.iso.org/iso/catalogue_detail.htm?csnumber=16883

Ivantysynova, L. (2008). *RFID in Manufacturing: Mapping the Shop Floor to IT-Enabled Business Processes*. Humboldt-Universität zu Berlin, Berlin.

Jaenen, V., Tummel, C., & Henning, K. (2010). Benefits of RFID for the Production of Hybrid Micro Systems in Flexible Production Networks of SMEs. In V. Mahadevan & Z. Jianhong (Eds.), *2nd International Conference on Computer and Automation Engineering (ICCAE)* (pp. 185–189). February 26, Singapore.

Johnson, M. W., Christensen, C. M., & Kagermann, H. (2008). Reinventing Your Business Model. *Harvard Business Review*. December.

Jones, M. C., & Beatty, R. C. (1998). Towards the Development of Measures of Perceived Benefits and Compatibility of EDI: A Comparative Assessment of

Competing First Order Factor Models. *European Journal of Information Systems*, 7(3), 210–220.

Joshi, K., & Pant, S. (2008). Development of a Framework to Assess and Guide IT Investments: An Analysis Based on a Discretionary-Mandatory Classification. *International Journal of Information Management*, 28(3), 181–193.

Kaplan, R. S. (1996). Using the Balanced Scorecard as a Strategic Management System. *Harvard Business Review*, 74, 75–85.

Kaplan, R. S., & Norton, D. P. (1992). The Balanced Scorecard - Measures that Drive Performance. *Harvard Business Review*, 70(1).

Kaplan, R. S., & Norton, D. P. (1993). Putting the Balanced Scorecard to Work. *Harvard Business Review*, 71(5), 134–147.

King, J. L., & Schrems, E. L. (1978). Cost-Benefit Analysis in Information Systems Development and Operation. *ACM Computing Surveys (CSUR)*, 10(1), 19–34.

Klein, R., & Permenter, K. (2010). *Item-Level RFID Tagging in Retail*. Aberdeen Group. Retrieved from http://www.aberdeen.com/aberdeen-library/6504/RA-rfid-retail-inventory-visibility.aspx

Klose, K., Knackstedt, R., & Beverungen, D. (2007). Identification of Services - A Stakeholder Based Approach to SOA Development and its Application in the Area of Production Planning. *European Conference on Information Systems (ECIS)* (pp. 1802–1814). June 7, St. Gallen, Switzerland.

Ko, R. K. L., Lee, S. S. G., & Lee, E. W. (2009). Business Process Management (BPM) Standards: A Survey. *Business Process Management Journal*, 15(5), 744–791.

Kogut, P., Cranefield, S., Hart, L., Dutra, M., Baclawski, K., Kokar, M., & Smith, J. (2002). UML for Ontology Development. *The Knowledge Engineering Review*, 17(1), 61–64.

Kovar, J. F. (2010, October 11). Oracle Cuts Former Sun Partners From Maintenance Renewals Business. *CRN*. October 11. Retrieved from http://www.crn.com/news/channel-programs/227700450/oracle-cuts-former-sun-partners-from-maintenance-renewals-business.htm

Kröner, A. (2010). Digitales Produktgedächtnis. In K. Vieweg & H. Gerhäuser (Eds.), *Recht-Technik-Wirtschaft 105* (pp. 183–208). Carl Heymanss Verlag.

Lindner, M. A., Vaquero, L. M., Rodero-Merino, L., & Caceres, J. (2010). Cloud Economics: Dynamic Business Models for Business on Demand. *International Journal of Business Information Systems*, 5(4), 373–392.

Love, P. E. D., Irani, Z., & Edwards, D. J. (2004). Industry-centric Benchmarking of Information Technology Benefits, Costs and Risks for Small-to-Medium Sized Enterprises in Construction. *Automation in Construction*, *13*(4), 507–524.

MacInnes, I. (2005). Dynamic Business Model Framework for Emerging Technologies. *International Journal of Services Technology and Management*, *6*(1), 3–19.

Mahadevan, B. (2000). Business Models for Internet-based e-Commerce: An Anatomy. *California Management Review*, *42*(4), 55–69.

Mcauley, L., Doherty, N., & Keval, N. (2002). The Stakeholder Dimension in Information Systems Evaluation. *Journal of Information Technology*, *17*(4), 241–255.

Mendling, J. (2008). *Metrics for Process Models - Empirical Foundations of Verification, Error Prediction, and Guidelines for Correctness*. Lecture Notes in Business Information Processing (Vol. 6). Berlin Heidelberg: Springer.

Merriam-Webster. (2011). The Merriam-Webster Dictionary. Retrieved March 28, 2011, from http://www.merriam-webster.com/dictionary/criterion

Milis, K., & Mercken, R. (2004). The Use of the Balanced Scorecard for the Evaluation of Information and Communication Technology Projects. *International Journal of Project Management*, *22*, 87–97.

Mills, R. W. (1988). Capital Budgeting Techniques Used in the UK and the USA. *Management Accounting*, *66*, 26–27.

Mirani, R., & Lederer, A. L. (1998). An Instrument for Assessing the Organizational Benefits of IS Projects. *Decision Sciences*, *29*(4), 803–838.

Morris, M., Schindehutte, M., & Allen, J. (2005). The Entrepeneur's Business Model: Toward a Unified Perspective. *Journal of Business Research*, *58*(6), 726–735.

Nardi, D., & Brachman, R. (2003). An Introduction to Description Logics. *The Description Logic Handbook*. Cambridge: Cambridge University Press.

Nielsen, J. (1993). *Usability Engineering*. Mountain View, CA, USA: Morgan Kaufman.

Norman, D. A. (2009). Compliance and Tolerance. *Interactions*, *16*(3), 61–65.

Norman, D. A., & Draper, S. W. (1986). *User-Centered System Design: New Perspectives on Human-Computer Interaction*. Hillsdale, NJ, USA: Lawrence Earlbaum Associates.

Noy, N. F., & McGuinness, D. L. (2001). *Ontology Development 101: A Guide to Creating Your First Ontology* (Stanford Technical Report No. SMI-2001-0880). Stanford: Stanford University. Retrieved from http://protege.stanford.edu/publications/ontology_development/ontology10 1-noy-mcguinness.html

Object Management Group. (2010). *Business Motivation Model (Version 1.1)* (No. formal/2010-05-01). May. Retrieved from http://www.omg.org/spec/BMM/1.1/

Object Management Group. (2011). Unified Modeling Language (UML). Retrieved April 5, 2011, from http://www.uml.org

OMG. (2010). BPMN 2.0 Beta 2. Retrieved from http://www.omg.org/cgi-bin/doc?dtc/10-06-04

Osterwalder, A, & Pigneur, Y. (2003). Towards Strategy and Information Systems Alignment through a Business Model Ontology. *23rd Annual Conference of the Strategic Management Society*. November, Baltimore.

Osterwalder, Alexander, Pigneur, Y., & Tucci, C. L. (2005). Clarifying Business Models: Origins, Present, and Future of the Concept. *Communications of the Association for Information Systems*, *16*(1), 1–25.

Papazoglou, M. P., & v.d. Heuvel, W.-J. (2006). Service-Oriented Design and Development Methodology. *International Journal of Web Engineering and Technology*, *2*(4), 412–442.

Parker, M., & Benson, R. (1989). Enterprisewide Information Economics: Latest Concepts. *Information Systems Management*, *6*(4), 7–13.

Parker, M. M., Benson, R. J., & Trainor, H. E. (1988). *Information Economics: Linking Business Performance to Information Technology*. Englewood Cliffs, NJ: Prentice-Hall.

Peppard, J., Ward, J., & Daniel, E. (2007). Managing the Realization of Business Benefits from IT Investments. *MIS Quarterly Executive*, *6*(1), 1–11.

Porter, M. E. (2008). The Five Competitive Forces That Shape Strategy. *Harvard Business Review*. January.

Project RAN. (2011). RFID-based Automotive Network (RAN). Retrieved from www.autoran.de

Reinhart, G., Irrenhauser, T., Reinhardt, S., Reisen, K., & Schellmann, H. (2011). Wirtschaftlicher und ressourceneffizienter durch RFID? Methode für eine unternehmensübergreifende Bewertung der Wirtschaftlichkeit und der Ressourceneffizienz. *Zeitschrift für Wirtschaftlichen Fabrikbetrieb*, *106*(4), 225–230.

Renkema, T. J. W., & Berghout, E. W. (1997). Methodologies for Information Systems Investment Evaluation at the Proposal Stage: a Comparative Review. *Information and Software Technology, 39*(1), 1 – 13.

Riehle, D., & Züllighoven, H. (1996). Understanding and Using Patterns in Software Development. *Theory and Practice of Object Systems, 2*(1), 3–13.

Ross, J. W., & Beath, C. M. (2002). Beyond the Business Case: New Approaches to IT Investment. *MIT Sloan Management Review, 43*(2), 51–59.

Russell, N., Ter Hofstede, A. H. M., Edmond, D., & Van der Aalst, W. M. P. (2005). Workflow Data Patterns: Identification, Representation and Tool Support. In L. Delcambre, C. Kop, H. C. Mayr, J. Mylopoulos, & O. Pastor (Eds.), *Conceptual Modeling - ER 2005*, LNCS (Vol. 3716, pp. 353–368). Berlin Heidelberg: Springer-Verlag.

Ryan, S. D., & Harrison, D. A. (2000). Considering Social Subsystem Costs and Benefits in Information Technology Investment Decisions: A View from the Field on Anticipated Payoffs. *Journal of Management Information Systems, 16*(4), 11–40.

Salipante, P., Notz, W., & Bigelow, J. (1982). A Matrix Approach to Literature Reviews. In B. M. Staw & L. L. Cummings (Eds.), *Research in Organizational Behavior* (pp. 321–348). Greenwich, CT: JAI Press.

SAP AG. (2011). Value Lifecycle Manager. Retrieved from https://sapvalueengineering.com/VLM2/client.page

Sassone, P. G. (1988). Cost Benefit Analysis of Information Systems: A Survey of Methodologies. *Conference on Supporting Group Work, ACM SIGOIS and IEEECS TC-OA*. Palo Alto, CA, USA.

Schmidt, M. J. (2003). *The IT Business Case: Keys to Accuracy and Credibility*. Solution Matrix Ltd. Retrieved from www.solutionmatrix.com/publications.html

Schmidt, M. J. (2009). *Business Case Essentials: A Guide to Structure and Content* (3rd ed.). Boston, MA, USA: Solution Matrix, Ltd.

Schmitz, M., Baus, J., & Dörr, R. (2008). The Digital Sommelier: Interacting with Intelligent Products. *The Internet of Things: 1st International Conference* (pp. 247–262). March 26, Zurich, Switzerland: Springer-Verlag.

Schryen, G. (2010). Preserving Knowledge on IS Business Value. *Business & Information Systems Engineering*, (4), 233–244.

SemProM. (2010). Retrieved from http://www.semprom.org

Serafeimidis, V., & Smithson, S. (1999). Rethinking the Approaches to Information Systems Investment Evaluation. *Logistics Information Management, 12*(1/2), 94–107.

Serafeimidis, V., & Smithson, S. (2000). Information Systems Evaluation in Practice: A Case Study of Organizational Change. *Journal of Information Technology, 15*(2), 93–105.

Simon, H. A. (1996). *The Sciences of the Artificial* (3rd ed.). Cambridge, Massachusetts: The MIT Press.

Smithson, S., & Angell, I. O. (1991). *Information Systems Management: Opportunities and Risks*. Basingstoke: Macmillan Press.

Smithson, S., & Hirschheim, R. (1998). Analysing Information System Evaluation: Another Look at an Old Problem. *European Journal of Information Systems, 7*(3), 158–174.

SolutionMatrix Ltd. (2010). FREE Excel Financial Metrics Calculator. Retrieved from http://www.solutionmatrix.com/download-center.html

Staab, S., Studer, R., Schnurr, H.-P., & Sure, Y. (2001). Knowledge Processes and Ontologies. *IEEE Intelligent Systems, 16*(1), 26–34.

Strassmann, P. (1985). *Information Payoff: The Transformation of Work in the Electronic Age*. New York: The Free Press.

Timmers, P. (1998). Business Models for Electronic Markets. *Journal on Electronic Markets, 8*(2), 3–8.

Urbach, N., Smolnik, S., & Riempp, G. (2009). The State of Research on Information Systems Success - A Review of Existing Multidimensional Approaches. *Business & Information Systems Engineering, 4*, 315–325.

Vaccaro, V. L., & Cohn, D. Y. (2004). The Evolution of Business Models and Marketing Strategies in the Music Industry. *International Journal on Media Management, 6*(1/2), 46–58.

Van der Aalst, W. M. P., Ter Hofstede, A., Kiepuszewski, B., & Barros, A. P. (2003). Workflow Patterns. *Distributed and Parallel Databases, 14*(1), 5–51.

Van der Aalst, W. M. P., & Weijters, A. J. M. M. (2005). Process Mining. In M. Dumas, W. M. P. Van der Aalst, & A. H. M. Ter Hofstede (Eds.), *Process-Aware Information Systems: Bridging People end Software through Process Technology* (pp. 235–255). Wiley & Sons.

Van Putten, B.-J., Brecht, F., & Günther, O. (2011). Challenges in Business Case Development and Requirements for Business Case Frameworks. *5th European*

Conference on Information Management and Evaluation (ECIME). September 8, Como, Italy.

Van Putten, B.-J., Irrenhauser, T., & Meijler, T. D. (2012). Supporting Dynamic Reuse in Business Case Development. *20th European Conference on Information Systems (ECIS)*. June 10, Barcelona, Spain.

VDMA. (2009). *Manufacturing Execution Systems (MES) Kennzahlen* (No. 66412-1). Retrieved from http://www.vdma.org/

Venkatesh, V., & Bala, H. (2008). Technology Acceptance Model 3 and a Research Agenda on Interventions. *Decision Sciences, 39*(2), 273–315. May.

Venkatesh, V., & Davis, F. D. (2000). A Theoretical Extension of the Technology Acceptance Model: Four Longitudinal Field Studies. *Management Science, 46*, 186–204.

Venkatesh, V., Morris, M. G., Davis, G. B., & Davis, F. D. (2003). User Acceptance of Information Technology: Toward a Unified View. *MIS Quarterly, 27*(3).

vom Brocke, J., Simons, A., Niehaves, B., Riemer, K., Plattfaut, R., & Cleven, A. (2009). Reconstructing the Giant: On the Importance of Rigour in Documenting the Literature Search Process. *17th European Conference on Information Systems (ECIS)*. Verona, Italy.

W3C. (2004). Resource Description Framework (RDF). Retrieved April 6, 2011, from http://www.w3.org/standards/techs/rdf

W3C. (2009). Web Ontology Language (OWL). Retrieved April 6, 2011, from http://www.w3.org/standards/techs/owl

Wahlster, W., Kröner, A., Schneider, M., & Baus, J. (2008). Sharing Memories of Smart Products and their Consumers in Instrumented Environments. *Information Technology, 50*(1), 45–49.

Walter, S. G., & Spitta, T. (2004). Approaches to the Ex-ante Evaluation of Investments into Information Systems. *Wirtschaftsinformatik, 46*(3), 171–180.

Ward, J., Daniel, E., & Peppard, J. (2008). Building Better Business Cases for IT Investments. *MIS Quarterly Executive, 7*(1), 1–15.

Ward, J. M. (1990). A Portfolio Approach to Evaluating Information Systems Investments and Setting Priorities. *Journal of Information Technology, 5*(4), 222–231.

Ward, J., Taylor, P., & Bond, P. (1996). Evaluation and Realization of IS/IT Benefits: An Empirical Study of Current Practice. *European Journal of Information Systems, 4*, 214–225.

Webster, J., & Watson, R. T. (2002). Analyzing the Past to Prepare for the Future: Writing a Literature Review. *MIS Quarterly, 26*(2), xiii–xxiii.

Weill, P., & Vitale, M. (2002). What IT Infrastructure Capabilities are Needed to Implement E-Business Models? *MIS Quarterly, 1*(1), 17–34.

Weiner, N., Renner, T., & Kett, H. (2010). *Geschäftsmodelle im Internet de Dienste*. Fraunhofer IAO. http://www.itbusinessmodels.org/downloads/weiner_renner_kett_2010_gesc haeftsmodelle.pdf.

Weston, R. H., Chatka, K. A., & Ajaefobi, J. O. (2004). Process Thinking in Support of System Specification and Selection. *Advanced Engineering Informatics, 18*(4), 217–229.

Willcocks, L., & Lester, S. (1991). Information Systems Investments: Evaluation at the Feasibility Stage of Projects. *Technovation, 11*(5), 283–302.

Willcocks, L. P., & Lester, S. (1994). Evaluating the Feasibility of Information Systems Investments: Recent UK Evidence and New Approaches. In L. P. Willcocks (Ed.), *Information Management: The Evaluation of Information Systems Investments*. London: Chapman & Hall.

Wolstenholme, E. F., Henderson, S., & Gavine, A. (1993). *The Evaluation of Management Information Systems: a Dynamic and Holistic Approach*. Chichester: Wiley.

A Interview Protocol (Ch. 2)

This appendix belongs to Chapter 2 and shows the protocol that was used for the semi-structured interviews with business case developers.

SemProM Business Case Interview

version: 20.01.2010 (v16)

date:

Introduction

The decision for or against investments in companies needs a well-founded basis. To support investment decision makers, business cases are often used. The goal of this survey is to determine challenges and requirements for business cases and business case frameworks in general, and for SemProM in particular.

Personalia

A1. Name:

A2. Organization:

A3. Job title:

A4. Role in SemProM:

Your organization

B1. Please select all the roles that your organization plays or will play in the context of SemProM:

Provider of SemProM as part of or attached to a product,

☐ external: providing to third parties

☐ internal: providing to internal organization

Provider of SemProM independent of a product (e.g., RFID tag with storage),

☐ external: providing to third parties

☐ internal: providing to internal organization

Customer of SemProM,

☐ external: buying from third party

☐ internal: 'buying' from internal organization

Other role? Please describe:

B2. Please describe the main industry in which your organization is active:

Business cases in your organization

A business case is an analysis of costs, benefits, and risks of each proposed investment alternative. In the case of SemProM, the investment could concern buying SemProM hardware or software (i.e., the customer perspective) and related investments, e.g. for organizational change. The investment could also concern productizing, selling, and supporting SemProM hardware or software (i.e., the provider perspective) and related investments, e.g. for organizational change.

Business case development is the process before investment, consisting of collecting and structuring information, writing documents, composing spreadsheets, collaborating with stakeholders, etc.

Business case evaluation is the process of analysing the investment alternative(s) as proposed by the business case and deciding if an investment will be made.

C1. My organization actively uses business cases.

strongly disagree	disagree	neither agree nor disagree	agree	strongly agree	no opinion
☐	☐	☐	☐	☐	☐

Explanation:

C2. If applicable, please describe the main business cases in your organization. Please mention:
- Goal (why is there a business case):
- Scope (suitable for which domain):
- Format (Word, Excel, Powerpoint, combination, ?):
- Users (who are using it):
- Other remarks:

C3. I have actively supported the development of a business case.

strongly disagree	disagree	neither agree nor disagree	agree	strongly agree	no opinion
☐	☐	☐	☐	☐	☐

Explanation:

C4. I have actively supported the evaluation of a business case.

strongly disagree	disagree	neither agree nor disagree	agree	strongly agree	no opinion
☐	☐	☐	☐	☐	☐

Explanation:

C5. I am a business case development expert.

strongly disagree	disagree	neither agree nor disagree	agree	strongly agree	no opinion
☐	☐	☐	☐	☐	☐

Explanation:

C6. I am a business case evaluation expert.

strongly disagree	disagree	neither agree nor disagree	agree	strongly agree	no opinion
☐	☐	☐	☐	☐	☐

Explanation:

C7. A business case is useful.

strongly disagree	disagree	neither agree nor disagree	agree	strongly agree	no opinion
☐	☐	☐	☐	☐	☐

Explanation:

C8. My organization has developed a business case for SemProM.

strongly disagree	disagree	neither agree nor disagree	agree	strongly agree	no opinion
☐	☐	☐	☐	☐	☐

Explanation:

C9. My organization is developing a business case for SemProM.

strongly disagree	disagree	neither agree nor disagree	agree	strongly agree	no opinion
☐	☐	☐	☐	☐	☐

Explanation:

C10. My organization will develop a business case for SemProM.

strongly disagree	disagree	neither agree nor disagree	agree	strongly agree	no opinion
☐	☐	☐	☐	☐	☐

Explanation:

Business case frameworks in your organization

A business case framework (BCF) is meant to support the development of business cases. A common form is an Excel sheet, but it can also be a PowerPoint template, a guideline in Word, or any other kind of tool or method to make business case development easier or better.

D1. My organization actively uses a BCF.

strongly disagree	disagree	neither agree nor disagree	agree	strongly agree	no opinion
☐	☐	☐	☐	☐	☐

Explanation:

D2. If applicable, please describe the main BCF(s) in your organization. Please mention:
- Goal (why is there a framework):
- Scope (suitable for which domain):
- Format (Word, Excel, Powerpoint, combination, ?):
- Users (who are using it):
- Other remarks:

D3. I have actively used a BCF.

strongly disagree	disagree	neither agree nor disagree	agree	strongly agree	no opinion
☐	☐	☐	☐	☐	☐

Explanation:

D4. A BCF is useful.

strongly disagree	disagree	neither agree nor disagree	agree	strongly agree	no opinion
☐	☐	☐	☐	☐	☐

Explanation:

A SemProM specific BCF is meant to support the development of business cases, to decide on investment in SemProM products or services (provider perspective or customer perspective). A SemProM specific BCF could for example include suggestions for benefits, costs, and risks, specific to the use cases of SemProM.

D5. My organization already has a useful SemProM specific BCF.

strongly disagree	disagree	neither agree nor disagree	agree	strongly agree	no opinion
☐	☐	☐	☐	☐	☐

Explanation:

D6. My organization is interested in a SemProM specific BCF.

strongly disagree	disagree	neither agree nor disagree	agree	strongly agree	no opinion
☐	☐	☐	☐	☐	☐

Explanation:

D7. My organization would use a SemProM specific BCF.

strongly disagree	disagree	neither agree nor disagree	agree	strongly agree	no opinion
☐	☐	☐	☐	☐	☐

Explanation:

Challenges & Requirements

Please deal with the following statements in the context of business cases and BCF *in general*. Thus, we are not asking about SemProM specific business cases or BCF.

For each of the topics an example is available. Please only refer to the example if the topic is unclear, and consider that we are researching your opinion on the more general concept, rather than your opinion on the specific example.

For each of the topics we will also ask you for an explanation.

Reuse of Content

The content of a business case is composed of all items of information, which can be qualitative, or quantitative, and presented in any form, such as text, figures, images, etc.

E1. Content from earlier business cases should be reusable in later business cases.

strongly disagree	disagree	neither agree nor disagree	agree	strongly agree	no opinion
☐	☐	☐	☐	☐	☐

Explanation:

E2. Reusing content from an earlier business case in a later one is a challenge.

strongly disagree	disagree	neither agree nor disagree	agree	strongly agree	no opinion
☐	☐	☐	☐	☐	☐

Explanation:

E3. A BCF should support reuse of content.

strongly disagree	disagree	neither agree nor disagree	agree	strongly agree	no opinion
☐	☐	☐	☐	☐	☐

Explanation:

Reuse of Structure

The structure of a business cases defines which content items are presented, in which order they are presented, and how content items can be aggregated into other content items (e.g., calculation methods).

F1. Structure from earlier business cases should be reusable in later business cases. (table left out to save space in this dissertation)

F2. Reusing structure from an earlier business case in a later one is a challenge. etc.

F3. A BCF should support reuse of structure.

Aggregation

G1. Specific business cases sometimes need to be aggregated to more general business cases.

G2. Aggregating more specific business cases to more general business cases is a challenge.

G3. A BCF should support aggregation of business cases.

Comparison

H1. A later business case should be comparable with an earlier business case in the same domain.

H2. Comparing a later business case with an earlier business case is a challenge.

H3. A BCF should support comparison of business cases.

Provider vs. Customer Perspective

I1. A provider perspective business case should include a customer perspective.

I2. Including a customer perspective in a provider perspective business case is a challenge.

I3. A BCF should support including a customer perspective in a provider perspective business case.

Market Potential Estimation

J1. A provider perspective business case should include a market potential estimation.

J2. Estimating the market potential for a product or service is a challenge.

J3. A BCF should support the estimation of market potential.

Changing Assumptions

K1. A business case should be adapted after assumptions have changed.

K2. After assumptions have changed, adapting a business case is a challenge.

K3. A BCF should support adaptation after assumptions have changed.

Product Innovation Lifecycle

L1. A provider perspective business case should be useful throughout the product innovation lifecycle.

L2. Adapting a business case to changing factors during the product innovation lifecycle is a challenge.

L3. A BCF should support adaptation to changing factors during the product innovation lifecycle.

Business Model Adaptivity

A business model describes the rationale of how an organization creates, delivers, and captures value, e.g., through buyers, suppliers, and pricing.

M1. A provider perspective business case should be adapted to the provider's business model.

M2. Adapting a business case to a changing business model is a challenge.

M3. A BCF should support adaptation to a changing business model.

Clarifying Reasoning

N1. The assumptions and reasoning behind a business case should be clear to all stakeholders.

N2. Clarifiying the assumptions and reasoning behind a business case to all stakeholders is a challenge.

N3. A BCF should support clarification of assumptions and reasoning.

Stakeholders' Opinions

O1. The opinions of stakeholders should be recorded and comparable in a business case.

O2. Recording and comparing stakeholders' opinions is a challenge.

O3. A BCF should support the recording and comparison of stakeholders' opinions.

Information Sources

P1. The sources of information in a business case should be clear.

P2. Finding out the sources of information in a business case is a challenge.

P3. A BCF should support finding out the sources of information.

Information Quality

Q1. The quality of information in a business case should be clear.

Q2. Determining the quality of information in a business case is a challenge.

Q3. A BCF should support the determination of the quality of information.

Sharing

R1. A business case shoud be shared with partners in the value network.

R2. Sharing a business case with partners in the value network is a challenge.

R3. A BCF should support sharing in the value network.

Security

S1. Parts of a business case should only be accessible to authorized users.

S2. Protecting parts of a business case against unauthorized access is a challenge.

S3. A BCF should support the definition of access restrictions for certain users.

Remarks

If you have any further questions or remarks concerning business cases, BCF, SemProM, or this interview, please express them here:

B Literature Review: Concept Matrix (Ch. 3)

This appendix belongs to Chapter 3 and shows screenshots of the concept matrix.

Year	Authors	Criteria	Methods	Efficiency & Effectiveness	Comparison & Benchmarking	Usage & Acceptance	Understanding & Learning
				Reusable Components		**Arguments**	
1992	Bacon	p.338 (Tbl 1)	0	p.337, 344	0	p.343,345	p.343, 344
1996	Ballantine et al.	0	0	0	0	0	0
1998	Ballantine & Stray	0	p.4 (Tbl 1) p.5 (Tbl 2) p.8 (Tbl 4) p.11 (Tbl 9)	0	0	p.4 (Tbl 1) p.5 (Tbl 2) p.8 (Tbl 4) p.9	0
2005	Berghout & Remenyi	0	p.84	0	0	0	0
1982	Chandler	0	p.62, 63	0	0	0	0
1992	Farbey et al.	p.111	p.113	0	0	0	0
1995	Farbey et al.	0	0	0	0	0	0
1999	Farbey et al.	0	p.191, 199	0	0	0	0
2009	Gadatsch	0	p.260	0	0	0	0
1990	Hochstrasser	0	0	0	0	0	0
2002	Irani	p.18 (Tbl 2) p.20 (Tbl 3)	0	0	0	0	0
2000	Irani & Love	p.168 (Tbl 1,2) p.169 (Tbl 3) p.173 (Tbl 4,5)	0	0	0	0	0
2006	Irani et al.	p.1107 (Tbl 3)	p.1105 (Tbl 2)	p.1119	0	p.1104 (Fig 1)	p.1104 (Fig 1) p.1119
2008	Joshi & Pant	p.182, 183	0	p.182	0	0	p.183
1992	Kaplan & Norton	p.72 (Fig 1)	0	p.79	p.74	0	0
1993	Kaplan & Norton	p.136 (Fig 2)	0	p.134	p.135, 141	0	p.142
1996	Kaplan	0	0	0	0	p.1, 3, 5	p.1, 3
1978	King & Schrems	p.21 p.23 (Tbl 1) p.24 (Tbl 2)	p.22-27	0	0	0	0
2004	Milis & Mercken	p.95 (Fig 2)	p.88 (Tbl 1)	0	0	p.96	p.96
1989	Parker & Benson	0	p.10	0	0	0	0
1997	Renkema & Berghout	p.2, 4	p.3-7, 10-11	0	0	0	p.9
2002	Ross & Beath	0	0	0	0	0	0
1988	Sassone	0	p.127-131	0	0	0	0
2010	Schryen	p.234, 236	p.237, 240	0	0	0	0
2000	Serafeimidis & Smithson	p.99	p.94, 95, 99	0	p.95	0	p.97
2009	Urbach et al.	p.316, 317	p.321	0	0	0	0
2004	Walter & Spitta	p.172	p.174-176	0	0	0	p.175, 178
2008	Ward et al.	0	p.3-10	0	0	0	0
2005	Wehrmann & Zimmermann	p.249	p.248	0	0	0	0
2006	Wehrmann et al.	p.235, 236	p.236-239	p.235	p.234-245	p.236, 244	p.244
1991	Willcocks & Lester	p.293 (Tbl 7)	0	p.289	0	0	p.298

Figure B.1: The reviewed literature (1 of 3): Reusable Components and Arguments

Year	Authors	Formality	Reliability	Familiarity	Usability	Applicability	Guidelines
1992	Bacon	p.343	p.343	0	p.342,344	p.342	0
1996	Ballantine et al.	0	0	p.138	0	0	0
1998	Ballantine & Stray	0	0	p.9	p.9	p.8-10	0
2005	Berghout & Remenyi	0	0	0	0	0	0
1982	Chandler	0	0	0	0	0	0
1992	Farbey et al.	p.113	0	0	0	p.116	p.117
1995	Farbey et al.	0	0	0	0	0	p.49
1999	Farbey et al.	p.193	0	0	0	p.194	p.191
2009	Gadatsch	0	0	0	0	p.260	0
1990	Hochstrasser	p.220	0	0	0	0	p.216
2002	Irani	0	0	0	0	0	0
2000	Irani & Love	0	0	p.167	0	p.163, 166, 167, 174	0
2006	Irani et al.	p.1119	0	0	0	0	p.1105
2008	Joshi & Pant	p.182	0	0	0	p.182, 183, 191	p.181-192
1992	Kaplan & Norton	0	0	0	0	0	0
1993	Kaplan & Norton	0	0	0	0	p.141	0
1996	Kaplan	0	0	0	0	0	0
1978	King & Schrems	0	p.31	0	0	p.33	0
2004	Milis & Mercken	0	p.87, 96	0	p.92	p.89, 96	p.96
1989	Parker & Benson	0	0	0	0	p.12	p.10
1997	Renkema & Berghout	0	p.9	0	p.7, 8, 9	p.9	0
2002	Ross & Beath	0	0	0	0	0	p.54
1988	Sassone	0	p.127-131	0	p.127-131	p.126	p.127-131
2010	Schryen	0	0	0	0	p.240, 241	0
2000	Serafeimidis & Smithson	p.95	p.95	p.101	0	p.93	p.97
2009	Urbach et al.	0	0	0	0	0	0
2004	Walter & Spitta	0	p.172	0	p.176-178	p.174-176	p.178
2008	Ward et al.	0	0	0	0	0	0
2005	Wehrmann & Zimmermann	p.247, 257	0	0	0	p.248	p.248, 256
2006	Wehrmann et al.	0	0	0	0	0	0
1991	Willcocks & Lester	p.290, 296	p.295	p.294	0	0	p.292, 299

Figure B.2: The reviewed literature (2 of 3): Challenges and Guidelines

Year	Authors	Methodology	Behavioral Science	Design Science	Literature Review	Argumentative	Journal
1992	Bacon	survey (80)	0	0	0		MIS Quarterly
1996	Ballantine et al.	survey (97)	0	0	0		J. of Information Technology
1998	Ballantine & Stray	survey (97)	0	X	0		J. of Information Technology
2005	Berghout & Remenyi	0	0	X	0		Electronic J. of IS Evaluation
1982	Chandler	0	X	0	0		MIS Quarterly
1992	Farbey et al.	case studies (16)	X	0	0		J. of Information Technology
1995	Farbey et al.	0	0	0	X		Eu. J. of Information Systems
1999	Farbey et al.	0	0	0	X		J. of Strategic Information Systems
2009	Gadatsch	0	0	X	0		Business & Information Systems Engineering
1990	Hochstrasser	case studies (34 companies, 60+ interviews)	0	0	X		J. of Information Technology
2002	Irani	case study (1)	0	0	0		Information & Management
2000	Irani & Love	case study (1)	0	0	0		J. of Management Information Systems
2006	Irani et al.	0	0	X	0		Eu. J. of Operational Research
2008	Joshi & Pant	interviews (3)	X	0	X		Int. J. of Information Management
1992	Kaplan & Norton	case studies (12)	0	0	0		Harvard Business Review
1993	Kaplan & Norton	case studies (3)	0	0	0		Harvard Business Review
1996	Kaplan	case studies (100)	0	0	0		Harvard Business Review
1978	King & Schrems	0	0	X	0		ACM Computing Surveys
2004	Milis & Mercken	0	0	0	X		Int. J. of Project Management
1989	Parker & Benson	0	0	0	X		Information Systems Management
1997	Renkema & Berghout	0	0	X	0		Information and Software Technology
2002	Ross & Beath	case studies (30 companies, 48 interviews)	0	0	0		MIT Sloan Management Review
1988	Sassone	0	0	X	0		ACM Conference
2010	Schryen	0	0	X	0		Business & Information Systems Engineering
2000	Serafeimidis & Smithson	case study + interviews	0	0	X		J. of Information Technology
2009	Urbach et al.	0	0	X	0		Business & Information Systems Engineering
2004	Walter & Spitta	0	0	X	0		Wirtschaftsinformatik
2008	Ward et al.	case studies (20), case studies (5), survey (102)	0	0	0		MIS Quarterly Executive
2005	Wehrmann & Zimmermann	0	X	0	0		Wirtschaftsinformatik
2006	Wehrmann et al.	0	X	0	0		Wirtschaftsinformatik
1991	Willcocks & Lester	survey + interviews (50)	0	0	0		Technovation

Figure B.3: The reviewed literature (3 of 3): Methodology

C Applications of Business Case Ontology (Ch. 4)

This appendix belongs to Chapter 4 and shows how the Business Case Ontology (BCO) can be applied to describe some well-known models.

Financial and Non-financial Criteria

According to Irani and Love (2008), "choosing an evaluation approach that seeks to go beyond the traditional boundaries of financial evaluation is increasingly important, and many factors associated with developing a robust IS requires a business, user and technology context. Therefore, providing decision-makers with direct cost analysis, cash flow projections, financial figures etc., will not be enough, as there are other strategic (grounded in long-term objectives), softer, political and social factors that need to be considered during the evaluation process." Therefore, it is common to evaluate a set of financial and non-financial criteria in IS business cases. For example, Bacon (1992) defined a list of 15 criteria for his research on the usage and application of IS investment criteria (**Figure C.1**).

Financial Criteria

Discounted Cash Flow (DCF)
1. Net Present Value
2. Internal Rate of Return
3. Profitability Index Method

Other Financial
4. Average/Accounting Rate of Return
5. Payback Method
6. Budgetary Constraint

Management Criteria
7. Support Explicit Business Objectives
8. Support Implicit Business Objectives
9. Response to Competitve Systems
10. Support Management Decision Making
11. Probability of Achieving Benefits
12. Legal/Government Requirements

Development Criteria
13. Technical/System Requirements
14. Introduce/Learn New Technology
15. Probability of Project Completion

Figure C.1: IS investment criteria considered by Bacon (1992)

In terms of BCO, the criteria should obviously be modeled as instances of the class Criterion. The headers should be modeled as groups. 'Discounted Cash Flow (DCF)' and 'Other Financial' are sub-groups of 'Financial Criteria'. Using Description Logic this would look as follows:

```
"Net Present Value", "Internal Rate of Return", … ∈ Criterion
"Financial Criteria", "Discounted Cash Flow (DCF)", … ∈ Group
memberOf("Discounted Cash Flow (DCF)", "Financial Criteria")
memberOf("Net Present Value", "Discounted Cash Flow (DCF)")
etc.
```

To obtain a value for these criteria, most of them are probably associated with a method. The financial criteria are probably related to quantification methods, while for the other criteria other types of methods are applied. If we consider two cases (i.e., instances of class Case), case "vendor A database" and "vendor B database", this could be described as follows using Description Logic:

```
"vendor A database", "vendor B database" ∈ Case
"Net Present Value" ∈ Criterion
"NPV Calculation" ∈ Quantification
"MethodApplication X" ∈ MethodApplication
"MethodApplication Y" ∈ MethodApplication
applies("MethodApplication X", "NPV Calculation")
appliedToCase("MethodApplication X", "vendor A database")
appliedToCriterion("MethodApplication X", "Net Present Value")
applies("MethodApplication Y", "NPV Calculation")
appliedToCase("MethodApplication Y", "vendor B database")
appliedToCriterion("MethodApplication Y", "Net Present Value")
```

Just like Bacon, there are many authors who provide lists of criteria. For example, Gunasekaran et al. (2001) structure criteria along Strategic Considerations, Tactical Considerations, Operational Considerations, Intangibles (such as Competitive Advantage), Tangible Considerations (with subgroups Financial and Non-Financial). In many models, competitive advantage is part of the 'intangible', 'strategic' or 'management' criteria. In the next sub-section a common method for valuating competitive advantage will be described.

Competitive Advantage

A well-known model for explaining the competitive advantage and thus the strategy of a firm is Porter's Five Forces model (Porter, 2008), **Figure C.2**. The rivalry among existing competitors is determined by the bargaining power of suppliers, the bargaining power of buyers, the threat of new entrants and the threat of substitute products or services. Together, these make up the 'five forces'. The five forces may be used as criteria in a business case that is expected to have strategic impact, such as those proposing the investment in strategic information systems.

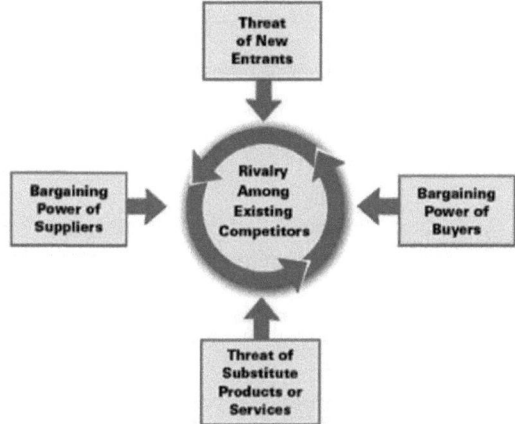

Figure C.2: The five competitive forces that shape strategy, adopted from Porter (2008)

Porter's model can be described using BCO, by modeling all five forces as criteria, whereby the „rivalry among existing competitors" is affected by the other four criteria. In Description Logic:

"Threat of New Entrants" ∈ Criterion

"Bargaining Power of Buyers" ∈ Criterion

"Threat of Substitute Products or Services" ∈ Criterion

"Bargaining Power of Suppliers" ∈ Criterion

"Rivalry Among Existing Competitors" ∈ Criterion

hasEffectOn("Threat of New Entrants", "Rivalry Among Existing Competitors")

hasEffectOn("Bargaining Power...", "Rivalry Among Existing Competitors")

etc.

Together, these five criteria can be seen as an indication for the criterion 'Competitive Advantage':

"Competitive Advantage" ∈ Criterion
"Comp_Adv_Indicators" ∈ Indication
uses("Comp_Adv_Indicators", "Threat of New Entrants")
uses("Comp_Adv_Indicators", "Bargaining Power of Buyers")
etc.

Balanced Scorecard

Another famous method, which does not just consider financial criteria, is the balanced scorecard (Kaplan & Norton, 1992). It helps top management to select a set of measures that provide an integrated look at a company. Four 'scorecards' of measurable items are proposed:

The *financial scorecard* contains the traditional financial performance measures. The company should set financial goals and select a limited set of financial measures.

The *customer scorecard* deals with the question "how do customers see us?" Again, goals are set and measures are selected.

The *internal business scorecard* provides goals and measures concerning the internal operations. The underlying question here is "What should we excel at?".

The fourth scorecard deals with the *innovation and learning* perspective. Can we continue to improve and create value?

It is relatively easy to tailor the balanced scorecard framework to the specific needs of IT investment evaluation (Milis & Mercken, 2004). Willcocks and Lester (1994) illustrate this with a case, based on their experience with a major European ferry company (**Figure C.3**). These four scorecards can be described with BCO. The names (Financial perspective etc.) are modelled as first level criteria. The measurable items are modelled as second level criteria, making the first level criteria more specific. In Description Logic:

"Financial perspective" ∈ Criterion
"return on investment/equity" ∈ Criterion
"profitability per employee" ∈ Criterion
"Finan_Persp_Indicators" ∈ Indication
uses("Finan_Persp_Indicators", "return on investment/equity")
uses("Finan_Persp_Indicators", "profitability per employee")
etc.

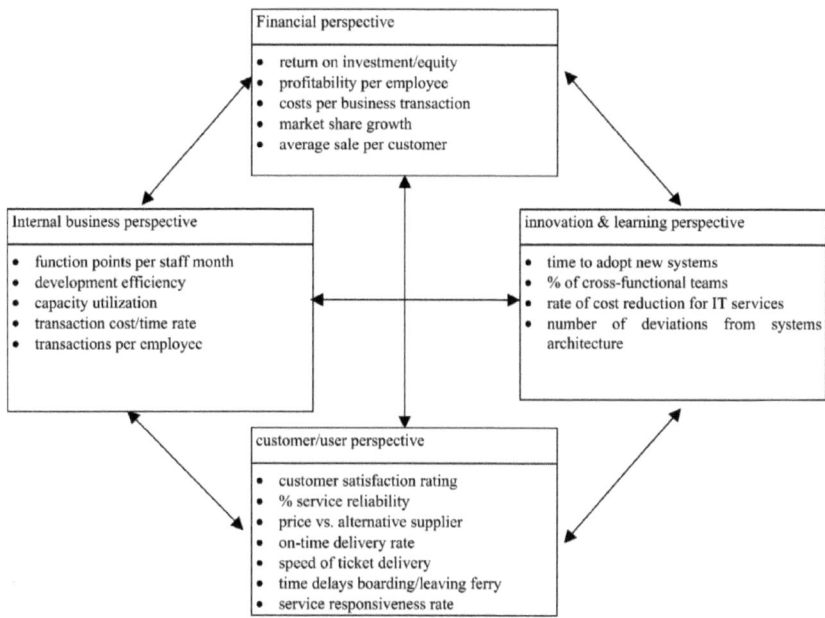

Figure C.3: A balanced scorecard applied to IT investment evaluation at a European ferry company, adopted from Willcocks and Lester (1994)

An alternative to modeling the 'perspectives' as criteria is to model them as groups and to then relate the other criteria to these groups. The arrows in the diagram show dependencies between the scorecards, which we interpreted as 'everything has an influence on everything else'. Describing this in BCO would require a large amount of 'hasEffectOn' relations, namely for each pair of criteria.

Benefit-Dependency Network

As part of their benefits management approach, Peppard et al. (2007) propose the benefit-dependency network (BDN): "The BDN provides a framework for explicitly linking the overall investment objectives and the requisite benefits with the business changes which are necessary to deliver those benefits and the essential IT functionality to both drive and enable these changes to be made".

Figure C.4 shows an example of such a network that was used by a large European paper manufacturer to evaluate a customer relationship management (CRM) system.

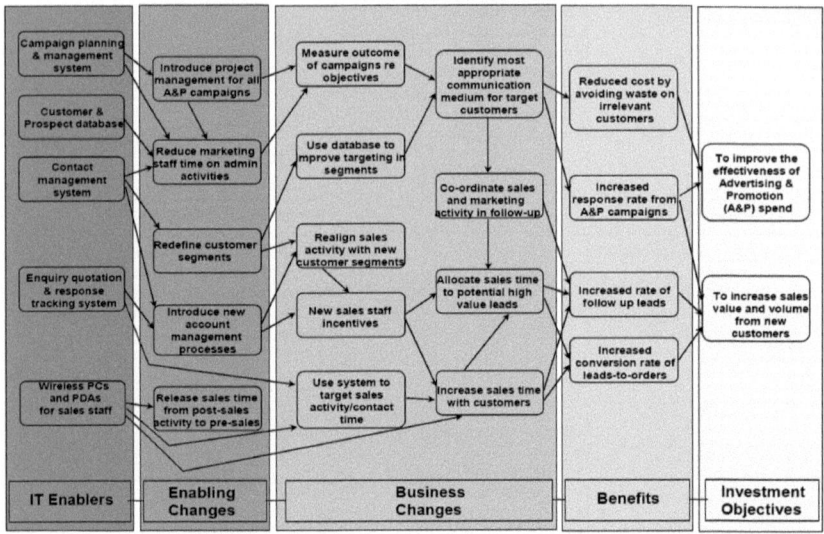

Figure C.4: An example of a (partial) benefits-dependency network for a new CRM system for a European paper manufacturer, adopted from Peppard et al. (2007)

We believe that all 'benefits', i.e., rectangles with rounded corners, can be modelled as criteria using BCO. Although the BDN categorizes 'Increase sales time with customers' as a Business Change and not as a Benefit, this is arguably also a benefit and thus a criterion. Similarly, 'To increase sales value and volume from new customers' can be seen as a benefit, albeit on a slightly more abstract level than the benefits that have a direct relation to this benefit. Although we can not claim that a 'Contact management system' is a benefit by itself, from our point of view it is also a criterion because it is a concept that is being evaluated through the business case. E.g., in a business case one could compare two cases: a contact management systems from provider A and another contact management system from provider B. These may have different effects on the Enabling Changes, which need to be evaluated as well and are thus also criteria. Concluding, we argue that all five categories of 'benefits' in the BDN are criteria, albeit on different levels of abstraction. In Description Logic:

"Investment Objectives", "Benefits", … ∈ Group
"To improve the effectiveness of Advertising…", "Reduced cost by avoiding waste…", … ∈ Criterion
memberOf("To improve the effectiveness of Advertising…", "Investment Objectives")

```
memberOf("Reduced cost by avoiding waste…", "Benefits")
etc.
hasEffectOn("Reduced cost by avoiding waste…", "To improve the
effectiveness of Advertising…")
hasEffectOn("Identify most appropriate communication…", "Co-
ordinate sales and marketing…")
etc.
```

D Laboratory Experiment: Recommender Algorithm (Ch. 6)

This appendix belongs to Chapter 6 and shows two of the most important parts of the recommender algorithm. It is written in PHP.

```php
function buildCriteriaRecommendations() {
    global $dbconn, $numRecommendations, $lang,
    $exemplaryCriterion_EN, $exemplaryCriterion_DE;
    if ($lang == "DE") {
        $lang_instruction = "Die folgenden Vorteile, die
        möglicherweise Ihrem neuen Business Case zugehörig sind,
        wurden in unserer Datenbank von vorherigen Business Cases
        gefunden. Um einen Vorteil in die obige Liste aufzunehmen,
        drücken Sie den Knopf davor.";
        $lang_noRecommendations = "Neue Empfehlungen konnten
        aufgrund Ihres vorherigen Eingabe nicht gefunden werden.";
        $lang_include = "Einfügen";
    }
    else {
        $lang_instruction = "The following benefits, which are
        possibly related to your new business case, have been
        found in our database of earlier business cases. To
        include a benefit in the list above, press the button in
        front of it.";
        $lang_noRecommendations = "No recommendations could be
        found based on your input above.";
        $lang_include = "Include";
    }
    // create an array of the new criteria texts
    $newCriteria = getNewCriteria();
    // if a criterion occurs multiple times in the new BC, it
    should be considered only once
    $newCriteria = array_unique($newCriteria);
    // create an array of weighted old criteria
    // initialize the array
    $weightedCriteria = array();
    $weightingScopes[] = "siblings";
    $weightingScopes[] = "children";
    $weightingScopes[] = "parents";
    $weightingScopes[] = "grandchildren";
```

```php
$weightingScopes[] = "grandparents";
$weightingScopes[] = "others";
foreach ($newCriteria as $criterionText) {
    $relatedBusinessCases = getRelatedBusinessCases($criterionText);
    // relatedBusinessCases has been undoubled, because we want to weigh the criteria in each related BC only once for each new criterion
    // however, if a new criterion occurs N times in one of those related BC, all criteria in that BC will be weighted N times
    // because the weights are relative to the position, I need to make sure that the weighting is done starting from the right position
    foreach ($relatedBusinessCases as $bcID) {
        // each old criterion should be added to the array of weightedCriteria (if it is not already in)
        // and it should get a weight based on its position relative to the position of the new criterion in the old BC
        // if there are multiple related BCs in which a certain old criterion occurs, the weight of that criterion will be the sum of the weights in all those BCs
        // therefore, if the criterion is already in the weightedCriteria, its weight should be increased (not replaced or something)
        // find the place where the old BC matched, to use this as a starting point for weighing
        $query = "SELECT criterionID, relParentID FROM criterion WHERE criterionText_$lang = '$criterionText' AND relBusinessCaseID = $bcID";
        $result = mysql_query($query, $dbconn);
        if ($result) {
            // it is possible that the $result contains multiple (N) rows, if the new criterion occurs on N places in the old BC
            // that is OK, because in that case we want to weigh the criteria N times
            while ($row = mysql_fetch_array($result)) {
                // this is the ID of the new criterion in the criteria base (groundtruth)
                $criterionID = $row["criterionID"];
                $parentID = $row["relParentID"];
```

```
                    foreach ($weightingScopes as
                $weightingScope) {
                        $weightedCriteria =
                        increaseWeights($newCriteria,
                        $weightedCriteria, $bcID,
                        $criterionID, $parentID,
                        $weightingScope);
                }
            }
        }
        else {
            error(mysql_errno($dbconn),mysql_error($dbconn)
            );
        }
    }
}
$output = "<p>$lang_instruction</p>\n";
if (empty($weightedCriteria)) {
    $output .= "<p>$lang_noRecommendations</p>";
}
else {
    $output .= "<table id=\"criteria_recommendations\">";
}
// sort weightedCriteria by weight, descending
arsort($weightedCriteria);
// reduce the list to the number of criteria that need to be recommended
$weightedCriteria = array_slice($weightedCriteria, 0,
$numRecommendations);
$rank = 1;
foreach ($weightedCriteria as $critText => $critWeight) {
    $output .= "<tr><td class=\"include\"><input
    type=\"hidden\" id=\"criterion_include$rank\"
    value=\"$critText\" /><input type=\"button\"
    name=\"include\" value=\"$lang_include\"
    onclick=\"includeAndSubmit($rank);\"
    /></td><td>$critText</td></tr>\n";
    $rank++;
}
if (!empty($weightedCriteria)) {
    $output .= "</table>";
}
```

197

```
        return $output;
}


// returns the array of weighted criteria, after updating their
weights
function increaseWeights($newCriteria, $weightedCriteria, $bcID,
$criterionID, $parentID, $weightingScope) {
     global $dbconn, $lang;
     // create a string of all criteria (texts) in SQL format
     $newCriteria = "'".implode("','", $newCriteria)."'";
     // the abstract criteria occur so often in the groundtruth that
     we need to ignore them to give the other criteria a chance to
     show up in the top 10 recommendations
     // this is a work-around for a much more complex algorithm that
     would not just take the frequency of occurence of criteria into
     account, but also their distinctiveness
     $ignoreCriteria = "
     'Quality', 'Qualität',
     'Reliability', 'Zuverlässigkeit',
     'Information',
     'Process automation', 'Prozess-automation',
     'Process control', 'Prozess-steuerung',
     'Process efficiency', 'Prozesseffizienz',
     'Process robustness', 'Prozess-sicherheit',
     'Process technology', 'Prozesstechnik'
     ";
     switch ($weightingScope) {
           // siblings have the same parentID
           case "siblings":
           $query = "SELECT criterionID, criterionText_$lang FROM
           criterion WHERE criterionText_$lang NOT IN ($newCriteria,
           $ignoreCriteria) AND relBusinessCaseID = $bcID AND
           relParentID = $parentID";
           $addWeight = 4;
           break;
           // children: parentID is ID of new criterion
           case "children":
           $query = "SELECT criterionID, criterionText_$lang FROM
           criterion WHERE criterionText_$lang NOT IN ($newCriteria,
           $ignoreCriteria) AND relBusinessCaseID = $bcID AND
           relParentID = $criterionID";
           $addWeight = 3;
```

```
        break;
    // parents: ID is the parentID of new criterion
    case "parents":
        $query = "SELECT criterionID, criterionText_$lang FROM
criterion WHERE criterionText_$lang NOT IN ($newCriteria,
$ignoreCriteria) AND relBusinessCaseID = $bcID AND
criterionID = $parentID";
        $addWeight = 3;
        break;
    // grandchildren: parentID is the ID of a child
    case "grandchildren":
        $query = "SELECT criterionID, criterionText_$lang FROM
criterion WHERE criterionText_$lang NOT IN ($newCriteria,
$ignoreCriteria) AND relParentID IN (SELECT criterionID
FROM criterion WHERE relBusinessCaseID = $bcID AND
relParentID = $criterionID)";
        $addWeight = 2;
        break;
    // grandparents: ID is the parentID of a parent
    case "grandparents":
        $query = "SELECT criterionID, criterionText_$lang FROM
criterion WHERE criterionText_$lang NOT IN ($newCriteria,
$ignoreCriteria) AND criterionID IN (SELECT relParentID
FROM criterion WHERE relBusinessCaseID = $bcID AND
criterionID = $parentID)";
        $addWeight = 2;
        break;
    // others: all IDs not included in one of the beforementioned sets
    // the 'criterionText NOT IN ($newCriteria' needs to be
    added outside of a NOT IN... otherwise the system may
    recommend new criteria
    // the 'relBusinessCaseID = $bcID' needs to be added
    outside of a NOT IN... otherwise the system may recommend
    from un-related BCs
    case "others":
        $query = "SELECT criterionID, criterionText_$lang FROM
criterion WHERE
        criterionText_$lang NOT IN ($newCriteria,
$ignoreCriteria) AND
        relBusinessCaseID = $bcID AND
        criterionID NOT IN (SELECT criterionID FROM criterion
WHERE relBusinessCaseID = $bcID AND relParentID =
$parentID) AND
```

```php
                    criterionID NOT IN (SELECT criterionID FROM criterion
                    WHERE relBusinessCaseID = $bcID AND relParentID =
                    $criterionID) AND
                    criterionID NOT IN (SELECT criterionID FROM criterion
                    WHERE relBusinessCaseID = $bcID AND criterionID =
                    $parentID) AND
                    criterionID NOT IN (SELECT criterionID FROM criterion
                    WHERE relParentID IN (SELECT criterionID FROM criterion
                    WHERE relBusinessCaseID = $bcID AND relParentID =
                    $criterionID)) AND
                    criterionID NOT IN (SELECT criterionID FROM criterion
                    WHERE criterionID IN (SELECT relParentID FROM criterion
                    WHERE relBusinessCaseID = $bcID AND criterionID =
                    $parentID))";
                    $addWeight = 1;
                    break;
            }
            $result = mysql_query($query, $dbconn);
            if ($result) {
                    while ($row = mysql_fetch_array($result)) {
                            $critText = $row["criterionText_$lang"];
                            // if the criterion is already in the array, we
                            should update its weight
                            if (array_key_exists($critText, $weightedCriteria))
                            {
                                    // get the criterion's current weight
                                    $oldWeight = $weightedCriteria[$critText];
                                    // update the criterion's weight
                                    $newWeight = $oldWeight + $addWeight;
                                    $weightedCriteria[$critText] = $newWeight;
                                    // reset variables for next iteration
                                    unset($oldWeight, $newWeight);
                            }
                            // if the criterion is not yet in the array of
                            weighted criteria, we should add it
                            else {
                                    $weightedCriteria[$critText] = $addWeight;
                    } } return $weightedCriteria; }
            else {
                    error(mysql_errno($dbconn),mysql_error($dbconn));
            }
    }
}
```

E Laboratory Experiment: Screenshots (Ch. 6, 7)

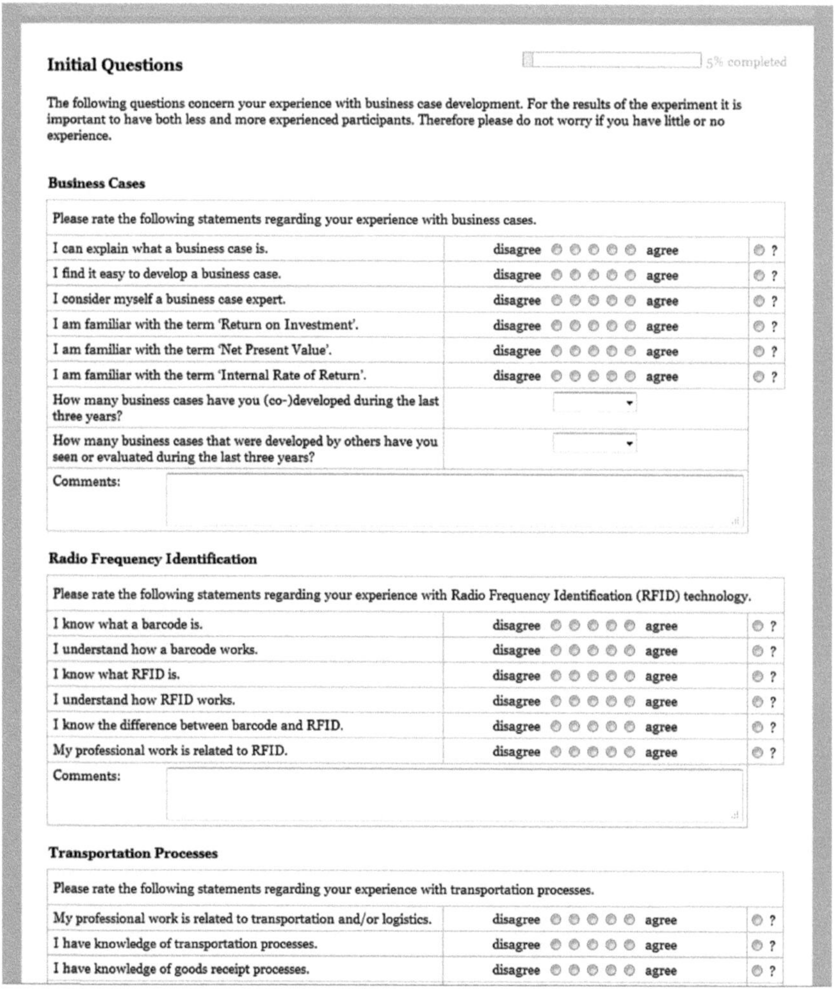

This appendix belongs to Chapters 6 and 7 and shows screenshots of the system that was developed for the laboratory experiment.

Figure E.1: The pre-test questionnaire

I am familiar with the term 'Return on Investment'.	disagree ○ ○ ○ ○ ○ agree	○ ?
I am familiar with the term 'Net Present Value'.	disagree ○ ○ ○ ○ ○ agree	○ ?
I am familiar with the term 'Internal Rate of Return'.	disagree ○ ○ ○ ○ ○ agree	○ ?
How many business cases have you (co-)developed during the last three years?	▼	
How many business cases that were developed by others have you seen or evaluated during the last three years?	▼	
Comments:		

Radio Frequency Identification

Please rate the following statements regarding your experience with Radio Frequency Identification (RFID) technology.

I know what a barcode is.	disagree ○ ○ ○ ○ ○ agree	○ ?
I understand how a barcode works.	disagree ○ ○ ○ ○ ○ agree	○ ?
I know what RFID is.	disagree ○ ○ ○ ○ ○ agree	○ ?
I understand how RFID works.	disagree ○ ○ ○ ○ ○ agree	○ ?
I know the difference between barcode and RFID.	disagree ○ ○ ○ ○ ○ agree	○ ?
My professional work is related to RFID.	disagree ○ ○ ○ ○ ○ agree	○ ?
Comments:		

Transportation Processes

Please rate the following statements regarding your experience with transportation processes.

My professional work is related to transportation and/or logistics.	disagree ○ ○ ○ ○ ○ agree	○ ?
I have knowledge of transportation processes.	disagree ○ ○ ○ ○ ○ agree	○ ?
I have knowledge of goods receipt processes.	disagree ○ ○ ○ ○ ○ agree	○ ?
I have knowledge of warehousing processes.	disagree ○ ○ ○ ○ ○ agree	○ ?
Comments:		

Personal Data

What is your gender?	▼
What is your age?	▼
What is your highest level of education?	▼
In which country do you normally work?	▼

[Continue]

Figure E.2: The pre-test questionnaire (continued)

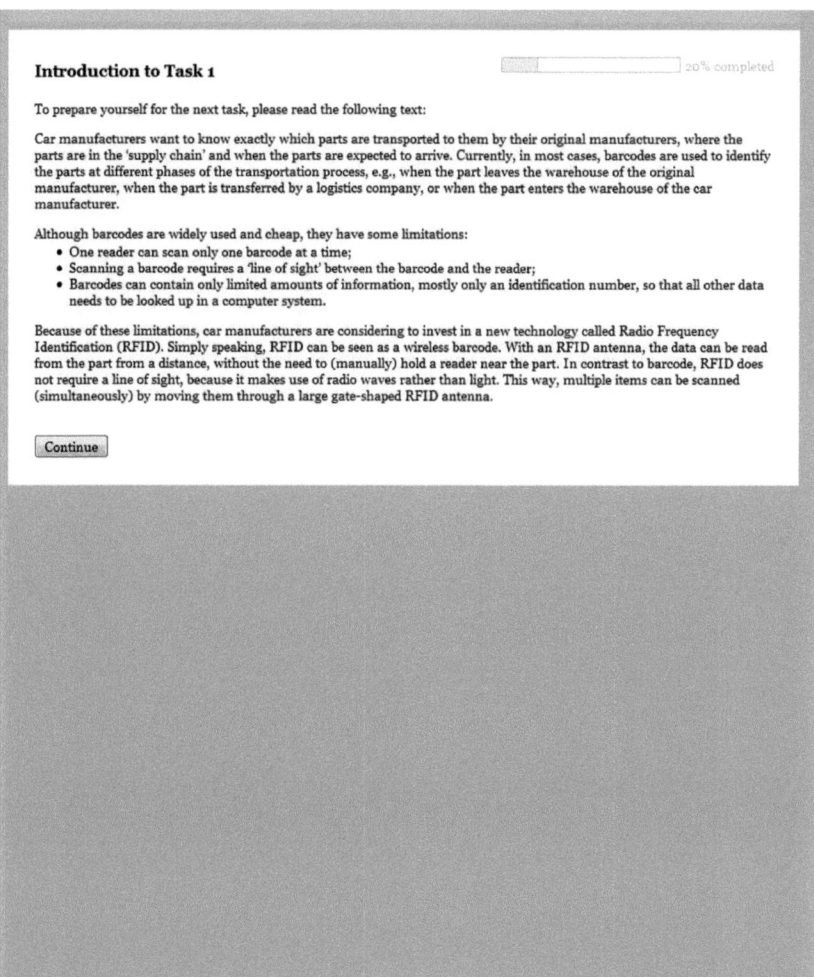

Figure E.3: The introduction to the task

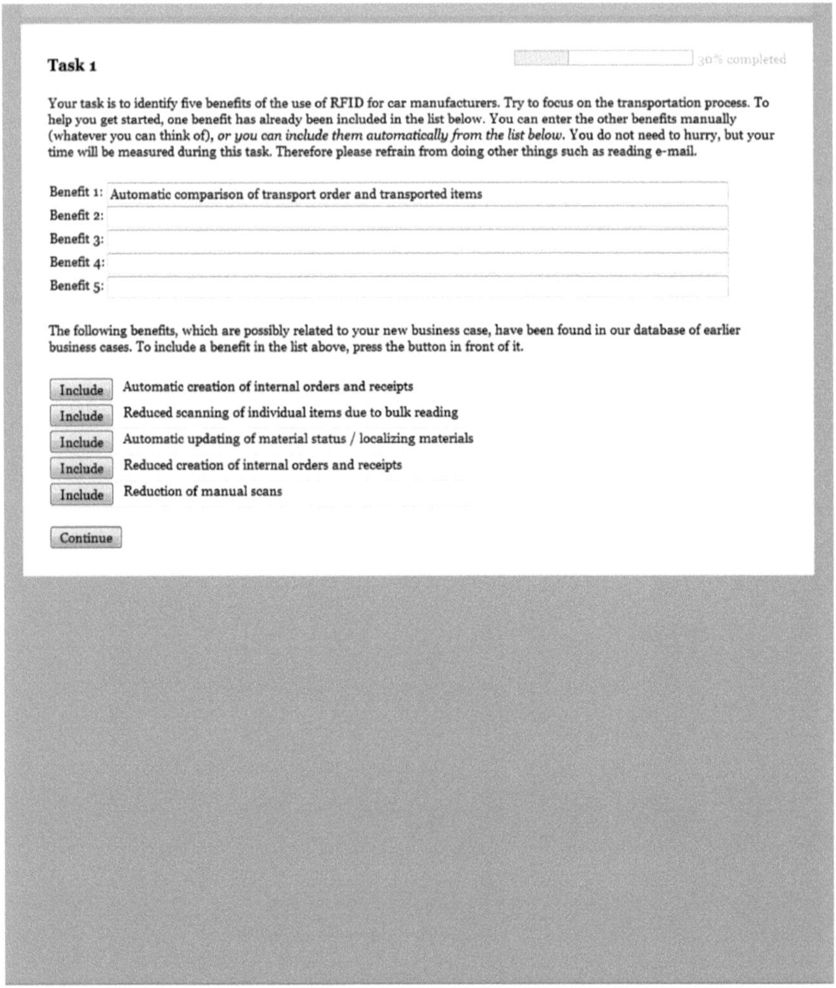

Task 1 ▭▭▭ 30% completed

Your task is to identify five benefits of the use of RFID for car manufacturers. Try to focus on the transportation process. To help you get started, one benefit has already been included in the list below. You can enter the other benefits manually (whatever you can think of), *or you can include them automatically from the list below*. You do not need to hurry, but your time will be measured during this task. Therefore please refrain from doing other things such as reading e-mail.

Benefit 1: Automatic comparison of transport order and transported items
Benefit 2: _____
Benefit 3: _____
Benefit 4: _____
Benefit 5: _____

The following benefits, which are possibly related to your new business case, have been found in our database of earlier business cases. To include a benefit in the list above, press the button in front of it.

[Include] Automatic creation of internal orders and receipts
[Include] Reduced scanning of individual items due to bulk reading
[Include] Automatic updating of material status / localizing materials
[Include] Reduced creation of internal orders and receipts
[Include] Reduction of manual scans

[Continue]

Figure E.4: The task in the recommendations-condition

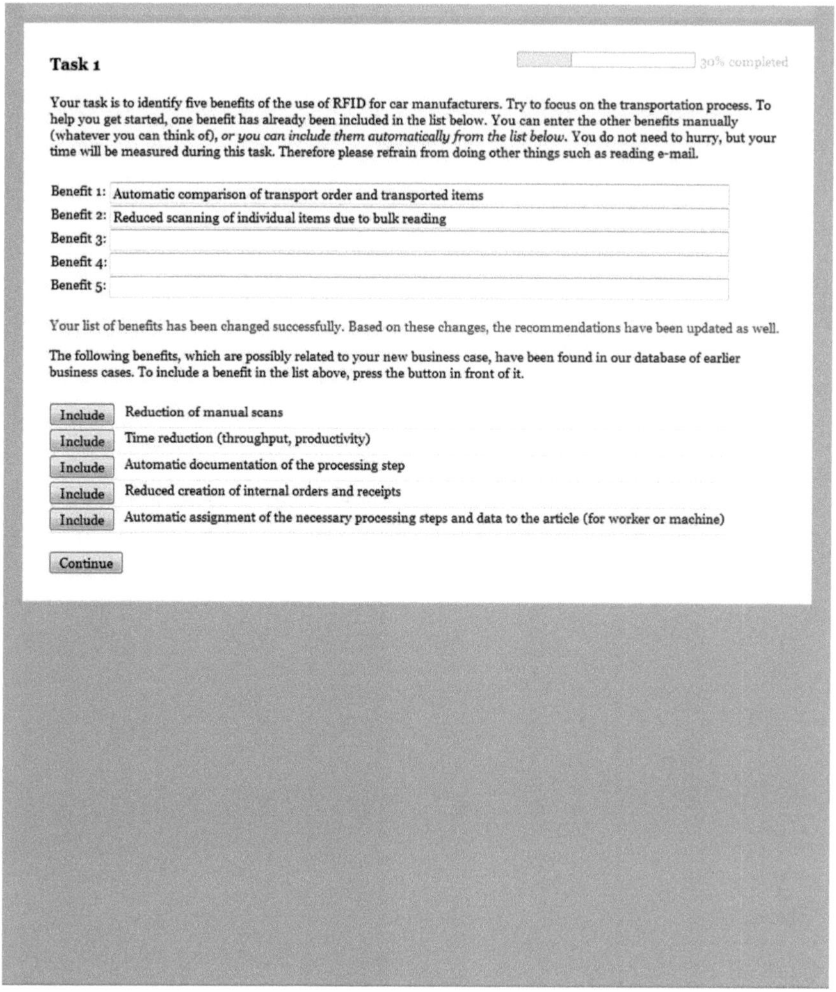

Task 1   30% completed

Your task is to identify five benefits of the use of RFID for car manufacturers. Try to focus on the transportation process. To help you get started, one benefit has already been included in the list below. You can enter the other benefits manually (whatever you can think of), *or you can include them automatically from the list below*. You do not need to hurry, but your time will be measured during this task. Therefore please refrain from doing other things such as reading e-mail.

Benefit 1: Automatic comparison of transport order and transported items
Benefit 2: Reduced scanning of individual items due to bulk reading
Benefit 3:
Benefit 4:
Benefit 5:

Your list of benefits has been changed successfully. Based on these changes, the recommendations have been updated as well.
The following benefits, which are possibly related to your new business case, have been found in our database of earlier business cases. To include a benefit in the list above, press the button in front of it.

[Include] Reduction of manual scans
[Include] Time reduction (throughput, productivity)
[Include] Automatic documentation of the processing step
[Include] Reduced creation of internal orders and receipts
[Include] Automatic assignment of the necessary processing steps and data to the article (for worker or machine)

[Continue]

Figure E.5: The task in the recommendations-condition (continued)

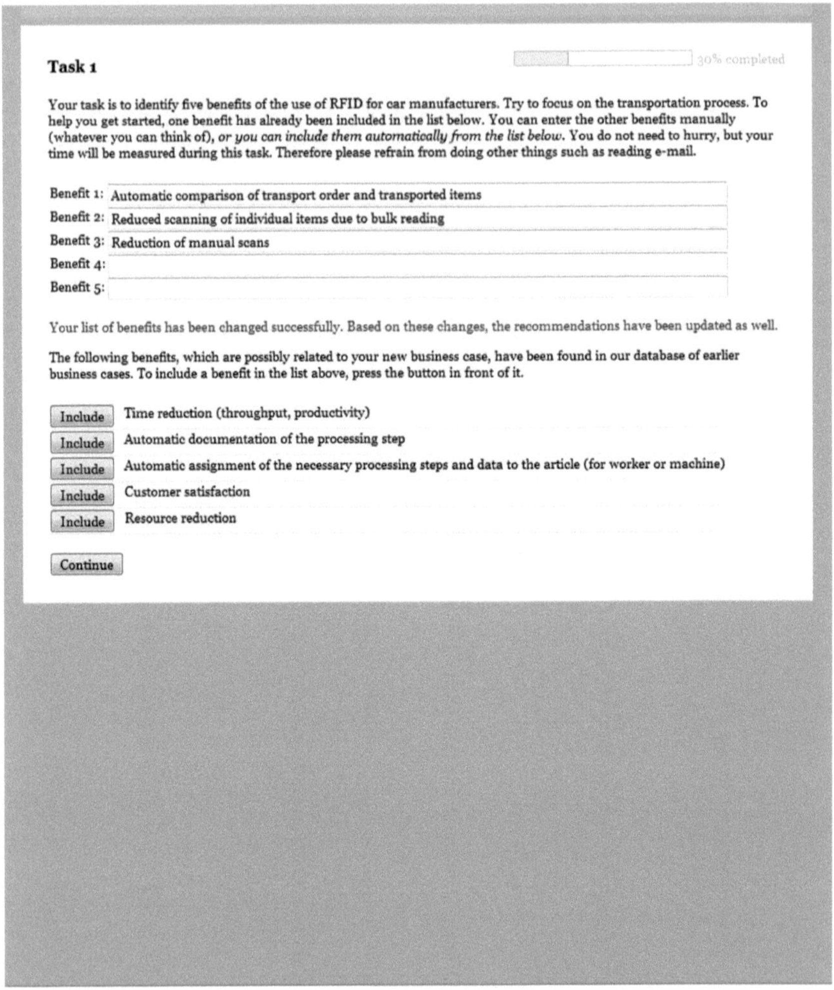

Task 1 ☐☐☐☐☐ 30% completed

Your task is to identify five benefits of the use of RFID for car manufacturers. Try to focus on the transportation process. To help you get started, one benefit has already been included in the list below. You can enter the other benefits manually (whatever you can think of), *or you can include them automatically from the list below*. You do not need to hurry, but your time will be measured during this task. Therefore please refrain from doing other things such as reading e-mail.

Benefit 1: Automatic comparison of transport order and transported items
Benefit 2: Reduced scanning of individual items due to bulk reading
Benefit 3: Reduction of manual scans
Benefit 4:
Benefit 5:

Your list of benefits has been changed successfully. Based on these changes, the recommendations have been updated as well.

The following benefits, which are possibly related to your new business case, have been found in our database of earlier business cases. To include a benefit in the list above, press the button in front of it.

[Include] Time reduction (throughput, productivity)
[Include] Automatic documentation of the processing step
[Include] Automatic assignment of the necessary processing steps and data to the article (for worker or machine)
[Include] Customer satisfaction
[Include] Resource reduction

[Continue]

Figure E.6: The task in the recommendations-condition (continued)

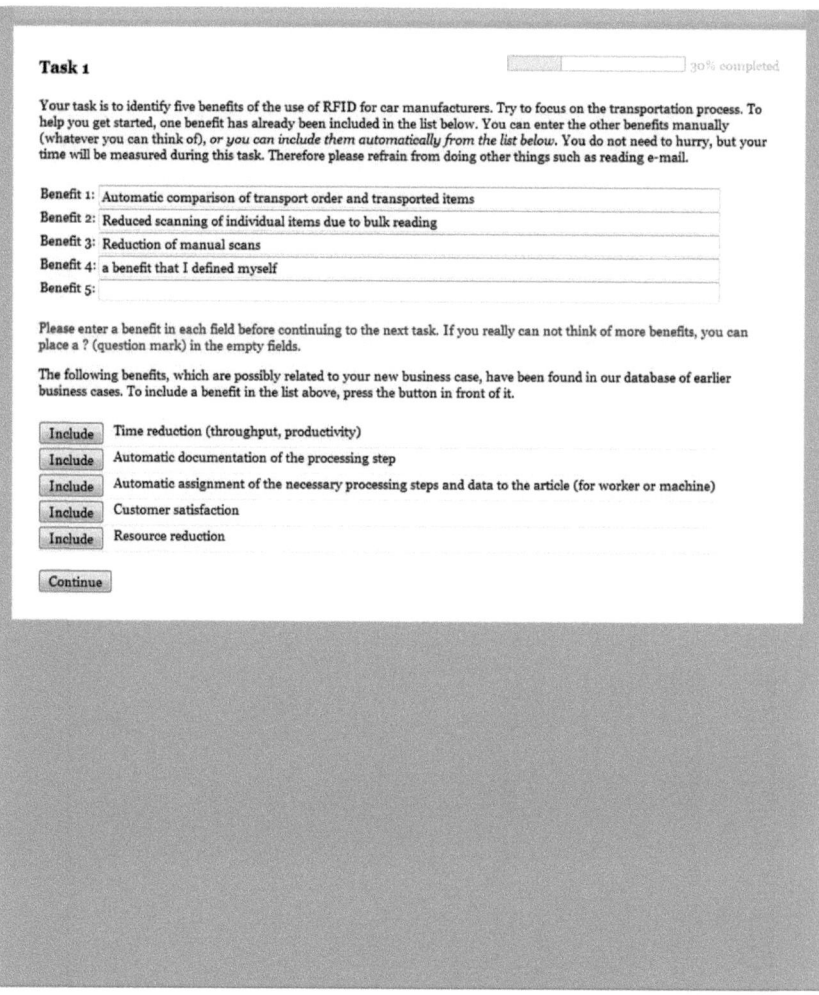

Figure E.7: The task in the recommendations-condition (continued)

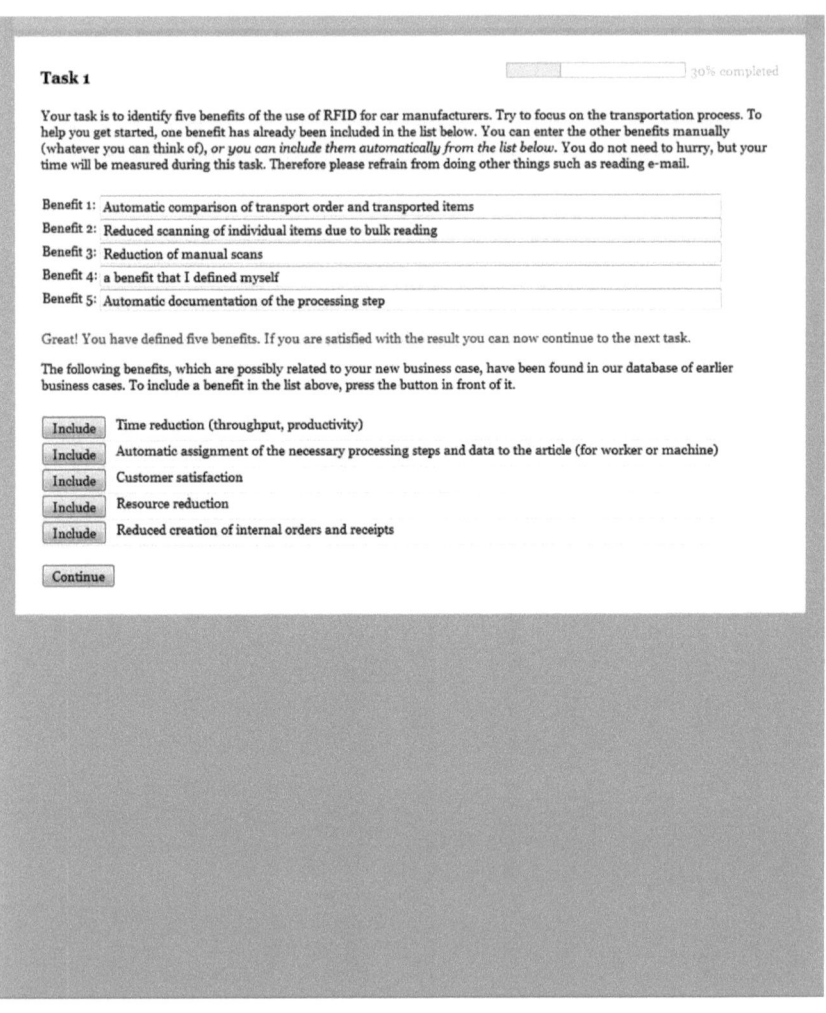

Figure E.8: The task in the recommendations-condition (continued)

Task 1

30% completed

Your task is to identify five benefits of the use of RFID for car manufacturers. Try to focus on the transportation process. To help you get started, one benefit has already been included in the list below. You can enter the other benefits manually (whatever you can think of), *or you can include them automatically from the list below*. You do not need to hurry, but your time will be measured during this task. Therefore please refrain from doing other things such as reading e-mail.

Benefit 1: Automatic comparison of transport order and transported items
Benefit 2:
Benefit 3:
Benefit 4:
Benefit 5:

The following benefits, which are possibly related to your new business case, have been found in our database of earlier business cases. To include a benefit in the list above, press the button in front of it.

Goods Receipt

Include	Process efficiency
Include	Time reduction (throughput, productivity)
Include	Process automation
Include	Automatic assignment of products to supply information (through ASN)
Include	Reduced scanning of individual items due to bulk reading
Include	Reduction of manual scans
Include	Automatic updating of stock data / goods receipt booking (if not realized in a different manner)
Include	Automatic comparison of supply data / completeness testing
Include	Automatic creation of internal orders and receipts
Include	Reduced creation of internal orders and receipts
Include	Automatic feedback to suppliers
Include	Increase of throughput (as overall result)
Include	Process robustness
Include	Reduction of errors in goods receipt
Include	Reduction of errors in booking received containers
Include	Reduction of errors in internal material distribution
Include	Process control
Include	Automatic process control by direct assignment of object and transport order
Include	Automatic back ordering/reclamation in case of incorrect/incomplete supplies
Include	Resource reduction
Include	Process technology
Include	Reduced creation of internal orders and receipts (saves paper, printing, labels)

Figure E.9: The task in the templates-condition

Task 1   30% completed

Your task is to identify five benefits of the use of RFID for car manufacturers. Try to focus on the transportation process. To help you get started, one benefit has already been included in the list below. You can enter the other benefits manually (whatever you can think of), *or you can include them automatically from the list below*. You do not need to hurry, but your time will be measured during this task. Therefore please refrain from doing other things such as reading e-mail.

Benefit 1: Automatic comparison of transport order and transported items
Benefit 2: Reduced scanning of individual items due to bulk reading
Benefit 3:
Benefit 4:
Benefit 5:

Your list of benefits has been changed successfully.

The following benefits, which are possibly related to your new business case, have been found in our database of earlier business cases. To include a benefit in the list above, press the button in front of it.

Goods Receipt

Include	Process efficiency
Include	Time reduction (throughput, productivity)
Include	Process automation
Include	Automatic assignment of products to supply information (through ASN)
Include	Reduced scanning of individual items due to bulk reading (already included)
Include	Reduction of manual scans
Include	Automatic updating of stock data / goods receipt booking (if not realized in a different manner)
Include	Automatic comparison of supply data / completeness testing
Include	Automatic creation of internal orders and receipts
Include	Reduced creation of internal orders and receipts
Include	Automatic feedback to suppliers
Include	Increase of throughput (as overall result)
Include	Process robustness
Include	Reduction of errors in goods receipt
Include	Reduction of errors in booking received containers
Include	Reduction of errors in internal material distribution
Include	Process control
Include	Automatic process control by direct assignment of object and transport order
Include	Automatic back ordering/reclamation in case of incorrect/incomplete supplies
Include	Resource reduction
Include	Process technology

Figure E.10: The task in the templates-condition (continued)

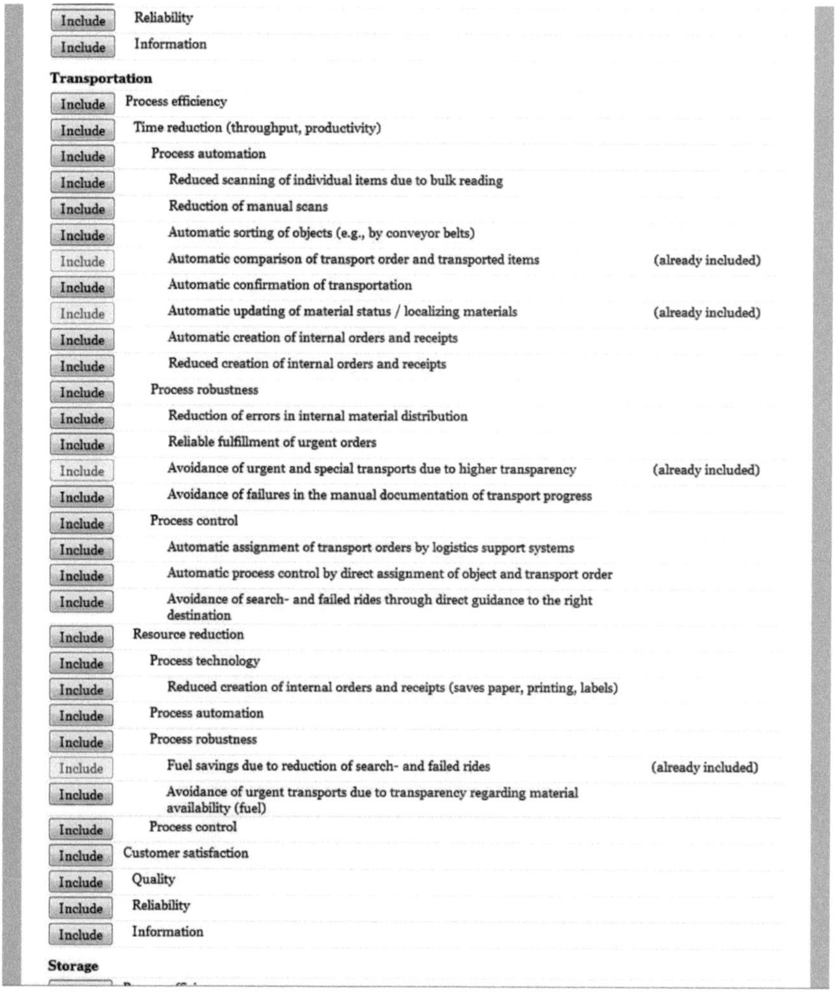

| Include | Reliability |
| Include | Information |

Transportation

Include	Process efficiency	
Include	Time reduction (throughput, productivity)	
Include	Process automation	
Include	Reduced scanning of individual items due to bulk reading	
Include	Reduction of manual scans	
Include	Automatic sorting of objects (e.g., by conveyor belts)	
Include	Automatic comparison of transport order and transported items	(already included)
Include	Automatic confirmation of transportation	
Include	Automatic updating of material status / localizing materials	(already included)
Include	Automatic creation of internal orders and receipts	
Include	Reduced creation of internal orders and receipts	
Include	Process robustness	
Include	Reduction of errors in internal material distribution	
Include	Reliable fulfillment of urgent orders	
Include	Avoidance of urgent and special transports due to higher transparency	(already included)
Include	Avoidance of failures in the manual documentation of transport progress	
Include	Process control	
Include	Automatic assignment of transport orders by logistics support systems	
Include	Automatic process control by direct assignment of object and transport order	
Include	Avoidance of search- and failed rides through direct guidance to the right destination	
Include	Resource reduction	
Include	Process technology	
Include	Reduced creation of internal orders and receipts (saves paper, printing, labels)	
Include	Process automation	
Include	Process robustness	
Include	Fuel savings due to reduction of search- and failed rides	(already included)
Include	Avoidance of urgent transports due to transparency regarding material availability (fuel)	
Include	Process control	
Include	Customer satisfaction	
Include	Quality	
Include	Reliability	
Include	Information	

Storage

Figure E.11: The task in the templates-condition (continued)

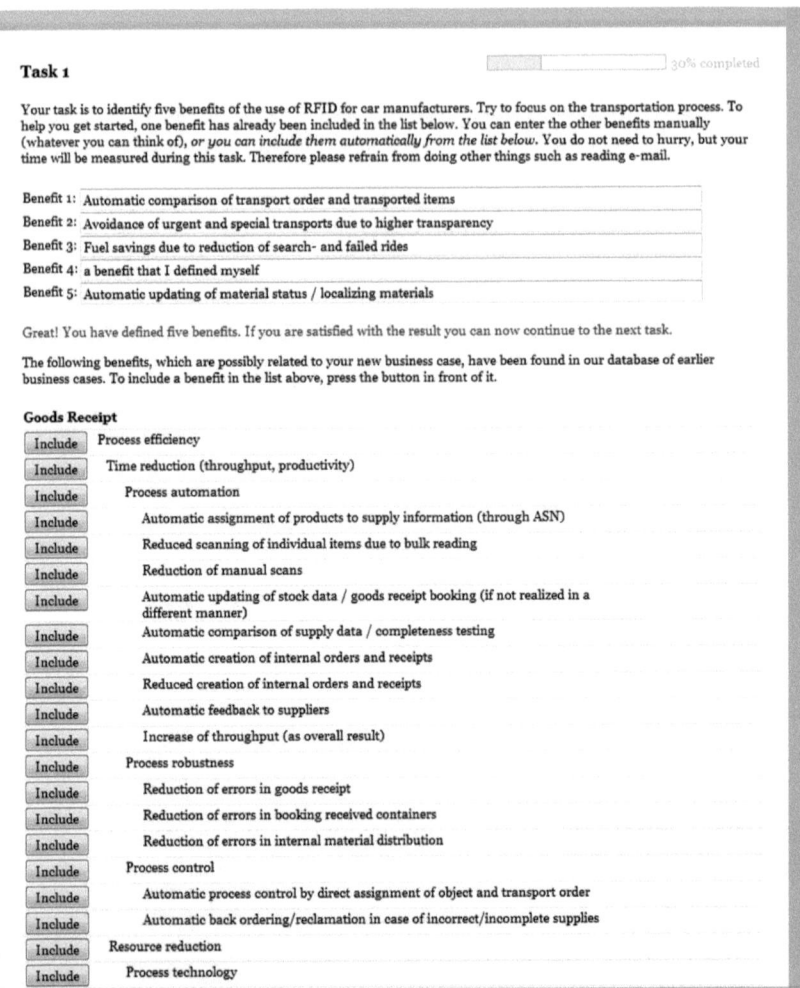

Figure E.12: The task in the templates-condition (continued)

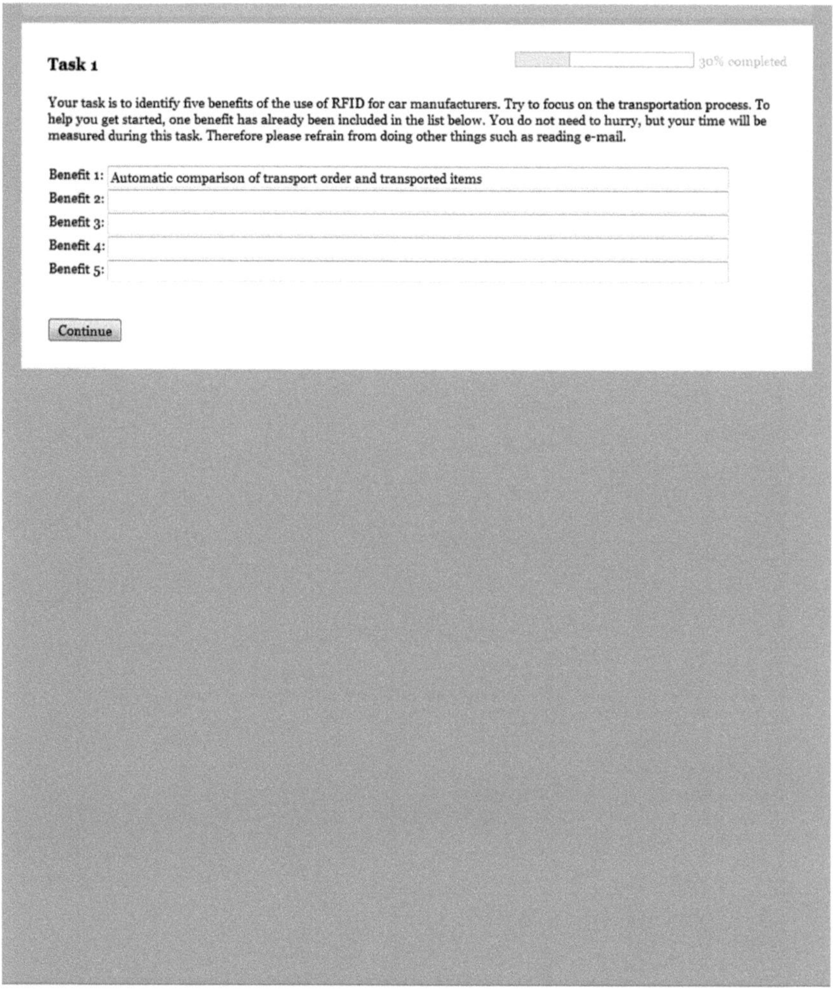

Task 1   30% completed

Your task is to identify five benefits of the use of RFID for car manufacturers. Try to focus on the transportation process. To help you get started, one benefit has already been included in the list below. You do not need to hurry, but your time will be measured during this task. Therefore please refrain from doing other things such as reading e-mail.

Benefit 1: Automatic comparison of transport order and transported items
Benefit 2:
Benefit 3:
Benefit 4:
Benefit 5:

[Continue]

Figure E.13: The task in the control-condition

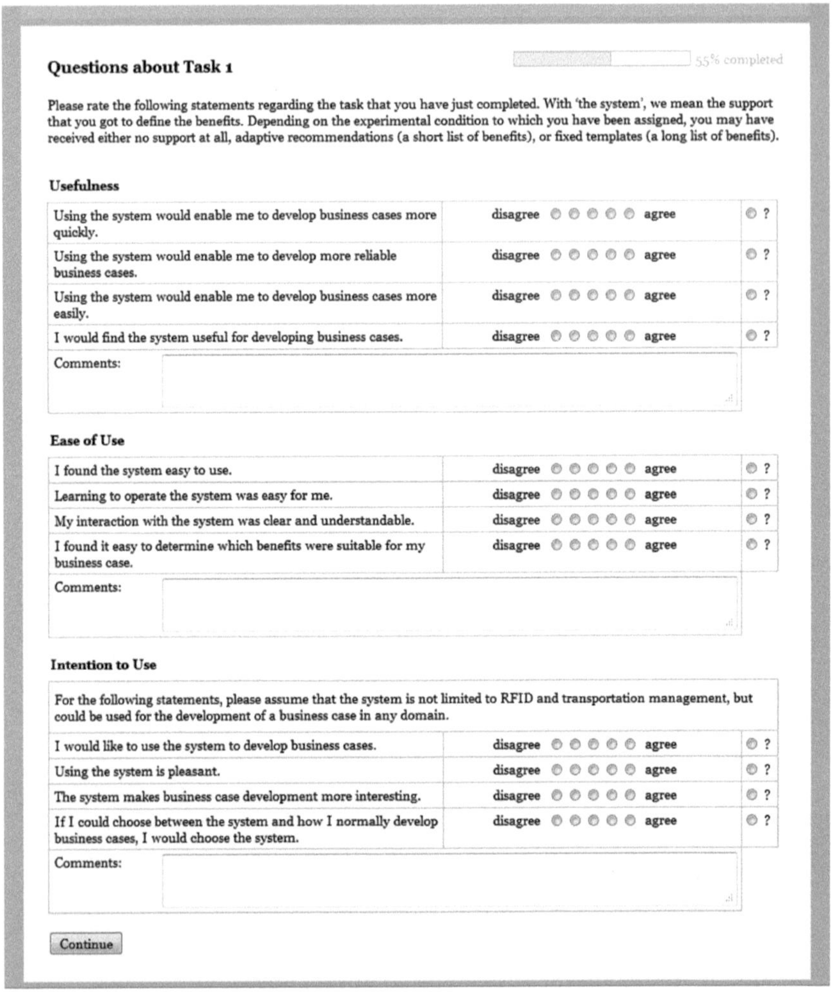

Questions about Task 1

[_____] 55% completed

Please rate the following statements regarding the task that you have just completed. With 'the system', we mean the support that you got to define the benefits. Depending on the experimental condition to which you have been assigned, you may have received either no support at all, adaptive recommendations (a short list of benefits), or fixed templates (a long list of benefits).

Usefulness

Using the system would enable me to develop business cases more quickly.	disagree ○ ○ ○ ○ ○ agree	○ ?
Using the system would enable me to develop more reliable business cases.	disagree ○ ○ ○ ○ ○ agree	○ ?
Using the system would enable me to develop business cases more easily.	disagree ○ ○ ○ ○ ○ agree	○ ?
I would find the system useful for developing business cases.	disagree ○ ○ ○ ○ ○ agree	○ ?
Comments: [_____]		

Ease of Use

I found the system easy to use.	disagree ○ ○ ○ ○ ○ agree	○ ?
Learning to operate the system was easy for me.	disagree ○ ○ ○ ○ ○ agree	○ ?
My interaction with the system was clear and understandable.	disagree ○ ○ ○ ○ ○ agree	○ ?
I found it easy to determine which benefits were suitable for my business case.	disagree ○ ○ ○ ○ ○ agree	○ ?
Comments: [_____]		

Intention to Use

For the following statements, please assume that the system is not limited to RFID and transportation management, but could be used for the development of a business case in any domain.

I would like to use the system to develop business cases.	disagree ○ ○ ○ ○ ○ agree	○ ?
Using the system is pleasant.	disagree ○ ○ ○ ○ ○ agree	○ ?
The system makes business case development more interesting.	disagree ○ ○ ○ ○ ○ agree	○ ?
If I could choose between the system and how I normally develop business cases, I would choose the system.	disagree ○ ○ ○ ○ ○ agree	○ ?
Comments: [_____]		

[Continue]

Figure E.14: The post-test for the task

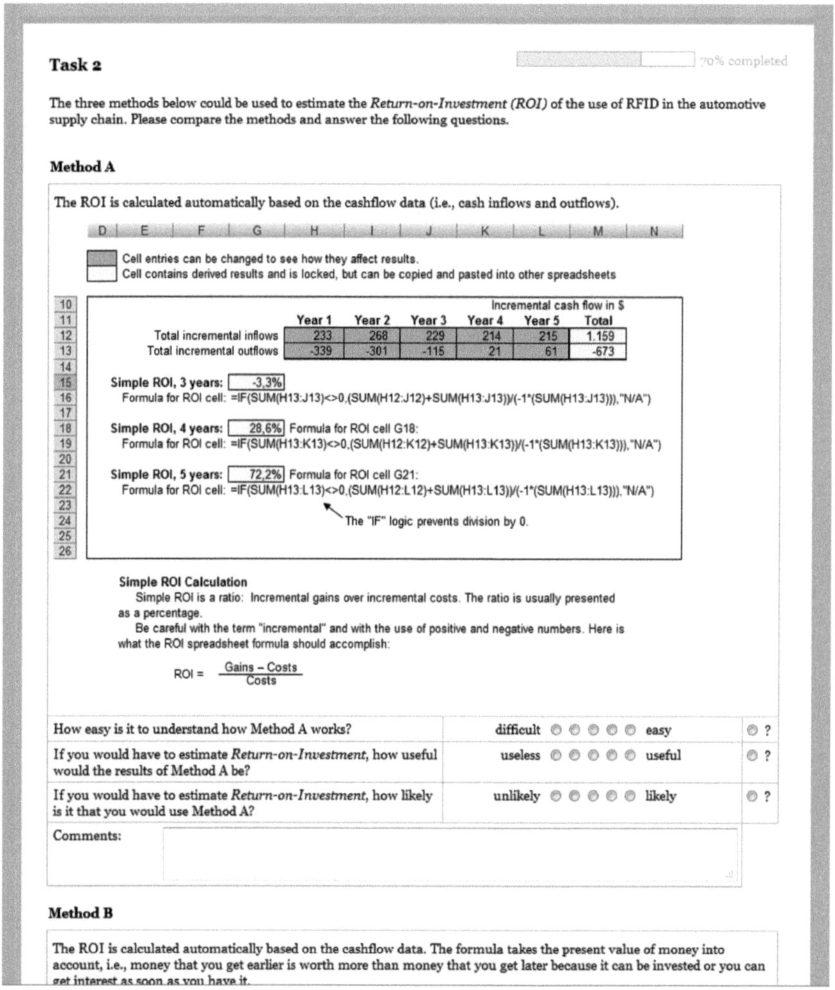

Task 2 70% completed

The three methods below could be used to estimate the *Return-on-Investment (ROI)* of the use of RFID in the automotive supply chain. Please compare the methods and answer the following questions.

Method A

The ROI is calculated automatically based on the cashflow data (i.e., cash inflows and outflows).

Cell entries can be changed to see how they affect results.
Cell contains derived results and is locked, but can be copied and pasted into other spreadsheets

Incremental cash flow in $

	Year 1	Year 2	Year 3	Year 4	Year 5	Total
Total incremental inflows	233	268	229	214	215	1.159
Total incremental outflows	-339	-301	-115	21	61	-673

Simple ROI, 3 years: -3,3%
Formula for ROI cell: =IF(SUM(H13:J13)<>0,(SUM(H12:J12)+SUM(H13:J13))/(-1*(SUM(H13:J13))),"N/A")

Simple ROI, 4 years: 28,6% Formula for ROI cell G18:
Formula for ROI cell: =IF(SUM(H13:K13)<>0,(SUM(H12:K12)+SUM(H13:K13))/(-1*(SUM(H13:K13))),"N/A")

Simple ROI, 5 years: 72,2% Formula for ROI cell G21:
Formula for ROI cell: =IF(SUM(H13:L13)<>0,(SUM(H12:L12)+SUM(H13:L13))/(-1*(SUM(H13:L13))),"N/A")

The "IF" logic prevents division by 0.

Simple ROI Calculation

Simple ROI is a ratio: Incremental gains over incremental costs. The ratio is usually presented as a percentage.

Be careful with the term "incremental" and with the use of positive and negative numbers. Here is what the ROI spreadsheet formula should accomplish:

$$ROI = \frac{Gains - Costs}{Costs}$$

How easy is it to understand how Method A works?	difficult ○ ○ ○ ○ ○ easy	○ ?
If you would have to estimate *Return-on-Investment*, how useful would the results of Method A be?	useless ○ ○ ○ ○ ○ useful	○ ?
If you would have to estimate *Return-on-Investment*, how likely is it that you would use Method A?	unlikely ○ ○ ○ ○ ○ likely	○ ?

Comments:

Method B

The ROI is calculated automatically based on the cashflow data. The formula takes the present value of money into account, i.e., money that you get earlier is worth more than money that you get later because it can be invested or you can get interest as soon as you have it.

Figure E.15: Method A, an FML method, in the Return-on-Investment condition

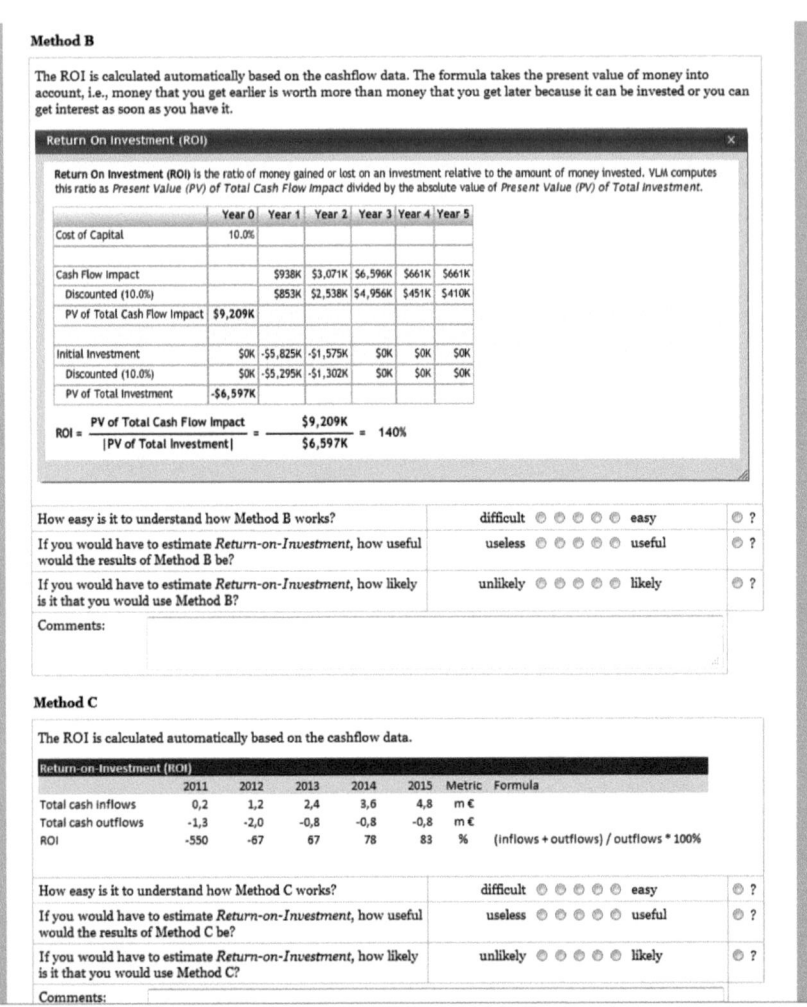

Figure E.16: Method B, a VLM method, in the Return-on-Investment condition

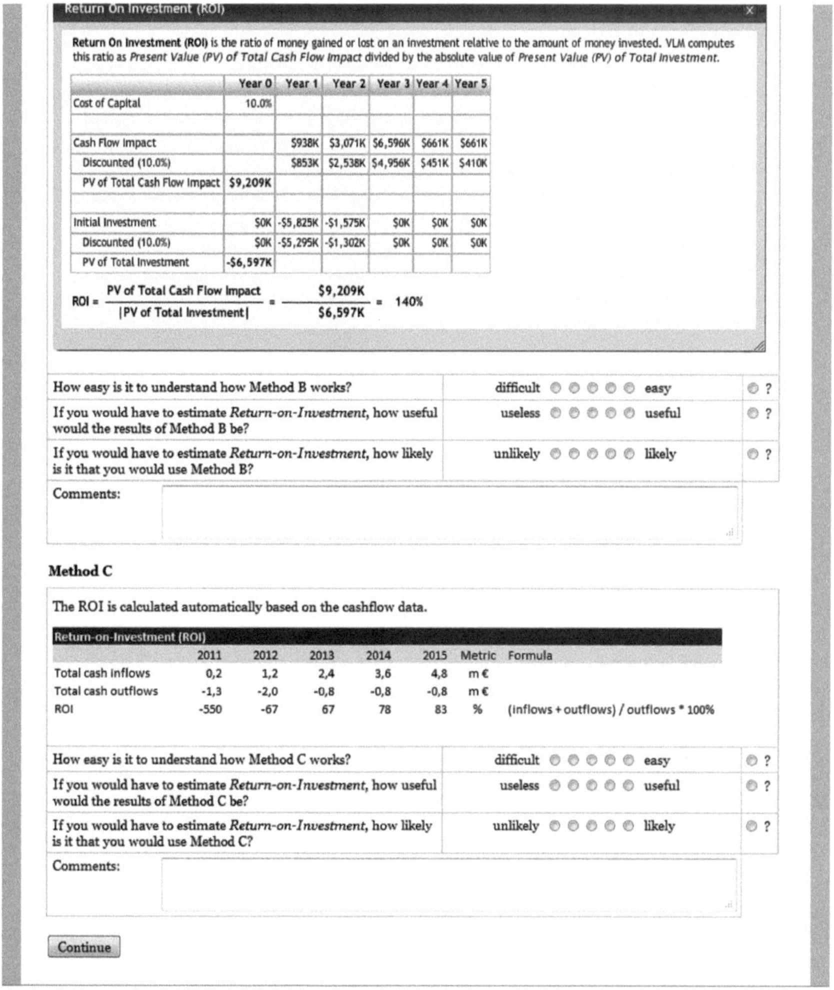

Return On Investment (ROI)

Return On Investment (ROI) is the ratio of money gained or lost on an investment relative to the amount of money invested. VLM computes this ratio as *Present Value (PV) of Total Cash Flow Impact* divided by the absolute value of *Present Value (PV) of Total Investment*.

	Year 0	Year 1	Year 2	Year 3	Year 4	Year 5
Cost of Capital	10.0%					
Cash Flow Impact		$938K	$3,071K	$6,596K	$661K	$661K
Discounted (10.0%)		$853K	$2,538K	$4,956K	$451K	$410K
PV of Total Cash Flow Impact	$9,209K					
Initial Investment	$0K	-$5,825K	-$1,575K	$0K	$0K	$0K
Discounted (10.0%)	$0K	-$5,295K	-$1,302K	$0K	$0K	$0K
PV of Total Investment	-$6,597K					

$$ROI = \frac{PV\ of\ Total\ Cash\ Flow\ Impact}{|PV\ of\ Total\ Investment|} = \frac{\$9,209K}{\$6,597K} = 140\%$$

How easy is it to understand how Method B works?	difficult ○ ○ ○ ○ ○ easy	○ ?
If you would have to estimate *Return-on-Investment*, how useful would the results of Method B be?	useless ○ ○ ○ ○ ○ useful	○ ?
If you would have to estimate *Return-on-Investment*, how likely is it that you would use Method B?	unlikely ○ ○ ○ ○ ○ likely	○ ?
Comments:		

Method C

The ROI is calculated automatically based on the cashflow data.

Return-on-Investment (ROI)

	2011	2012	2013	2014	2015	Metric	Formula
Total cash inflows	0,2	1,2	2,4	3,6	4,8	m €	
Total cash outflows	-1,3	-2,0	-0,8	-0,8	-0,8	m €	
ROI	-550	-67	67	78	83	%	(inflows + outflows) / outflows * 100%

How easy is it to understand how Method C works?	difficult ○ ○ ○ ○ ○ easy	○ ?
If you would have to estimate *Return-on-Investment*, how useful would the results of Method C be?	useless ○ ○ ○ ○ ○ useful	○ ?
If you would have to estimate *Return-on-Investment*, how likely is it that you would use Method C?	unlikely ○ ○ ○ ○ ○ likely	○ ?
Comments:		

[Continue]

Figure E.17: Method C, a new method, in the Return-on-Investment condition

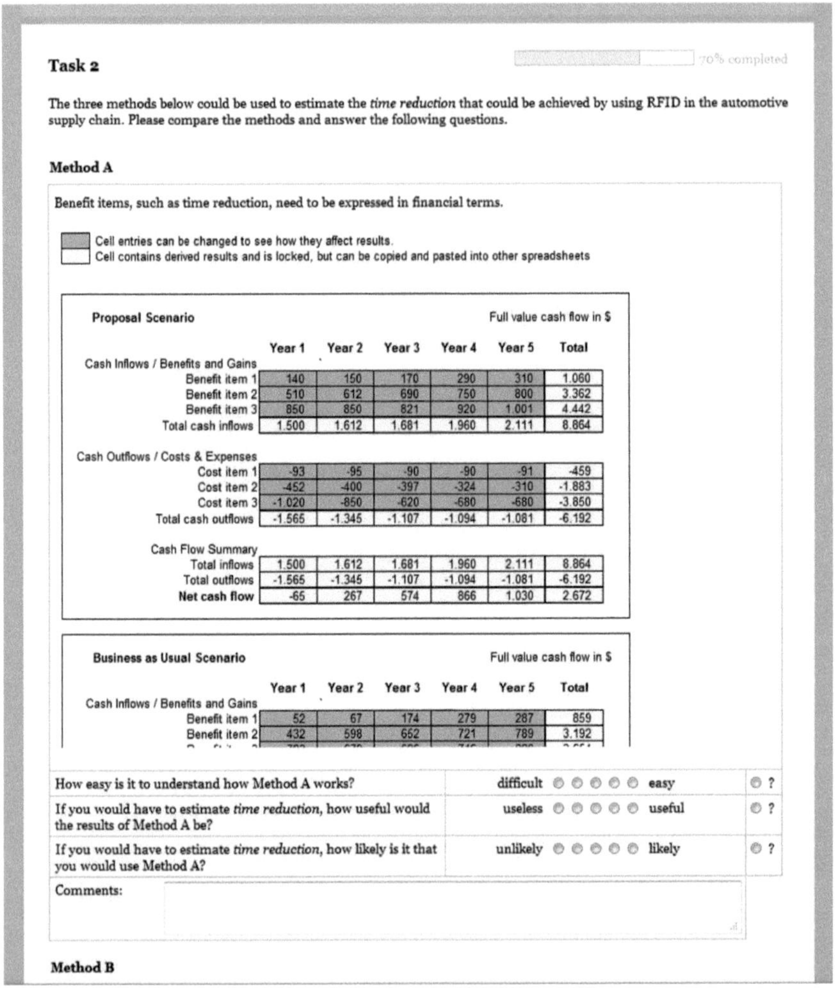

Figure E.18: Method A, an FML method, in the Time Reduction condition

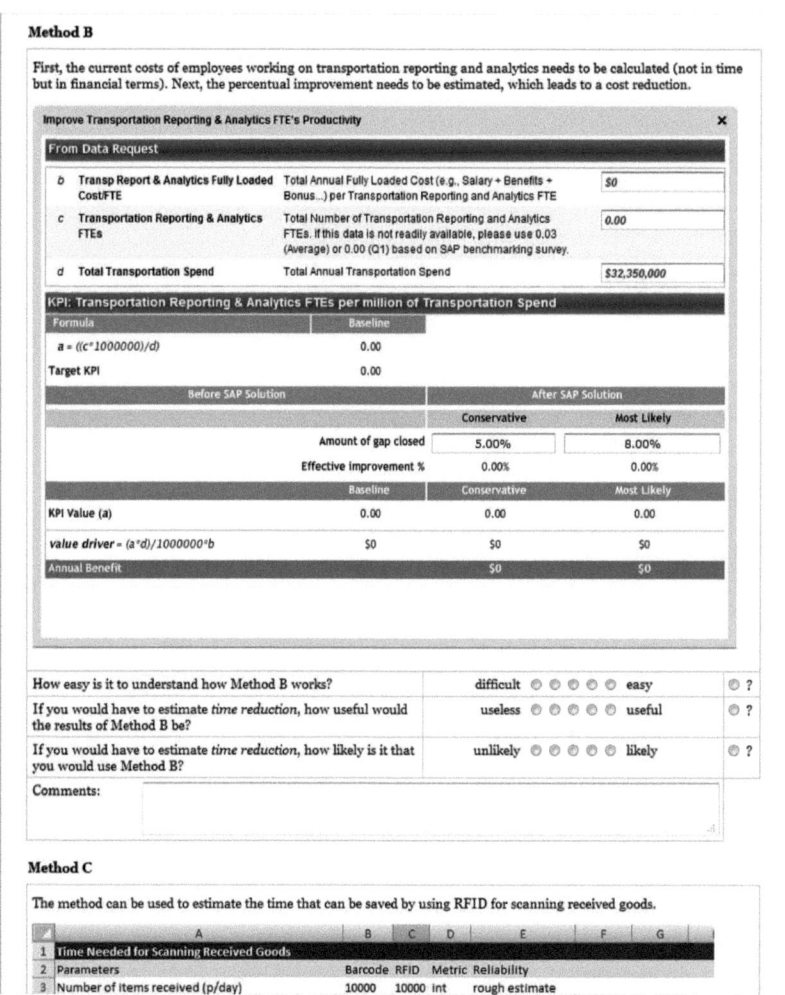

Figure E.19: Method B, a VLM method, in the Time Reduction condition

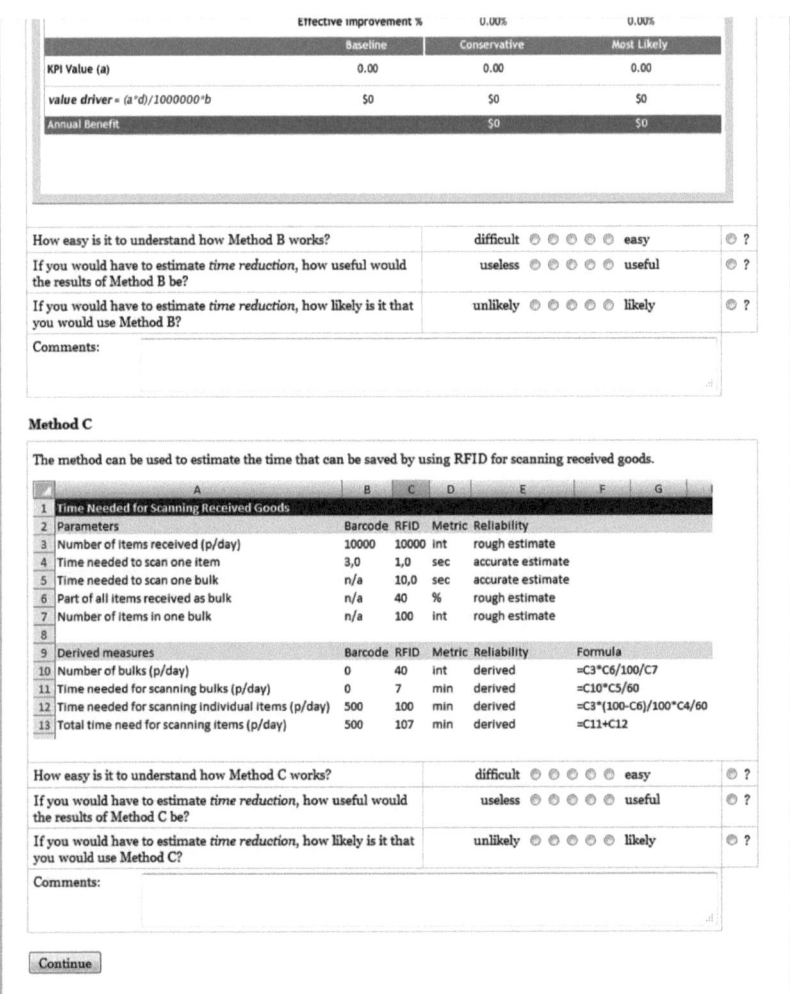

Figure E.20: Method C, a new method, in the Time Reduction condition

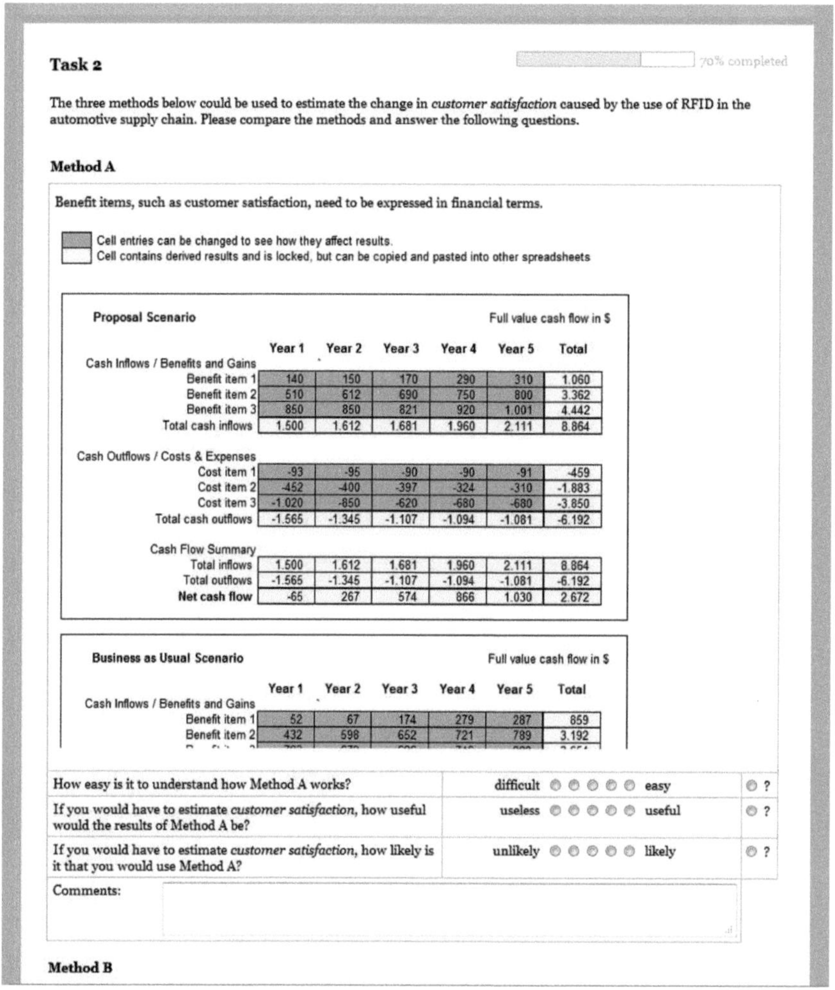

Task 2   70% completed

The three methods below could be used to estimate the change in *customer satisfaction* caused by the use of RFID in the automotive supply chain. Please compare the methods and answer the following questions.

Method A

Benefit items, such as customer satisfaction, need to be expressed in financial terms.

▨ Cell entries can be changed to see how they affect results.
▨ Cell contains derived results and is locked, but can be copied and pasted into other spreadsheets

Proposal Scenario Full value cash flow in $

	Year 1	Year 2	Year 3	Year 4	Year 5	Total
Cash Inflows / Benefits and Gains						
Benefit item 1	140	150	170	290	310	1.060
Benefit item 2	510	612	690	750	800	3.362
Benefit item 3	850	850	821	920	1.001	4.442
Total cash inflows	1.500	1.612	1.681	1.960	2.111	8.864
Cash Outflows / Costs & Expenses						
Cost item 1	-93	-95	-90	-90	-91	-459
Cost item 2	-452	-400	-397	-324	-310	-1.883
Cost item 3	-1.020	-850	-620	-680	-680	-3.850
Total cash outflows	-1.565	-1.345	-1.107	-1.094	-1.081	-6.192
Cash Flow Summary						
Total inflows	1.500	1.612	1.681	1.960	2.111	8.864
Total outflows	-1.565	-1.345	-1.107	-1.094	-1.081	-6.192
Net cash flow	-65	267	574	866	1.030	2.672

Business as Usual Scenario Full value cash flow in $

	Year 1	Year 2	Year 3	Year 4	Year 5	Total
Cash Inflows / Benefits and Gains						
Benefit item 1	52	67	174	279	287	859
Benefit item 2	432	598	652	721	789	3.192

How easy is it to understand how Method A works?	difficult ◉ ◉ ◉ ◉ ◉ easy	◉ ?
If you would have to estimate *customer satisfaction*, how useful would the results of Method A be?	useless ◉ ◉ ◉ ◉ ◉ useful	◉ ?
If you would have to estimate *customer satisfaction*, how likely is it that you would use Method A?	unlikely ◉ ◉ ◉ ◉ ◉ likely	◉ ?
Comments:		

Method B

Figure E.21: Method A, an FML method, in the Customer Satisfaction condition

Method B

First, customer satisfaction needs to be estimated as a percentual value. Next, the percentual improvement needs to be estimated.

Improve Customer Satisfaction			✕
From Data Request			
b Customer Satisfaction (in %)	Current Customer Satisfaction (in %). Customer satisfaction is a sum total of "Very Satisfied" customer and "Satisfied" customer.		0.0%

Strategic KPI: Customer Satisfaction (in %)			
Formula	Baseline		
a - b	0.0%		
Target KPI	0.0%		
	Before SAP Solution	After SAP Solution	
		Conservative	Most Likely
	Amount of gap closed	0.00%	0.00%
	Effective Improvement %	0.00%	0.00%
	Baseline	Conservative	Most Likely
KPI Value (a)	0.0%	0.0%	0.0%

How easy is it to understand how Method B works?	difficult ○ ○ ○ ○ ○ easy	○ ?
If you would have to estimate *customer satisfaction*, how useful would the results of Method B be?	useless ○ ○ ○ ○ ○ useful	○ ?
If you would have to estimate *customer satisfaction*, how likely is it that you would use Method B?	unlikely ○ ○ ○ ○ ○ likely	○ ?
Comments:		

Method C

Different stakeholders need to be asked for their opinion. They should rate from 1 (low) to 5 (high) what the level of customer satisfaction currently is and how it is expected to change when using RFID.

Customer Satisfaction				
Parameters	Barcode	RFID	Metric	Reliability
Delivery time				

Figure E.22: Method B, a VLM method, in the Customer Satisfaction condition

How easy is it to understand how Method B works?	difficult ○ ○ ○ ○ ○ easy	○ ?
If you would have to estimate *customer satisfaction*, how useful would the results of Method B be?	useless ○ ○ ○ ○ ○ useful	○ ?
If you would have to estimate *customer satisfaction*, how likely is it that you would use Method B?	unlikely ○ ○ ○ ○ ○ likely	○ ?
Comments:		

Method C

Different stakeholders need to be asked for their opinion. They should rate from 1 (low) to 5 (high) what the level of customer satisfaction currently is and how it is expected to change when using RFID.

Customer Satisfaction				
Parameters	Barcode	RFID	Metric	Reliability
Delivery time				
opinion Frank (warehousing)	3	4	1-5	guess
opinion Clara (goods receipt)	2	3	1-5	guess
opinion Steve (shipping)	4	4	1-5	guess
opinion Sarah (planning & control)	4	3	1-5	guess
Transparency of order status and item location				
opinion Frank (warehousing)	3	5	1-5	guess
opinion Clara (goods receipt)	3	5	1-5	guess
opinion Steve (shipping)	4	5	1-5	guess
opinion Sarah (planning & control)	3	4	1-5	guess
Delivery of the correct items in the correct quantity				
opinion Frank (warehousing)	3	3	1-5	guess
opinion Clara (goods receipt)	2	2	1-5	guess
opinion Steve (shipping)	5	4	1-5	guess
opinion Sarah (planning & control)	4	5	1-5	guess

Derived measures	Barcode	RFID	Metric	Reliability	Formula
Delivery time: average opinion	3,3	3,5	int	derived	=AVERAGE
Transparency: average opinion	3,3	4,8	int	derived	=AVERAGE
Correct items/quantity: average opinion	3,5	3,5	int	derived	=AVERAGE

How easy is it to understand how Method C works?	difficult ○ ○ ○ ○ ○ easy	○ ?
If you would have to estimate *customer satisfaction*, how useful would the results of Method C be?	useless ○ ○ ○ ○ ○ useful	○ ?
If you would have to estimate *customer satisfaction*, how likely is it that you would use Method C?	unlikely ○ ○ ○ ○ ○ likely	○ ?
Comments:		

[Continue]

Figure E.23: Method C, a new method, in the Customer Satisfaction condition

Von der Promotion zum Buch

WWW.GABLER.DE

Sie haben eine wirtschaftswissenschaftliche Dissertation bzw. Habilitation erfolgreich abgeschlossen und möchten sie als Buch veröffentlichen?

Zeigen Sie, was Sie geleistet haben.
Publizieren Sie Ihre Dissertation als Buch bei Gabler Research.
Ein Buch ist nachhaltig wirksam für Ihre Karriere.
Nutzen Sie die Möglichkeit mit Ihrer Publikation bestmöglich sichtbar und wertgeschätzt zu werden – im Umfeld anerkannter Wissenschaftler und Autoren.
Qualitative Titelauswahl sowie namhafte Herausgeber renommierter Schriftenreihen bürgen für die Güte des Programms.

Ihre Vorteile:

- Kurze Produktionszyklen: Drucklegung in 6-8 Wochen
- Dauerhafte Lieferbarkeit print und digital: Druck + E-Book in SpringerLink Zielgruppenrechter Vertrieb an Wissenschaftler, Bibliotheken, Fach- und Hochschulinstitute und (Online-)Buchhandel
- Umfassende Marketingaktivitäten: E-Mail-Newsletter, Flyer, Kataloge, Rezensionsexemplar-Versand an nationale und internationale Fachzeitschriften, Präsentation auf Messen und Fachtagungen etc.

▶ Möchten Sie Autor beim Gabler Verlag werden? Kontaktieren Sie uns!

Ute Wrasmann | Lektorat Wissenschaftliche Monografien
Tel. +49 (0)611.7878-239 | Fax +49 (0)611.7878-78-239 | ute.wrasmann@gabler.de

KOMPETENZ IN SACHEN WIRTSCHAFT

If you have any concerns about our products,
you can contact us on
ProductSafety@springernature.com

In case Publisher is established outside the EU,
the EU authorized representative is:
**Springer Nature Customer Service Center GmbH
Europaplatz 3, 69115 Heidelberg, Germany**

Printed by Libri Plureos GmbH
in Hamburg, Germany